D0850675

BLOOM'S

HOW TO WRITE ABOUT

William Faulkner

ANNA PRIDDY

Introduction by
HAROLD BLOOM

BLOOM'S
LITERARY CRITICISM
An imprint of Infobase Publishing

Bloom's How to Write about William Faulkner

Copyright © 2010 by Infobase Publishing
Introduction © 2010 by Harold Bloom

Bloom's Literary Criticism
An imprint of Infobase Publishing
132 West 31st Street
New York NY 10001

Library of Congress Cataloging-in-Publication Data

Priddy, Anna.
  Bloom's how to write about William Faulkner / Anna Priddy ; introduction by
Harold Bloom.
    p. cm.— (Bloom's how to write about literature)
  Includes bibliographical references and index.
  ISBN 978-0-7910-9742-7 (hardcover)
  1. Faulkner, William, 1897–1962—Criticism and interpretation. 2. Criticism—
Authorship. I. Bloom, Harold. II. Title. III. Title: How to write about William
Faulkner. IV. Series.
  PS3511.A86Z94645 2009
  813'.52—dc22   2009001158

Text design by Annie O'Donnell
Cover design by Ben Peterson

Printed in the United States of America

MP MSRF 10 9 8 7 6 5 4 3 2 1

This book is printed on acid-free paper.

CONTENTS

SERIES INTRODUCTION

BLOOM's How to Write about Literature series is designed to inspire students to write fine essays on great writers and their works. Each volume in the series begins with an introduction by Harold Bloom, meditating on the challenges and rewards of writing about the volume's subject author. The first chapter then provides detailed instructions on how to write a good essay, including how to find a thesis; how to develop an outline; how to write a good introduction, body text, and conclusion; how to cite sources; and more. The second chapter provides a brief overview of the issues involved in writing about the subject author and then a number of suggestions for paper topics, with accompanying strategies for addressing each topic. Succeeding chapters cover the author's major works.

The paper topics suggested within this book are open-ended, and the brief strategies provided are designed to give students a push forward in the writing process rather than a road map to success. The aim of the book is to pose questions, not answer them. Many different kinds of papers could result from each topic. As always, the success of each paper will depend completely on the writer's skill and imagination.

HOW TO WRITE ABOUT WILLIAM FAULKNER: INTRODUCTION

by Harold Bloom

EACH TIME that I have written about Faulkner, I have gone back to my first reading of him. The novel was *Light in August,* and it captured me instantly. I was 15 and was overcome by the *strangeness* of the story and its characters. Lena Grove and Joe Christmas seemed to emanate from different worlds, while the racist thug Percy Grimm prophesied Hitler's storm troopers, as Faulkner noted in a letter to Malcolm Cowley.

A year later, on my birthday, July 11, 1946, I purchased Cowley's very valuable *The Portable Faulkner,* then just published. The book remains in print, and I recommend it as a still fresh and useful introduction to the major American novelist since Henry James.

Cowley's introduction sees Faulkner as primarily a storyteller, most himself in short fiction such as "The Bear," "Old Man" (from *The Wild Palms*), and "Spotted Horses" (from *The Hamlet*). Certainly Faulkner invents marvelous stories, but he seems to me at his strongest where he is most original, in *As I Lay Dying, Sanctuary*, and *Light in August. The Sound and the Fury* perhaps owes too much to Conrad and to Joyce, while *Absalom, Absalom!* cannot seem to contain its own gothicism. Still, both the Compsons' and Sutpens' sagas would be major achievements for all but a few novelists.

Writing about Faulkner is not akin to writing about Joyce and Proust but has expected affinities with the rewards and hazards of commenting on the fictions of Joseph Conrad. Conrad's and Faulkner's men and women are doom-eager. They might like to wait for their doom to live, but it will not. Quentin Compson and his beloved sister, Caddy, in *The Sound and the Fury* scarcely resist their all-starred destinies. They do not just come down from the past; it comes down upon them. Darl Bundren, the central consciousness of *As I Lay Dying*, knows implicitly what the great Shakespearean protagonists utter explicitly: Reality is an abyss, and all families are catastrophes. Through Darl Bundren, the reader senses the larger issues, literary and experiential, that always seem to haunt Faulkner's novels during his Great Decade of 1928–1938. *That* Faulkner affirmed nothing and questioned everything, as Quentin Compson does in the mode of Joyce's Stephen, who himself imitates Hamlet.

One element of Faulkner for which you need to be on watch is the flaring out of epiphanies—Paterian, Conradian, Joycean—flashes of light as the spirit flares out against darkening backgrounds. In *Sanctuary*, which Faulkner deprecated as a thriller and yet created through it a lurid heterocosm wholly persuasive, these epiphanies abound. Impressionism in Conrad and Stephen Crane is a source for Faulkner, and any writing about the tale-teller of Oxford, Mississippi, involves coming to terms with the aims and techniques of literary impressionism.

Family romance in Faulkner, as in life, often a disaster, was for him an endless resource. Incest haunts his imagined land and is fecund in all his narratives. John T. Irwin, one of the best Faulkner critics, lists four major genealogical patterns in the novels and stories: doubling, incest, repetition, revenge. All repay close attention in writing about Faulkner. That these four patterns fuse together is not a malaise or defect but a virtue in Faulkner's best fictions.

In writing about Faulkner, it is best not to disentangle what he so richly weaves together. Like Balzac and Dickens, Faulkner constructs a human comedy founded on tragic farce. The hilarious and unsettling Snopes clan, ranging from the relentless Flem Snopes to the hapless Wall Street Panic Snopes, are Faulkner's grand contribution to the mythology of his nation. Dickens would have adored them. They seem to me a true challenge for all who would write about Faulkner. Our public life is thronged with them. I once thought of writing an essay about Reagan Revolution Snopes. How about Newt Gingrich Snopes or Sarah Palin Snopes? One use of good writing about Faulkner is to set forth the illuminating power of the Snopsian clan and vision.

HOW TO WRITE
A GOOD ESSAY

By Laurie A. Sterling and Anna Priddy

WHILE THERE are many ways to write about literature, most assignments for high school and college English classes call for analytical papers. In these assignments, you are presenting your interpretation of a text to your reader. Your objective is to interpret the text's meaning in order to enhance your reader's understanding and enjoyment of the work. Without exception, strong papers about the meaning of a literary work are built upon a careful, close reading of the text or texts. Careful, analytical reading should always be the first step in your writing process. This volume provides models of such close, analytical reading, and these should help you develop your own skills as a reader and as a writer.

As the examples throughout this book demonstrate, attentive reading entails thinking about and evaluating the formal (textual) aspects of the author's works: theme, character, form, and language. In addition, when writing about a work, many readers choose to move beyond the text itself to consider the work's cultural context. In these instances, writers might explore the historical circumstances of the time period in which the work was written. Alternatively, they might examine the philosophies and ideas that a work addresses. Even in cases where writers explore a work's cultural context, though, papers must still address the more formal aspects of the work itself. A good interpretative essay that evaluates Charles Dickens's use of the philosophy of utilitarianism in his novel *Hard Times,* for example, cannot adequately address the author's treatment of the philosophy without firmly grounding this discussion in the book itself. In other words, any analytical paper about a text, even one that seeks to evaluate the work's cultural context, must also have a firm handle on the work's themes, characters, and language. You must look for and evaluate these aspects of a work, then, as you read a text and as you prepare to write about it.

WRITING ABOUT THEMES

Literary themes are more than just topics or subjects treated in a work; they are attitudes or points about these topics that often structure other elements in a work. Writing about theme therefore requires that you not just identify a topic that a literary work addresses but also discuss what that work says about that topic. For example, if you were writing about the culture of the American South in William Faulkner's famous story "A Rose for Emily," you would need to discuss what Faulkner says, argues, or implies about that culture and its passing.

When you prepare to write about thematic concerns in a work of literature, you will probably discover that, like most works of literature, your text touches upon other themes in addition to its central theme. These secondary themes also provide rich ground for paper topics. A thematic paper on "A Rose for Emily" might consider gender or race in the story. While neither of these could be said to be the central theme of the story, they are clearly related to the passing of the "old South" and could provide plenty of good material for papers.

As you prepare to write about themes in literature, you might find a number of strategies helpful. After you identify a theme or themes in the story, you should begin by evaluating how other elements of the story—such as character, point of view, imagery, and symbolism—help develop the theme. You might ask yourself what your own responses are to the author's treatment of the subject matter. Do not neglect the obvious, either: What expectations does the title set up? How does the title help develop thematic concerns? Clearly, the title "A Rose for Emily" says something about the narrator's attitude toward the title character, Emily Grierson, and all she represents.

WRITING ABOUT CHARACTER

Generally, characters are essential components of fiction and drama. (This is not always the case, though; Ray Bradbury's "August 2026: There Will Come Soft Rains" is technically a story without characters, at least any human characters.) Often, you can discuss character in poetry, as in T. S. Eliot's "The Love Song of J. Alfred Prufrock" or Robert Browning's "My Last Duchess." Many writers find that analyzing character is one of the most interesting and engaging ways to work with a piece of literature and to shape a paper. After all, characters generally are human, and we all know something about being human and living in the world. While it is always important to remember that these figures are not real people but creations of the writer's imagination, it can be fruitful to begin evaluating them as you might evaluate a real person. Often you can start with your own response to a character. Did you like or dislike the character? Did you sympathize with the character? Why or why not?

Keep in mind, though, that emotional responses like these are just starting places. To truly explore and evaluate literary characters, you need to return to the formal aspects of the text and evaluate how the author has drawn these characters. The 20th-century writer E. M. Forster coined the terms *flat* characters and *round* characters. Flat characters are static, one-dimensional characters that frequently represent a particular concept or idea. In contrast, round characters are fully drawn and much more realistic characters that frequently change and develop over the course of a work. Are the characters you are studying flat or round? What elements of the characters lead you to this conclusion? Why might the author have drawn characters like this? How does their development affect the meaning of the work? Similarly, you should explore the techniques the author uses to develop characters. Do we hear a character's own words, or do we hear only other characters' assessments of him or her? Or, does the author use an omniscient or limited omniscient narrator to allow us access to the workings of the characters' minds? If so, how does that help develop the characterization? Often you can even evaluate the narrator as a character. How trustworthy are the opinions and assessments of the narrator? You should also think about characters' names. Do they mean anything? If you encounter a hero named Sophia or Sophie, you should probably think about her wisdom (or lack thereof), since *sophia* means "wisdom" in Greek. Similarly, since the name Sylvia is derived from the word *sylvan,* meaning "of the wood," you might want to evaluate that character's relationship with nature. Once again, you might look to the title of the work. Does Herman Melville's "Bartleby, the Scrivener" signal anything about Bartleby himself? Is Bartleby adequately defined by his job as scrivener? Is this part of Melville's point? Pursuing questions such as these can help you develop thorough papers about characters from psychological, sociological, or more formalistic perspectives.

WRITING ABOUT FORM AND GENRE

Genre, a word derived from French, means "type" or "class." Literary genres are distinctive classes or categories of literary composition. On the most general level, literary works can be divided into the genres of drama, poetry, fiction, and essays, yet within those genres there are classifications that are also referred to as genres. Tragedy and comedy, for example, are genres of drama. Epic, lyric, and pastoral are genres of poetry. *Form,* on the other hand, generally refers to the shape or structure of a work. There are many clearly defined forms of poetry that follow specific patterns of meter, rhyme, and stanza. Sonnets, for example, are poems that follow a fixed form of 14 lines. Sonnets generally follow one of two basic sonnet forms, each with its own distinct rhyme scheme. Haiku is another example of poetic form, traditionally consisting of three unrhymed lines of five, seven, and five syllables.

While you might think that writing about form or genre might leave little room for argument, many of these forms and genres are very fluid. Remember that literature is evolving and ever changing, and so are its forms. As you study poetry, you may find that poets, especially more modern poets, play with traditional poetic forms, bringing about new effects. Similarly, dramatic tragedy was once quite narrowly defined, but over the centuries playwrights have broadened and challenged traditional definitions, changing the shape of tragedy. When Arthur Miller wrote *Death of a Salesman,* many critics challenged the idea that tragic drama could encompass a common man like Willy Loman.

Evaluating how a work of literature fits into or challenges the boundaries of its form or genre can provide you with fruitful avenues of investigation. You might find it helpful to ask why the work does or does not fit into traditional categories. Why might Miller have thought it fitting to write a tragedy of the common man? Similarly, you might compare the content or theme of a work with its form. How well do they work together? Many of Emily Dickinson's poems, for instance, follow the meter of traditional hymns. While some of her poems seem to express traditional religious doctrines, many seem to challenge or strain against traditional conceptions of God and theology. What is the effect, then, of her use of traditional hymn meter?

WRITING ABOUT LANGUAGE, SYMBOLS, AND IMAGERY

No matter what the genre, writers use words as their most basic tool. Language is the most fundamental building block of literature. It is essential that you pay careful attention to the author's language and word choice as you read, reread, and analyze a text. Imagery is language that appeals to the senses. Most commonly, imagery appeals to our sense of vision, creating a mental picture, but authors also use language that appeals to our other senses. Images can be literal or figurative. Literal images use sensory language to describe an actual thing. In the broadest terms, figurative language uses one thing to speak about something else. For example, if I call my boss a snake, I am not saying that he is literally a reptile. Instead, I am using figurative language to communicate my opinions about him. Since we think of snakes as sneaky, slimy, and sinister, I am using the concrete image of a snake to communicate these abstract opinions and impressions.

The two most common figures of speech are similes and metaphors. Both are comparisons between two apparently dissimilar things. Similes are explicit comparisons using the words *like* or *as*; metaphors are implicit comparisons. To return to the previous example, if I say, "My boss, Bob, was waiting for me when I showed up to work five minutes late today—the snake!" I have constructed a metaphor. Writing about his experiences fighting in World War I, Wilfred Owen begins his poem "Dulce et decorum est," with a string of similes: "Bent double, like old beggars under sacks, / Knock-kneed, coughing like hags, we cursed through sludge." Owen's goal was to undercut clichéd notions that war and dying in battle were glorious. Certainly, comparing soldiers to coughing hags and to beggars underscores his point.

"Fog," a short poem by Carl Sandburg, provides a clear example of a metaphor. Sandburg's poem reads:

> The fog comes
> on little cat feet.
>
> It sits looking
> over harbor and city
> on silent haunches
> and then moves on.

Notice how effectively Sandburg conveys surprising impressions of the fog by comparing two seemingly disparate things—the fog and a cat.

Symbols, by contrast, are things that stand for, or represent, other things. Often they represent something intangible, such as concepts or ideas. In everyday life we use and understand symbols easily. Babies at christenings and brides at weddings wear white to represent purity. Think, too, of a dollar bill. The paper itself has no value in and of itself. Instead, that paper bill is a symbol of something else, the precious metal in a nation's coffers. Symbols in literature work similarly. Authors use symbols to evoke more than a simple, straightforward, literal meaning. Characters, objects, and places can all function as symbols. Famous literary examples of symbols include Moby-Dick, the white whale of Herman Melville's novel, and the scarlet *A* of Nathaniel Hawthorne's *The Scarlet Letter*. As both of these symbols suggest, a literary symbol cannot be adequately defined or explained by any one meaning. Hester Prynne's Puritan community clearly intends her scarlet *A* as a symbol of her adultery, but as the novel progresses, even her own community reads the letter as representing not just *adultery*, but *able, angel,* and a host of other meanings.

Writing about imagery and symbols requires close attention to the author's language. To prepare a paper on symbolism or imagery in a work, identify and trace the images and symbols and then try to draw some conclusions about how they function. Ask yourself how any symbols or images help contribute to the themes or meanings of the work.

What connotations do they carry? How do they affect your reception of the work? Do they shed light on characters or settings? A strong paper on imagery or symbolism will thoroughly consider the use of figures in the text and will try to reach some conclusions about how or why the author uses them.

WRITING ABOUT HISTORY AND CONTEXT

As noted above, it is possible to write an analytical paper that also considers the work's context. After all, the text was not created in a vacuum. The author lived and wrote in a specific time period and in a specific cultural context and, like all of us, was shaped by that environment. Learning more about the historical and cultural circumstances that surround the author and the work can help illuminate a text and provide you with productive material for a paper. Remember, though, that when you write analytical papers, you should use the context to illuminate the text. Do not lose sight of your goal—to interpret the meaning of the literary work. Use historical or philosophical research as a tool to develop your textual evaluation.

Thoughtful readers often consider how history and culture affected the author's choice and treatment of his or her subject matter. Investigations into the history and context of a work could examine the work's relation to specific historical events, such as the Salem witch trials in 17th-century Massachusetts or the restoration of Charles II to the English throne in 1660. Bear in mind that historical context is not limited to politics and world events. While knowing about the Vietnam War is certainly helpful in interpreting much of Tim O'Brien's fiction, and some knowledge of the French Revolution clearly illuminates the dynamics of Charles Dickens's *A Tale of Two Cities,* historical context also entails the fabric of daily life. Examining a text in light of gender roles, race relations, class boundaries, or working conditions can give rise to thoughtful and compelling papers. Exploring the conditions of the working class in 19th-century England, for example, can provide a particularly effective avenue for writing about Dickens's *Hard Times.*

You can begin thinking about these issues by asking broad questions at first. What do you know about the time period and about the author? What does the editorial apparatus in your text tell you? These might be starting places. Similarly, when specific historical events or dynamics are particularly important to understanding a work but might be somewhat obscure to modern readers, textbooks usually provide notes to explain historical background. These are a good place to start. With this information, ask yourself how these historical facts and circumstances might have affected the author, the presentation of theme, and the presentation of character. How does knowing more about the work's specific historical context illuminate the work? To take a well-known example, understanding the complex attitudes toward slavery during the time Mark Twain wrote *Adventures of Huckleberry Finn* should help you begin to examine issues of race in the text. Additionally, you might compare these attitudes to those of the time in which the novel was set. How might this comparison affect your interpretation of a work written after the abolition of slavery but set before the Civil War?

WRITING ABOUT PHILOSOPHY AND IDEAS

Philosophical concerns are closely related to both historical context and thematic issues. Like historical investigation, philosophical research can provide a useful tool as you analyze a text. For example, an investigation into the working class in Dickens's England might lead you to a topic on the philosophical doctrine of utilitarianism in *Hard Times*. Many other works explore philosophies and ideas quite explicitly. Mary Shelley's famous novel *Frankenstein*, for example, explores John Locke's tabula rasa theory of human knowledge as she portrays the intellectual and emotional development of Victor Frankenstein's creature. As this example indicates, philosophical issues are somewhat more abstract than investigations of theme or historical context. Some other examples of philosophical issues include human free will, the formation of human identity, the nature of sin, or questions of ethics.

Writing about philosophy and ideas might require some outside research, but usually the notes or other material in your text will provide you with basic information, and often footnotes and bibliographies suggest places you can go to read further about the subject. If you have identified a philosophical theme that runs through a text, you might ask yourself how the author develops this theme. Look at character development and the interactions of characters, for example. Similarly, you might examine whether the narrative voice in a work of fiction addresses the philosophical concerns of the text.

WRITING COMPARISON AND CONTRAST ESSAYS

Finally, you might find that comparing and contrasting the works or techniques of an author provides a useful tool for literary analysis. A comparison and contrast essay might compare two characters or themes in a single work, or it might compare the author's treatment of a theme in two works. It might also contrast methods of character development or analyze an author's differing treatment of a philosophical concern in two works. Writing comparison and contrast essays, though, requires some special consideration. While they generally provide you with plenty of material to use, they also come with a built-in trap: the laundry list. These papers often become mere lists of connections between the works. As this chapter will discuss, a strong thesis must make an assertion that you want to prove or validate. A strong comparison/contrast thesis, then, needs to comment on the significance of the similarities and differences you observe. It is not enough merely to assert that the works contain similarities and differences. You might, for example, assert why the similarities and differences are important and explain how they illuminate the works' treatment of theme. Remember, too, that a thesis should not be a statement of the obvious. A comparison/contrast paper that focuses only on very obvious similarities or differences does little to illuminate the connections between the works. Often, an effective method of shaping a strong thesis and argument is to begin your paper by noting the similarities between the works but then to develop a thesis that asserts how these apparently similar elements are different. If, for example, you observe that Emily Dickinson wrote a number of poems about spiders, you might analyze how she uses spider imagery differently in two poems. Similarly, many scholars have noted that Hawthorne created many "mad scientist" characters, men who are so devoted to their science or their art that they lose perspective on all else. A good thesis comparing two of these characters—Aylmer of "The Birth-mark" and Dr. Rappaccini of "Rappaccini's Daughter," for example—might initially identify both characters as examples of Hawthorne's mad scientist type but then argue that their motivations for scientific experimentation differ. If you strive to analyze the similarities or differences, discuss significances, and move beyond the obvious, your paper should move beyond the laundry list trap.

PREPARING TO WRITE

Armed with a clear sense of your task—illuminating the text—and with an understanding of theme, character, language, history, and philosophy, you are ready to approach the writing process. Remember that good writing is grounded in good reading and that close reading takes time, attention, and more than one reading of your text. Read for comprehension first. As you go back and review the work, mark the text to chart the details of the work as well as your reactions. Highlight important passages, repeated words, and image patterns. "Converse" with the text through marginal notes. Mark turns in the plot, ask questions, and make observations about characters, themes, and language. If you are reading from a book that does not belong to you, keep a record of your reactions in a journal or notebook. If you have read a work of literature carefully, paying attention to both the text and the context of the work, you have a leg up on the writing process. Admittedly, at this point, your ideas are probably very broad and undefined, but you have taken an important first step toward writing a strong paper.

Your next step is to focus, to take a broad, perhaps fuzzy, topic and define it more clearly. Even a topic provided by your instructor will need to be focused appropriately. Remember that good writers make the topic their own. There are a number of strategies—often called "invention"—that you can use to develop your own focus. In one such strategy, called *freewriting*, you spend 10 minutes or so just writing about your topic without referring back to the text or your notes. Write whatever comes to mind; the important thing is that you just keep writing. Often this process allows you to develop fresh ideas or approaches to your subject matter. You could also try *brainstorming*: Write down your topic and then list all the related points or ideas you can think of. Include questions, comments, words, important passages or events, and anything else that comes to mind. Let one idea lead to another. In the related technique of *clustering*, or *mapping*, write your topic on a sheet of paper and write related ideas around it. Then list related subpoints under each of these main ideas. Many people then draw arrows to show connections between points. This technique helps you narrow your topic and can also help you organize your ideas. Similarly, asking journalistic questions— Who? What? Where? When? Why? and How?—can lead to ideas for topic development.

Thesis Statements

Once you have developed a focused topic, you can begin to think about your thesis statement—the main point or purpose of your paper. It is imperative that you craft a strong thesis; otherwise, your paper will likely be little more than random, disorganized observations about the text. Think of your thesis statement as a kind of road map for your paper. It tells your reader where you are going and how you are going to get there.

To craft a good thesis, you must keep a number of things in mind. First, as the title of this subsection indicates, your paper's thesis should be a statement, an assertion about the text that you want to prove or validate. Beginning writers often formulate a question that they attempt to use as a thesis. For example, a writer who wanted to understand what Faulkner intended the reader to think about the character Quentin Compson in *The Sound and the Fury* might ask, Why is Quentin so obsessed with the passing of time? While a question like this is a good strategy to use in the invention process to help narrow your topic and find your thesis, it cannot serve as the thesis statement because it does not tell your reader what you want to assert about Quentin Compson and time. You might shape this question into a thesis by instead proposing an answer to that question: In *The Sound and the Fury*, Quentin Compson wants to escape from time and the suffering of the world. Time, like suffering, however, proves inescapable, even by suicide. Notice that this thesis provides an initial plan or structure for the rest of the paper, and notice, too, that the thesis statement does not necessarily have to fit into one sentence. After discussing Quentin's uneasy relationship with time, you could examine the ways he attempts to escape it but cannot and also what Faulkner seems to convey to the reader about time; perhaps you could discuss, too, how Quentin's father's views on time color his son's thinking.

Second, remember that a good thesis makes an assertion that you need to support. In other words, a good thesis does not state the obvious.

If you tried to formulate a thesis about time by simply saying, Time is important to Quentin in *The Sound and the Fury,* you have done nothing but rephrase the obvious. Since Faulkner's novel emphasizes Quentin's uneasy relationship with time, there would be no point in spending three to five pages supporting the assertion that it is important to him. You might try to develop a thesis from that point by asking yourself some further questions: What does it mean to be "temporary" (Faulkner 178)? Does the novel seem to indicate that the passing of time should be resisted? Does it present time as an enemy or as a blessing? Such a line of questioning might lead you to a more viable thesis, like the one in the preceding paragraph.

As the comparison with the road map also suggests, your thesis should appear near the beginning of the paper. In relatively short papers (three to six pages) the thesis almost always appears in the first paragraph. Some writers fall into the trap of saving their thesis for the end, trying to provide a surprise or a big moment of revelation, as if to say, "TA-DA! I've just proved that time is important to Quentin Compson in *The Sound and the Fury.*" Placing a thesis at the end of an essay can seriously mar the essay's effectiveness. If you fail to define your essay's point and purpose clearly at the beginning, your reader will find it difficult to assess the clarity of your argument and understand the points you are making. When your argument comes as a surprise at the end, you force your reader to reread your essay in order to assess its logic and effectiveness.

Finally, you should avoid using the first person ("I") as you present your thesis. Though it is not strictly wrong to write in the first person, it is difficult to do so gracefully. While writing in the first person, beginning writers often fall into the trap of writing self-reflexive prose (writing *about* their paper *in* their paper). Often this leads to the most dreaded of opening lines: "In this paper I am going to discuss . . ." Not only does this self-reflexive voice make for very awkward prose, it frequently allows writers to boldly announce a topic while completely avoiding a thesis statement. An example might be a paper that begins as follows: As I Lay Dying is William Faulkner's novel about the Bundren family, who are traveling to Jefferson to bury Addie Bundren. In this paper I am going to discuss how this trip unfolds. The author of this paper has done little more than announce a general topic for the paper (the Bundrens' journey). While the last sentence might move toward a thesis, the writer fails to present an opinion about the significance of the journey. To improve this "thesis," the writer would need to back up a couple of steps. First, the announced topic of the paper is too broad; it largely seems to summarize the events in the novel without saying anything about the ideas in the novel. The writer should highlight what she considers the journey's meaning to be: What is the novel about? The writer might conclude that the journey represents Addie's final means of asserting herself against her husband, Anse. From here, the author could select the means by which Faulkner communicates this idea and then begin to craft a specific thesis. A writer who chooses to explore the ways Addie has asserted herself before might, for example, craft a thesis that reads, As I Lay Dying is a novel that explores how Addie Bundren attempts to assert herself against the world: beating her students when she is a teacher, having an affair with the minister during her marriage, and choosing to be buried far away from her husband and family.

Outlines

While developing a strong, thoughtful thesis early in your writing process should help focus your paper, outlining provides an essential tool for logically shaping that paper. A good outline helps you see—and develop—the relationships among the points in your argument and assures you that your paper flows logically and coherently. Outlining not only helps place your points in a logical order but also helps you subordinate supporting points, weed out any irrelevant points, and decide if there are any necessary points that are missing from your argument. Most of us are familiar with formal outlines that use numerical and letter designations for each point. However, there are different types of outlines; you may find that an informal outline is a more useful tool for you. What is important, though, is that you spend the time to develop some sort of outline—formal or informal.

Remember that an outline is a tool to help you shape and write a strong paper. If you do not spend sufficient time planning your supporting points and shaping the arrangement of those points, you will most likely construct a vague, unfocused outline that provides little, if any, help with the writing of the paper. Consider the following example.

Thesis: As I Lay Dying is a novel that explores how Addie Bundren attempts to assert herself against the world: beating her students when she is a teacher, having an affair with the minister during her marriage, and choosing to be buried far away from her husband and family when she dies.

    I. Introduction and thesis

   II. Addie
       A. Students
       B. Anse
       C. Children
       D. Words

  III. Whitfield (her lover)

  IV. Blood
       A. "Now you are aware of me! Now I am something in your secret and selfish life, who have marked your blood with my own for ever and ever." (170)

   V. Conclusion
       A. Addie forces her family to bury her in Jefferson in order to assert herself

This outline has a number of flaws. First, the major topics labeled with the roman numerals are not arranged in a logical order. If the paper's aim is to show how Addie attempts to assert herself, the writer should establish how she does this. Second, the thesis makes no reference to blood, but the writer includes it as a major section of this outline. As the partner Addie uses to assert herself against God, Whitfield may well have a place in this paper, but the writer fails to provide details about his place in the argument. Blood, too, though it might be another entity she asserts herself against, does not logically merit its own section. The writer could, however, discuss blood in another section of the essay. Third, the writer includes "words" as one of the lettered items in section II. Letters A, B, and C all refer to specific people Addie attempts to assert herself against; words do not belong on this list. The writer could argue that words are representative of all that Addie feels powerless against (therefore, words are all, finally, that she is asserting herself against), but this is still not an example of the people in Addie's life. A fourth problem is the inclusion of a section A in sections IV and V. An outline should not include an A without a B, a 1 without a 2, and so forth. The final problem with this outline is the overall lack of detail. None of the sections provides much information about the content of the argument, and it seems likely that the writer has not given sufficient thought to the content of the paper.

A better start to this outline might be the following:

Thesis: *As I Lay Dying* is a novel that explores how Addie Bundren attempts to assert herself against the world: beating her students when she is a teacher, having an affair with the minister during her marriage, and choosing to be buried far away from her husband and family when she dies.

I. Introduction and thesis

II. Addie asserts herself against people
    A. Her students
    B. Her husband
    C. Her children

III. Addie asserts herself against God
    A. She has a hatred of "blood"
    B. She has a hatred of "words"
    C. She has an affair with Whitfield, the minister

IV. Addie asserts herself against death
    A. "living was to get ready to stay dead a long time" (169)

B. "I knew that living was terrible" (171)

    C. She insists that she be buried in Jefferson

  V. Conclusion

This new outline would prove much more helpful when it came time to write the paper.

An outline like this could be shaped into an even more useful tool if the writer fleshed out the argument by providing specific examples from the text to support each point. Once you have listed your main point and your supporting ideas, develop this raw material by listing related supporting ideas and material under each of those main headings. From there, arrange the material in subsections and order the material logically.

For example, you might begin with one of the theses cited above: In *The Sound and the Fury*, Quentin Compson wants to escape from time and the suffering of the world. Time, like suffering, however, proves inescapable, even by suicide. As noted above, this thesis already gives you the beginning of an organization: Start by supporting the notion that Quentin wants to escape time and that he equates time with suffering. You might begin your outline, then, with four topic headings: (1) objects such as his grandfather's watch, Harvard's bells, and the sun keep Quentin aware of time; (2) he attempts to destroy the watch and escape the other indicators of time; (3) Quentin equates his suffering with being in the world; (4) eluding time becomes his justification for taking his life. Under each of those headings, you could list ideas that support the particular points. Be sure to include references to parts of the text that help build your case.

An informal outline might look like this:

Thesis: In *The Sound and the Fury*, Quentin Compson wants to escape from time and the suffering of the world. Time, like suffering, however, proves inescapable, even by suicide.

  1. In his final day, Quentin attempts to escape any reminders of time

- The sun rises, and he attempts to ignore it
- He ignores the bells that would summon him to class
- The season has changed to spring
- He breaks his grandfather's watch
  - The watch: "I give it to you not that you may remember time, but that you might forget it now and then for a moment and not spend all your breath trying to conquer it." (76)
  - He breaks it, but it continues to work: "I could hear my watch ticking away in my pocket and after a while I had all other sounds shut away, leaving only the watch in my pocket." (83)
  - "Father said clocks slay time" (85)

2. Without time, there would be no suffering
- Quentin seems to think that he suffers because of time
  - He would like to be out of time with Caddy
  - That would do away with her pregnancy
  - Incest might be enough to remove them from the normal progression of time
- Quentin equates time to the suffering of the Cross
  - States that Jesus was crucified by time
  - States that the clock's hands, like the Cross, hold all the suffering of the world
- Time holds all the past
  - This includes the sufferings of the slaves
  - And the South's loss of the war

- The past keeps intruding on his present
    - His mother's monologue about Caddy's pregnancy and how she has suffered seems to be remembered word for word and comes to him in the middle of the day

3. Time is inescapable
   - Everywhere he goes, Quentin is reminded of time
       - The clock continues to chime no matter how far he travels out of its range
       - He is also marking the movement of the sun
   - As the day goes on, the shadows change with the sun's movement, but the shadow on Quentin is also his impending death

4. Suicide is not the answer
   - Quentin knows this even as he considers his own suicide
       - "any live man is better than any dead man"
       - His father has told him that death will not fix things
   - His desire to commit suicide is more to negate himself than to negate his suffering

Conclusion:
   - Faulkner shows that Quentin's mind, in its derangement, is focused on time
   - The novel implies that time is inescapable, but that too much attention to time is dangerous
   - The novel makes it clear that suicide is not the answer to Quentin's suffering

You would set about writing a formal outline with a similar process, though in the final stages you would label the headings differently. A formal outline for a paper that argues the thesis about *As I Lay Dying* cited above—that Addie asserts herself against the world in various ways, culminating with the request for burial in Jefferson—might look like this:

Thesis: *As I Lay Dying* is a novel that explores how Addie Bundren attempts to assert herself against the world: beating her students when she is a teacher, having an affair with the minister during her marriage, and choosing to be buried far away from her husband and family when she dies.

    I. Introduction and thesis

   II. Addie asserts herself against people
     A. Her students
       1. "I would go down the hill to the spring where I could be quiet and hate them." (169)
       2. "I would think with each blow of the switch: Now you are aware of me!" (170)
     B. Her husband
       1. "So I took Anse" (171). She makes the decision to marry
       2. He is not alive to her: "He did not know he was dead, then." (172)
     C. Her children
       1. She does not say she loves them
       2. She withholds her milk from them when she says it is time

  III. Addie asserts herself against God
     A. She has a hatred of "blood" and "words"
       1. Addie is very concerned about what "blood" and "words" mean

    a. "I had been used to words for
       a long time. I know that that
       word was like the others: just
       a shape to fill a lack." (172)
    b. "I believed that the reason was
       the duty to the alive, to the
       terrible blood, the red bitter
       flood boiling through the land."
       (174)
  2. Both "blood" and "words" have a
    symbolic importance to Christianity
B. She has an affair with Whitfield, the
  minister
  1. The sin fascinates her
    a. "I would think of sin as the
       clothes we wore in the world's
       face." (174)
    b. "He was the instrument ordained
       by God who created the sin."
       (174)
    c. She considers Whitfield "more
       beautiful since the garment
       which he had exchanged for sin
       was sanctified." (175)
  2. He abandons her
  3. She is left pregnant with Jewel, who
    is her favorite child

IV. Addie asserts herself against death
  A. "living was to get ready to stay dead a
    long time." (169)
    1. Addie's father gives her a fatalistic
      view of life
    2. She repeats this three times in the
      course of her monologue
  B. "I knew that living was terrible" (171)
    1. She describes life as a lack

        2. She tells Cora: "My daily life is an acknowledgement and expiation of my sin." (167)

    C. She insists that she be buried in Jefferson

        1. She becomes ready to die after she gives birth to Darl

        2. She decides that having Anse take her to Jefferson will be her "revenge" upon him

V. Conclusion

    A. To Addie Bundren, aggression is the only way to feel really alive

    B. In spite of her attempts to make herself known in life, she is most felt when she is dead

        1. She has a voice in the book only after she dies

        2. Her revenge does not seem complete, because she is easily replaced at the end of the journey

As in the previous example outline, the thesis provided the seeds of a structure, and the writer was careful to arrange the supporting points in a logical manner, showing the relationships among the ideas in the paper.

Body Paragraphs

Once your outline is complete, you can begin drafting your paper. Paragraphs, units of related sentences, are the building blocks of a good paper, and as you draft you should keep in mind both the function and the qualities of good paragraphs. Paragraphs help you chart and control the shape and content of your essay, and they help the reader see your organization and your logic. You should begin a new paragraph whenever you move from one major point to another. In longer, more complex essays you might use a group of related paragraphs to support major points. Remember that in addition to being adequately developed, a good paragraph is both unified and coherent.

Unified Paragraphs:

Each paragraph must be centered around one idea or point, and a unified paragraph carefully focuses on and develops this central idea without including extraneous ideas or tangents. For beginning writers, the best way to ensure that you are constructing unified paragraphs is to include a topic sentence in each paragraph. This topic sentence should convey the main point of the paragraph, and every sentence in the paragraph should relate to that topic sentence. Any sentence that strays from the central topic does not belong in the paragraph and needs to be revised or deleted. Consider the following paragraph about Joe Christmas's flight from justice in *Light in August*. Notice how the paragraph veers from the main point—that Christmas's journey ends in light, reflective of the novel's title:

> Christmas's end has been read as everything from a lynching to a scapegoating, to the fall of a mythic hero or a retelling of the Crucifixion. Most accurately, his flight moves through darkness and light, and his death situates him firmly in the light. The reader has wondered if Christmas is black or white. At his death, it no longer matters. Faulkner first called his novel *Dark House*, and the character he began the novel with was Hightower (Minter 7). Hightower is a man removed from life; he lives in the shadows. Later, Faulkner chose to begin the novel with Lena Grove. In doing so, he positioned the living before the dead, the light before the dark.

Although the paragraph begins solidly, and the second sentence provides the central idea of the paragraph, the author soon goes on a tangent. If the purpose of the paragraph is to demonstrate that Christmas is on a journey that has symbolic meaning, from darkness into light, the sentences about how Faulkner first conceived of his novel are tangential here. They may find a place later in the paper, but they should be deleted from this paragraph.

Coherent Paragraphs:

In addition to shaping unified paragraphs, you must also craft coherent paragraphs, paragraphs that develop their points logically with sentences that flow smoothly into one another. Coherence depends on the order of your sentences, but it is not strictly the order of the sentences that is important to paragraph coherence. You also need to craft your prose to help the reader see the relationship among the sentences.

Consider the following paragraph about the possibility of lightness and darkness and Joe Christmas. Notice how the writer uses the same ideas as the paragraph above yet fails to help the reader see the relationships among the points:

> Christmas's end has been read as everything from a lynching to a scapegoating, to the fall of a mythic hero or a retelling of the Crucifixion. When he runs from the law, he travels from the white part of town to the black part on the outskirts, ending up at Hightower's house. Most accurately, his flight moves through darkness and light, and his death situates him firmly in the light. The question of Christmas's exact racial identity is always with the reader. The reader has wondered if Christmas is black or white. At his death, it no longer matters. Faulkner first called his novel *Dark House*, and the character that he began the novel with was Hightower (Minter 7). Hightower is a man removed from life; he lives in the shadows. Later, Faulkner chose to begin the novel with Lena Grove. In doing so, he positioned the living before the dead, the light before the dark. This novel is the story of life triumphing over death. Christmas ultimately journeys into light.

This paragraph demonstrates that unity alone does not guarantee paragraph effectiveness. The argument is hard to follow because the author fails both to show connections between the sentences and to indicate how they work to support the overall point.

A number of techniques are available to aid paragraph coherence. Careful use of transitional words and phrases is essential. You can use transitional flags to introduce an example or an illustration (*for example, for instance),* to amplify a point or add another phase of the same idea *(additionally, furthermore, next, similarly, finally, then)*, to indicate a conclusion or result *(therefore, as a result, thus, in other words)*, to signal a contrast or a qualification *(on the other hand, nevertheless, despite this, on the contrary, still, however, conversely)*, to signal a comparison *(likewise, in comparison, similarly)*, and to indicate a movement in time *(afterward, earlier, eventually, finally, later, subsequently, until)*.

In addition to transitional flags, careful use of pronouns aids coherence and flow. If you were writing about *The Wizard of Oz*, you would not want to keep repeating the phrase *the witch* or the name *Dorothy*. Careful substitution of the pronoun *she* in these instances can aid coherence. A word of warning, though: When you substitute pronouns for proper names, always be sure that your pronoun reference is clear. In a paragraph that discusses both Dorothy and the witch, substituting *she* could lead to confusion. Make sure that it is clear to whom the pronoun refers. Generally, the pronoun refers to the last proper noun you have used.

While repeating the same name over and over again can lead to awkward, boring prose, it is possible to use repetition to help your paragraph's coherence. Careful repetition of important words or phrases can lend coherence to your paragraph by reminding readers of your key points. Admittedly, it takes some practice to use this technique effectively. You may find that reading your prose aloud can help you develop an ear for an effective use of repetition.

To see how helpful transitional aids are, compare the paragraph below to the preceding paragraph about Joe Christmas's fate in *Light in August*. Notice how the author works with the same ideas and quotations but shapes them into a much more coherent paragraph whose point is clearer and easier to follow.

> Joe Christmas's death in William Faulkner's *Light in August* has been read as everything from a lynching to a sacrificial act, to the fall of a mythic hero or a retelling of the Crucifixion. Understanding his death is dependent on understanding the days that precede it. The seven days Christmas spends on the run before he is killed are representative of all of his life. He says of it: "I have been further in these seven days than in all of thirty years. . . . But I have never gotten

outside that circle. I have never broken out of the
ring of what I have already done and cannot ever undo"
(339). When he runs from the law, he travels from the
white part of town to the black part on the outskirts,
ending up at Hightower's house. He feels death creeping
upon him like darkness, and he experiences blackness
as a negative element. But his flight takes him through
darkness and light, while his death situates him firmly
in the light. At his death, the question of whether he
is black or white no longer matters. The novel insists
on his humanity, though his death is described in terms
of an apotheosis.

Similarly, the following paragraph from a paper on Addie Bundren's
need to assert herself in *As I Lay Dying* demonstrates both unity and
coherence. In it, the author argues that all of Addie's relationships are
marked by her aggressive need to prove herself.

Addie Bundren is in many ways powerless. She is without
family, so she becomes a teacher. But she regards her
students with hatred. She says that at the end of each
day she "would go down the hill to the spring where
[she] could be quiet and hate them" (169). She also
describes the pleasure she would get from beating them,
how she "would think with each blow of the switch: Now
you are aware of me!" (170). But where does this hatred
come from? She speaks of her blood and their blood
as separate and strange, but mingling when she whips
them, as if a connection has been forged between them.
It is possible that what Addie feels is a desire to
make a connection, even if the connection is rooted in
hatred or revenge. Teaching does not give her what she
desires, so she decides to marry. Addie says, "So I took
Anse" (171). It is clear from the language she uses that
the marriage was made by her, but also implicit in the
language is the sexual and aggressive connotation of the
word *took*. There might also be a sense of resignation,

because the marriage to Anse does not provide her with
the connection she seeks either. She thinks to kill
him, but then decides it is not his fault and that he
is not truly even alive: "He did not know he was dead,
then" (173). This feeling comes to her after her second
pregnancy. By then, she realizes that even motherhood
does not touch her. She feels that motherhood is only
a word, like love, and she does not tell her children
that she loves them (172). She gives them her body only
to the extent she feels it is her duty, refusing them
her milk when she says it is time.

Introductions

Introductions present particular challenges for writers. Generally, your introduction should do two things: capture your reader's attention and explain the main point of your essay. In other words, while your introduction should contain your thesis, it needs to do a bit more work than that. You are likely to find that starting that first paragraph is one of the most difficult parts of the paper. It is hard to face that blank page or screen, and as a result, many beginning writers, in desperation to start somewhere, start with overly broad, general statements. While it is often a good strategy to start with more general subject matter and narrow your focus, do not begin with broad sweeping statements such as Everyone likes to be creative and feel understood. Such sentences are nothing but empty filler. They begin to fill the blank page, but they do nothing to advance your argument. Instead, you should try to gain your readers' interest. Some writers like to begin with a pertinent quotation or with a relevant question. Or, you might begin with an introduction of the topic you will discuss. If you are writing about the way Addie attempts to assert herself in *As I Lay Dying,* for instance, you might begin by talking about how women are often portrayed as unassertive. Another common trap to avoid is depending on your title to introduce the author and the text you are writing about. Always include the work's author and title in your opening paragraph.

Compare the effectiveness of the following introductions:

1. Women are generally thought to be the gentler sex.
   Throughout history they are portrayed as soft and
   kind. Even today, there is something funny about

the woman who does not have a nurturing side. But when Faulkner created Addie Bundren, he showed that a woman could assert herself as well as a man. She asserts herself against her students, in her marriage, and in her death.

2. Some of the more memorable characters in literature are not altogether likable. Addie Bundren, of William Faulkner's *As I Lay Dying,* is such a character. In a novel entirely about transporting her corpse to her gravesite, Addie's voice is heard only in one small section. By the time she speaks, she has been dead for several days. Addie is not the stereotypical woman who is charmed by children or finds satisfaction in marriage and motherhood. Addie is of a time and circumstance that renders her relatively powerless (a woman alone and without means in rural Mississippi at the start of the 20th century), but she attempts, over and over again, to assert herself against her circumstances. She asserts herself against her students, in her marriage, and in her death. The ways she does this, however, reveal the unusual nature of this character and this novel, for Addie beats her students when she is a teacher, has an affair with the minister during her marriage, and chooses to be buried far away from her husband and family when she dies.

The first introduction begins with a vague, overly broad sentence; cites unclear, undeveloped examples; and then moves abruptly to the thesis. Notice, too, how a reader deprived of the paper's title does not know the title of the story that the paper will analyze. The second introduction works with the same material and thesis but provides more detail and is consequently much more interesting. It begins by discussing stereotypical conceptions of women, asserts that women who defy these stereotypes may not be perceived as likable, and gives specific examples of how Addie Bundren does not fit this conception. Notice, too, that the author and title of the work are given early in the paragraph.

The paragraph below provides another example of an opening strategy. It begins by introducing the author and the text it will analyze, and then it moves on by briefly introducing relevant details of the story in order to set up its thesis.

> In William Faulkner's novel *The Sound and the Fury,*
> Quentin Compson wants to escape from time and the
> suffering of the world. *The Sound and the Fury* is told
> in four parts, and each part has a different narrator.
> But the second section, belonging to Quentin Compson,
> is the most poignant, because the reader knows that he
> will soon take his own life. This section, titled "June
> Second, 1910," allows the reader access to Quentin's
> thoughts on what will be the last day of his life.
> The section begins with the sun's rise and Quentin's
> attempts to ignore it. He ignores the bells that would
> summon him to class and the reminders that the season
> has turned to spring. Finally, he tries to break his
> grandfather's watch. When his father gave the watch to
> him, he told Quentin: "I give it to you not that you
> may remember time, but that you might forget it now and
> then for a moment and not spend all your breath trying
> to conquer it" (76). But the watch has not allowed
> Quentin to forget time. Although Quentin shatters the
> glass, the watch continues to keep time. Throughout
> Quentin's final day, he finds that time is always with
> him. Time, like suffering, proves inescapable, even by
> suicide.

Conclusions

Conclusions present another series of challenges for writers. No doubt you have heard the old adage about writing papers: "Tell us what you are going to say, say it, and then tell us what you've said." While this formula does not necessarily result in bad papers, it does not often result in good ones either. It will almost certainly result in boring papers (especially boring conclusions). If you have done a good job establishing your points in the body of the paper, the reader already knows and understands your argument. There is no need to merely reiterate. Do not just summarize your main points in your conclusion. Such a boring and mechanical conclusion does nothing to advance your argument or interest your reader. Consider the following conclusion to the paper about time and Quentin Compson in *The Sound and the Fury.*

```
In conclusion, Faulkner shows that time is a fact of
life. Quentin attempts to escape time. He goes so far
as to kill himself, but time goes on without him. We
must all remember that suicide is never the answer to
our troubles.
```

Besides starting with a mechanical transitional device, this conclusion does little more than summarize the main points of the outline (and it does not even touch on all of them). It is incomplete and uninteresting (and a little too depressing).

Instead, your conclusion should add something to your paper. A good tactic is to build upon the points you have been arguing. Asking "why?" often helps you draw further conclusions. For example, in the paper on *The Sound and the Fury,* you might speculate about or explain how Quentin's desire is a perverse one, because Faulkner shows the reader that time has to be accepted and not fought. The movement of time is a function of the natural world and must be accepted, as suffering must, as a part of life. Scholars often discuss Quentin's obsessive nature, and your conclusion could discuss whether his focus on time is reflective or an extension of his personal obsessions, including his uneasy relationship with his sister, Caddy, his family history, and the South. Another method for successfully concluding a paper is to speculate on other directions in which to take your topic by tying it into larger issues. You might do this by envisioning your paper as just one section of a larger paper. Having established your points in this paper, how would you build on this argument? Where would you go next? In the following conclusion to the paper on Quentin in *The Sound and the Fury,* the author reiterates some of the main points of the paper but does so in order to amplify the discussion of the novel's central message and to connect it to other texts by William Faulkner:

In Quentin Compson's final day, the reader learns how futile his attempts to escape time are. Even in his final moments, Quentin returns to the mundane and quotidian aspects of living: brushing his teeth, cleaning his hat. The sun rises and sets on June Second, 1910, just as it will on the next day. That the very next chapter is set eighteen years into the future shows the reader how true this is. One of Faulkner's recurring themes is the passage of time and time's effects. Quentin Compson wrestles with time again in *Absalom, Absalom!* and it is difficult to find a work by Faulkner that does not somehow address time. Time is an important aspect of Faulkner's short stories and also his major novels: *Light in August*; *Go Down, Moses*; and *As I Lay Dying*; in addition to the two discussed above. In every case, the fact of time's passing must be accepted; because nothing stops it, not even death.

Similarly, in the following conclusion to a paper on the death of Joe Christmas in *Light in August,* the author draws a conclusion about what the novel is saying about death more broadly.

This is the end of the journey Christmas began even before his birth. Faulkner writes that Christmas's story "had already been written and worded" (448), even before the birth of his mother. He embodies the type Faulkner spoke of in *The Ink of Melancholy*, an example of "man's free will . . . against a Greek background of fate, . . . the free will to choose and the courage, the fortitude to die for his choice" (Bleikasten 38). In the final moments of Christmas's life, he is not identified as an African American or a murderer, not even as Christmas, but simply as a man. Christmas is not necessarily an admirable character; he killed Joanna Burden. But in his death he illustrates the immortality that Faulkner said could be gained when a man is "faced with a tragedy he can't beat and he still tries to do something about it" (Meriwether 89).

Citations and Formatting

Using Primary Sources:

As the examples included in this chapter indicate, strong papers on literary texts incorporate quotations from the text in order to support their points. It is not enough for you to assert your interpretation without providing support or evidence from the text. Without well-chosen quotations to support your argument you are, in effect, saying to the reader, "Take my word for it." It is important to use quotations thoughtfully and selectively. Remember that the paper presents *your* argument, so choose quotations that support *your* assertions. Do not let the author's voice overwhelm your own. With that caution in mind, there are some guidelines you should follow to ensure that you use quotations clearly and effectively.

Integrate Quotations:

Quotations should always be integrated into your own prose. Do not just drop them into your paper without introduction or comment. Otherwise, it is unlikely that your reader will see their function. You can integrate textual support easily and clearly with identifying tags, short phrases that identify the speaker. For example:

```
Cora says Addie's "eyes are like two candles when you
watch them gutter down into the sockets or iron candle-
sticks."
```

While this tag appears before the quotation, you can also use tags after or in the middle of the quoted text, as the following examples demonstrate:

```
"My mother is a fish," thought Vardaman.
```

```
"Living," Addie's father told her, "was to get ready to
stay dead a long time."
```

You can also use a colon to formally introduce a quotation:

```
Lena Grove thought to herself: "I have come from Alabama:
a fur piece. All the way from Alabama a-walking. A fur
piece."
```

When you quote brief sections of poems (three lines or fewer), use slash marks to indicate the line breaks in the poem:

> As the poem ends, Dickinson speaks of the power of the imagination: "The revery alone will do, / If bees are few."

Longer quotations (more than four lines of prose or three lines of poetry) should be set off from the rest of your paper in a block quotation. Double-space before you begin the passage, indent it 10 spaces from your left-hand margin, and double-space the passage itself. Because the indentation signals the inclusion of a quotation, do not use quotation marks around the cited passage. Use a colon to introduce the passage:

> Addie experiences her marriage and motherhood as so many meaningless words:
>
> > When I knew I had Cash, I knew that living was terrible and that this was the answer to it. That was when I learned that words are no good; that words don't ever fit even what they are trying to say at. When he was born I knew that motherhood was invented by someone who had to have a word for it because the ones that had the children didn't care whether there was a word for it or not.
>
> Addie feels that no word describes what she experiences, and no experience penetrates what she calls her "aloneness."

> The whole of Dickinson's poem speaks of the imagination:
>
> > To make a prairie it takes a clover and one bee,
> > One clover, and a bee,
> > And revery.
> > The revery alone will do,
> > If bees are few.

```
Clearly, she argues for the creative power of the mind.
```

It is also important to interpret quotations after you introduce them and explain how they help advance your point. You cannot assume that your reader will interpret the quotations the same way that you do.

Quote Accurately:

Always quote accurately. Anything within quotations marks must be the author's exact words. There are, however, some rules to follow if you need to modify the quotation to fit into your prose.

1. Use brackets to indicate any material that might have been added to the author's exact wording. For example, if you need to add any words to the quotation or alter it grammatically to allow it to fit into your prose, indicate your changes in brackets:

   ```
   Quentin thinks of "the instant when [he came]
   to realise that tragedy [was] second-hand."
   ```

2. Conversely, if you choose to omit any words from the quotation, use ellipses (three spaced periods) to indicate missing words or phrases:

   ```
   Christmas reflects that his life has been a
   circle he cannot escape from, thinking, "in
   all of thirty years . . . I have never gotten
   outside that circle. I have never broken out of
   the ring of what I have already done and cannot
   ever undo."
   ```

3. If you delete a sentence or more, use the ellipses after a period:

   ```
   Quentin looks about him when he leaves the jewelers,
   "shutting the door upon the ticking. . . . There
   were about a dozen watches in the window, a
   dozen different hours and each with the same
   assertive and contradictory assurance that mine
   had, without any hands at all."
   ```

4. If you omit a line or more of poetry, or more than one paragraph of prose, use a single line of spaced periods to indicate the omission:

```
To make a prairie it takes a clover and one bee,
.   .   .   .   .   .   .   .   .   .   .   .   .   .
And revery.
The revery alone will do,
If bees are few.
```

Punctuate Properly:

Punctuation of quotations often causes more trouble than it should. Once again, you just need to keep these simple rules in mind.

1. Periods and commas should be placed inside quotation marks, even if they are not part of the original quotation:

```
Quentin says to the little girl, "Come on,
Sister."
```

The only exception to this rule is when the quotation is followed by a parenthetical reference. In this case, the period or comma goes after the citation (more on these later in this chapter):

```
Quentin says to the little girl, "Come on,
Sister" (131).
```

2. Other marks of punctuation—colons, semicolons, question marks, and exclamation points—go outside the quotation marks unless they are part of the original quotation:

```
Why does Quentin keep thinking about "the good
Saint Francis that said Little Sister Death,
that never had a sister"?
```

```
Quentin asks the girl: "Which way do you
live?"
```

Documenting Primary Sources:

Unless you are instructed otherwise, you should provide sufficient information for your reader to locate material you quote. Generally, literature papers follow the rules set forth by the Modern Language Association (MLA). These can be found in the *MLA Handbook for Writers of Research Papers* (sixth edition). You should be able to find this book in the reference section of your library. Additionally, its rules for citing both primary and secondary sources are widely available from reputable online sources. One of these is the Online Writing Lab (OWL) at Purdue University. OWL's guide to MLA style is available at http://owl.english.purdue.edu/owl/resource/557/01/. The Modern Language Association also offers answers to frequently asked questions about MLA style on this helpful Web page: http://www.mla.org/style_faq. Generally, when you are citing from literary works in papers, you should keep a few guidelines in mind.

Parenthetical Citations:

MLA asks for parenthetical references in your text after quotations. When you are working with prose (short stories, novels, or essays), include page numbers in the parentheses:

```
Joe says to himself: "Something is going to happen to
me" (118).
```

When you are quoting poetry, include line numbers:

```
Dickinson's speaker tells of the arrival of a fly: "There
interposed a Fly— / With Blue—uncertain stumbling Buzz—
/ Between the light—and Me—" (12-14).
```

Works Cited Page:

These parenthetical citations are linked to a separate works cited page at the end of the paper. The works cited page lists works alphabetically by the authors' last names. An entry for the above reference to Faulkner's *Light in August* would read:

```
Faulkner, William. Light in August. New York: Vintage,
1990.
```

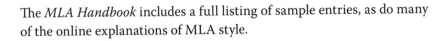

The *MLA Handbook* includes a full listing of sample entries, as do many of the online explanations of MLA style.

Documenting Secondary Sources:

To ensure that your paper is built entirely upon your own ideas and analysis, instructors often ask that you write interpretative papers without any outside research. If, on the other hand, your paper requires research, you must document any secondary sources you use. You need to document direct quotations, summaries, or paraphrases of others' ideas and factual information that is not common knowledge. Follow the guidelines above for quoting primary sources when you use direct quotations from secondary sources. Keep in mind that MLA style also includes specific guidelines for citing electronic sources. OWL's Web site provides a good summary: http://owl.english.purdue.edu/owl/resource/557/09/.

Parenthetical Citations:

As with the documentation of primary sources, described above, MLA guidelines require in-text parenthetical references to your secondary sources. Unlike the research papers you might write for a history class, literary research papers following MLA style do not use footnotes as a means of documenting sources. Instead, after a quotation, you should cite the author's last name and the page number:

```
"Quentin is really, as his sister knows, in love with
death itself" (Brooks 327).
```

If you include the name of the author in your prose, then you would include only the page number in your citation. For example:

```
Cleanth Brooks asserts, "Quentin is really, as his
sister knows, in love with death itself" (327).
```

If you are including more than one work by the same author, the parenthetical citation should include a shortened yet identifiable version of the title in order to indicate which of the author's works you cite. For example:

Michael Millgate writes, "Quentin is in some measure
a version of the artist, or at least the aesthete, as
hero" (*Achievement* 105).

Similarly, and just as important, if you summarize or paraphrase the
particular ideas of your source, you must provide documentation:

Christmas is a divided character, uncertain about
whether he is black or white, uncertain whether he
should live or die (Millgate, *New* 11).

Works Cited Page:

Like the primary sources discussed above, the parenthetical references
to secondary sources are keyed to a separate works cited page at the end
of your paper. Here is an example of a works cited page that uses the
examples cited above. Note that when two or more works by the same
author are listed, you should use three hyphens followed by a period in
the subsequent entries. You can find a complete list of sample entries in
the *MLA Handbook* or from a reputable online summary of MLA style.

WORKS CITED

Brooks, Cleanth. *William Faulkner: The Yoknapatawpha
    Country.* New Haven, CT: Yale UP, 1963.
Millgate, Michael, ed. *New Essays on Light in August.*
    New York: Cambridge University Press, 1987.
———. *The Achievement of William Faulkner.* New York:
    Random House, 1966.

Plagiarism:

Failure to document carefully and thoroughly can leave you open to
charges of stealing the ideas of others, which is known as plagiarism, and
this is a very serious matter. Remember that it is important to include
quotation marks when you use language from your source, even if you
use just one or two words. For example, if you wrote, Quentin is, as
his sister knows, in love with death itself, you would be
guilty of plagiarism, since you used Brooks's distinct language without
acknowledging him as the source. Instead, you should write: Quentin

does not love Caddy so much as he loves the idea of dying (Brooks 327). In this case, you have properly credited Brooks.

Similarly, neither summarizing the ideas of an author nor changing or omitting just a few words means that you can omit a citation. John T. Irwin's *Doubling and Incest/Repetition and Revenge* contains this discussion of the character of Quentin Compson:

> From *The Sound and the Fury* we know that Quentin is in love with his own sister Candace and that he is tormented by his inability to play the role of the avenging brother and kill her seducer. Of the many levels of meaning in *Absalom*, the deepest level is to be found in the symbolic identification of incest and miscegenation and in the relationship of this symbolic identification both to Quentin Compson's personal history in *The Sound and the Fury* and to the story that Quentin narrates in *Absalom, Absalom!*

Below are two examples of plagiarized passages:

> When Quentin Compson narrates the story of Judith and Bon, it relates directly to his own life as told in *The Sound and the Fury.* He sees in Henry the brother he could not be, because Henry kills his sister's lover. And he sees himself in Bon, too, because he is also in love with his sister.

> *The Sound and the Fury* shows us that Quentin is in love with Caddy and was unable to stand up for her as a brother should. *Absalom* in its deepest sense is about the taboos of incest and miscegenation and the way the life of Quentin in *The Sound and the Fury* resembles the story Quentin narrates in *Absalom, Absalom!* (Irwin 25–26).

While the first passage does not use Irwin's exact language, it does list the same ideas he proposes as critical to both novels without citing his work. Since this interpretation is Irwin's distinct idea, this constitutes plagiarism. The second passage has shortened his passage, changed some wording, and included a citation, but some of the phrasing is Irwin's. The first passage could be fixed with a parenthetical citation. Because some of the wording in the second remains the same, though, it would require the use of quotation marks, in addition to a parenthetical citation. The passage below represents an honestly and adequately documented use of the original passage:

> According to John T. Irwin, the key to understanding *Absalom, Absalom!* is in understanding Quentin Compson's character in *The Sound and the Fury*, for he, like Bon, is "*in love with his own sister*" (25). Irwin asserts that the greatest meaning in *Absalom, Absalom!* can be found in the "*symbolic identification* of incest and miscegenation and in the relationship of this symbolic identification . . . to Quentin Compson's personal history" (25).

This passage acknowledges that the interpretation is derived from Irwin while appropriately using quotations to indicate his precise language.

While it is not necessary to document well-known facts, often referred to as "common knowledge," any ideas or language that you take from someone else must be properly documented. Common knowledge generally includes the birth and death dates of authors or other well-documented facts of their lives. An often-cited guideline is that if you can find the information in three sources, it is common knowledge. Despite this guideline, it is, admittedly, often difficult to know if the facts you uncover are common knowledge or not. When in doubt, document your source.

Sample Essay

Alexander Kronick
Ms. Hadley
English 2008
December 10, 2009

THE JOURNEY TO THE LIGHT:
JOE CHRISTMAS IN *LIGHT IN AUGUST*

Joe Christmas's death in William Faulkner's *Light in August* has been read as everything from a lynching to a scapegoating, to the fall of a mythic hero or a retelling of the Crucifixion. Understanding his death is dependent on understanding the days that precede it. The seven days Christmas spends on the run before he is killed are representative of all his life. He says of it: "I have been further in these seven days than in all of thirty years. . . . But I have never gotten outside that circle. I have never broken out of the ring of what I have already done and cannot ever undo" (339). When he runs from the law, he travels from the white part of town to the black part on the outskirts, ending up at Hightower's house. He feels death creeping upon him like darkness, and he experiences blackness as a negative element. But while his flight takes him through darkness and light, his death situates him firmly in the light. At his death, the question of whether he is black or white no longer matters. The novel insists on his humanity, though his death is described in terms of an apotheosis.

Many critics see the title of *Light in August* as referring to Lena Grove. "To go light" is a phrase used by farmers when an animal foals, and Lena, who seems to maintain an aura of goodness about her in spite of her advanced pregnancy and unwed state, will bear her child in August. But death is also often described as going into "the light." The two central characters in *Light in August*, Joe Christmas and Lena Grove, begin their journeys to Jefferson with a climb through a window, which is another image of the passage through.

Deborah Clarke in *Robbing the Mother: Women in Faulkner* asks us to consider the trope of the journey and Lena's famous line: "A body does get around" (507) and what these might mean if applied to Joe Christmas. As Christmas travels through Jefferson, he is described in terms of "light." Faulkner writes, "He felt quite light" (333), and he moved "lightly" (333). But on his final day Christmas feels the "definite and ineradicable . . . black tide creeping up his legs moving from his feet upward as death moves" (339). The two opposites, light and dark, life and death, are still not reconciled in Christmas.

The first sign of Christmas after he kills Joanna Burden comes when a black man reports to the sheriff that the service at a black church was intruded on by a white man who took to the pulpit to curse God. Later, when men are searching for him with dogs, Christmas throws them off his trail by exchanging his shoes with a black woman. Christmas thinks: "It seemed to him that he could see himself being hunted by white men at last into the black abyss which had been waiting, trying, for thirty years to drown him" (331). As he continues to run, he finds that "time, the spaces of light and dark, [have] long since lost orderliness" (333).

Christmas is told as a child that his tragedy is that "he will never know" (384). Christmas will never learn if he did in fact have "black blood," and the novel provides no answer. When Christmas is castrated, and "the pent black blood" rushes out, this is not an indicator of race, because blood is described as black throughout *Light in August*. The description of his death is terrible, and it contains references to both the light and the dark:

> The man on the floor had not moved. He just lay there, with his eyes open and empty of everything save consciousness, and with something, a shadow, about his mouth. For a long moment he looked up at them with peaceful and unfathomable and unbearable eyes. Then his face, body, all, seemed to collapse, to fall in upon itself, and from out the slashed garments about his hips and loins the pent black blood seemed to rush like a released breath. It seemed to rush out of his pale body like the rush of sparks from a rising rocket; upon that black blast the man seemed to rise soaring into their memories forever and ever. (464–465)

Christmas travels into the memory of the town of Jefferson and the memories of those who read his story. His journey is not a straight line, ending with the knowledge of his race. It is a circle, and within the circle are both a "pale body" and the "black blood" (465), and both are less important than the man. Finally, Christmas at his death is described as "serene" and "triumphant" (465).

This is the end of the journey Christmas began even before his birth. Faulkner writes that Christmas's story "had already been written and worded" (448), even before the birth of his mother. He embodies the type Faulkner spoke of in *The Ink of Melancholy*, an example of "man's free will . . . against a Greek background of fate, . . . the free will to choose and the courage, the fortitude to die for his choice" (Bleikasten 38). In the final moments of Christmas's life, he is not identified as an African American or a murderer, not even as Christmas, but simply as a man. Christmas is not necessarily an admirable character; he killed Joanna Burden. But in his death he illustrates the immortality that Faulkner said could be gained when a man is "faced with a tragedy he can't beat and he still tries to do something about it" (Meriwether 89).

WORKS CITED

Bleikasten, Andre. *The Ink of Melancholy*. Bloomington: Indiana UP, 1990.

Clarke, Deborah. *Robbing the Mother: Women in Faulkner*. Jackson: UP of Mississippi, 1994.

Faulkner, William. *Light in August*. New York: Vintage International, 1990.

Meriwether, James B., and Michael Millgate, eds. *Lion in the Garden: Interviews with William Faulkner: 1926–1962*. Lincoln: U of Nebraska P, 1968.

HOW TO WRITE
ABOUT FAULKNER

WILLIAM FAULKNER was born on September 25, 1897, in New Albany, Mississippi. His family had once been prominent, and although their name continued to evoke that past, money was an issue for Faulkner all his life. His great-grandfather was William Clark Falkner. (It is not clear why the additional *u* was added to William Faulkner's name. Some stories have it that it was a typesetter's mistake that Faulkner chose to perpetuate. Another theory is that Faulkner himself added the extra letter. He was very interested in self-invention.) William Clark Falkner had served as a colonel in the Confederate Army, and some of his exploits and accomplishments are brought to life in Faulkner's creation of Colonel John Sartoris.

Faulkner did not show exceptional promise as a young person. He took classes at the University of Mississippi but never graduated. He worked for a while as a bank clerk. He wanted to fight in World War I, and although he was accepted into the Canadian Air Force, he never saw active duty. After various failed attempts at small jobs, one as a clerk in a bookstore in New York City and one as the postmaster at the University of Mississippi, Faulkner began to publish some of his poems and short stories. At that time, he wanted to be a poet.

During a trip to New Orleans, he fell in with the novelist Sherwood Anderson, who encouraged him in many ways, but particularly in his fiction and the idea of writing about the world that he knew. Faulkner also needed the money that a successful novel might bring. His first novel, *Soldier's Pay,* was published in 1926. *Mosquitoes* (1927), his second, came shortly after. With the publication of *Flags in the Dust* in 1929, which was published in an earlier, shorter version as *Sartoris,* Faulkner settled his literary world firmly in Jefferson, his fictionalized version of Oxford, Mississippi, where his family moved to when he was three.

By the time he published *The Sound and the Fury* (also in 1929), he had gained a strong grip on the public's imagination. His works were popular; he achieved critical acclaim as he seemed to have hit on a subject matter that was inexhaustible, the Oxford of his youth. Following *The Sound and the Fury* in quick succession were *As I Lay Dying* (1930), *Light in August* (1932), *Absalom, Absalom!* (1936), *The Wild Palms*, titled *If I Forget Thee, Jerusalem* without the inclusion of the story "Old Man" (1938), *The Hamlet* (1940), *Go Down, Moses* (1942), *Intruder in the Dust* (1948), *Requiem for a Nun* (1951), *A Fable* (1954), *The Town* (1957), *The Mansion* (1959), and *The Reivers* (1962).

He wrote short stories, he claimed, to supplement his income. Some of these were incorporated into his novels, while others, such as "A Rose for Emily," stand decidedly well on their own and do no disservice to their author's canon. For a time, Faulkner tried his hand at screenwriting in Hollywood, also in hopes of making money.

In 1949, Faulkner was awarded the Nobel Prize in literature. He died on July 6, 1962.

TOPICS AND STRATEGIES
Themes

One pleasure in reading Faulkner is that he returns to and enlarges on many of the same themes throughout his work. There are issues and ideas that he explored in his writing almost obsessively. Most of them are particularly southern. Slavery is one of the author's major preoccupations. You can find in Faulkner's work accounts of slavery before it was systematic in the country and accounts of the effects of slavery long after it had been abolished. Many of his characters labor under the stigma of slavery, giving rise to the idea that the institution is a curse to all people and perhaps to the entire nation as well.

Faulkner was a keen observer of the life and times immediately surrounding him, so that Mississippi emerges as another of his key subjects. Faulkner explores his landscape exhaustively. If one were to read all of Faulkner, one would know Yoknapatawpha (his fictionalized surrogate for his hometown of Oxford). Reading Faulkner you learn of the people, the land, its history, its society, and its economics. The characters, situations, and places in one Faulkner story may appear in another. There is a consistency among his works. The ponies from "Spotted Horses," for instance, are mentioned in several of his works, and one plays a significant role in *As I Lay Dying.*

Faulkner did not shy away from depicting the racism that existed in Mississippi. Readers have to remember that there is a difference between the depiction of racism and the author's views. Although some of Faulkner's characters are racists, they are not direct representatives of the author or directly expressing his views. Miscegenation, the sexual union of individuals from different races, is an important theme in Faulkner. Relationships that crossed color lines helped to blur those often rigid divisions. In *Absalom, Absalom!* the effects of miscegenation prove disastrous to the Sutpens. In *Go Down, Moses,* the existence of the "shadow family" of McCaslins is a source of shame to Isaac McCaslin, but the shadow family is also the future of that family.

Go Down, Moses illustrates another major theme of Faulkner's—the importance of the land. Isaac McCaslin denies his inheritance, in part because he believes that land cannot be owned. As in many other works by Faulkner, the author elevates if not romanticizes still wild and relatively untouched stretches of countryside. There is also a keen awareness that this land will not remain untouched. The wilderness of *Go Down, Moses* is sold off piece by piece. In *The Sound and the Fury,* Benjy's pasture becomes a golf course. In each case, there is the sense that this is a tremendous if not inevitable loss.

You might also notice such overarching themes as violence and its effects, the nature of love, the tragedy of death, or what happens to an individual in isolation from his community, among others. The themes listed below represent only a small sampling of the ideas and concerns that can be found in Faulkner's works.

Sample Topics:

1. **Racism:** How does Faulkner's work address racism in the American South?

   The work or works you choose to discuss will govern how you answer this question. For instance, if you were to concentrate on *Light in August*, you might find yourself talking about the violence that deep-seated racism engendered. You might talk about how some of Faulkner's characters are unabashedly racist, and this gives the reader insight into views perhaps never encountered before.

2. **Slavery:** What seems to be Faulkner's view of slavery?

Novels such as *Go Down, Moses* or *Light in August* concentrate more on the aftermath of slavery than the years before the war. What may seem curious to some readers at first is how the system of slavery persisted after the war, with so many slaves choosing in many cases to stay on with their former owners as servants. In many of his works, Faulkner's characters return to the idea that slavery is a stain on the South, a wrong so deeply felt that it would take years to try to expiate it.

3. **Miscegenation:** What does Faulkner's work reveal about miscegenation?

Absalom, Absalom! and *Go Down, Moses* are two of Faulkner's novels that confront the miscegenation that was a part of the system of slavery. *Light in August* also shows how miscegenation was condemned by whites and blacks both. For many, the idea of "shadow families" will perhaps be new or will be related by students to the life of Thomas Jefferson. Faulkner shows how widespread such interracial relationships were and how they were both condemned and accepted.

4. **Land:** What attitudes about land are expressed in Faulkner's work?

Faulkner's work shows a deep respect for the land, specifically the untouched wilderness, but also for the farmland that could feed a family. *Go Down, Moses* and the short story "The Bear" are illustrative of this. *As I Lay Dying* not only shows a family at odds with one another but also with the landscape they move through.

Character

Writing about character in Faulkner could be a relatively easy job since he created many memorable presences. If you decide to write an essay on a particular character, you might carefully analyze him or her. Why does he behave as he does? Is she likable? Is he a character of words or actions? How does she affect those around her? Such an essay needs to show its audience how the writer arrived at his or her opinions by quoting passages that are significant to an understanding of the character. Below are four broad categories of characters that might spur your thinking on the subject of Faulkner's fictive creations.

Just as you may at times hear Faulkner's work characterized as racist, you might also hear that it is misogynistic. He does have a habit of calling certain women "bovine"—the pregnant Lena Grove, Sarty Snopes's sisters, Eula Varner. But there is also a full assortment of strong women; perhaps "hard-headed" is another way to describe them. Emily Grierson of "A Rose for Emily" is a murderess, but also a lady; and there is no woman in literature quite like the dead Addie Bundren of *As I Lay Dying.*

Most literary works have a protagonist, often an admirable character that the reader can somehow root for. But when you consider Faulkner's work, it seems notably devoid of what you might otherwise term "heroes." For the work or works you are thinking about discussing, identify who the protagonist is and if that individual is someone you could admire.

Some of Faulkner's most heroic characters are the patriarchs of the great families of Yoknapatawpha. Colonel Sartoris, General Compson, and Thomas Sutpen, to name a few, are men of unusual strength and bearing. They are larger than life and accomplish much, not the least of which is establishing their names in history and legend. Yet, they are not heroes in the traditional ways we are used to thinking about that honorific. In spite of their legacies, they are deeply flawed people.

Mothers are also given special regard by Faulkner. Women who do not bear children, like Joanna Burden, are incomplete. Those who do bear children often fall into two categories. Young mothers are portrayed as fecund and fertile, animalistic in their ability to reproduce. Older mothers are often neurasthenic, bedridden, and weak.

Sample Topics:

1. **Women:** How would you characterize the women in Faulkner's work?

   Examine one woman or several in the works you are reading. Does it seem on the whole that the women are portrayed in different terms than the men? What particular characteristics do the women seem to have? Are they portrayed fairly?

2. **Heroes:** What constitutes a Faulknerian hero?

   Is there such a thing? Who is the hero of the story or novel you are reading? Is he or she a conventional hero? Is the character noble or strong or admirable? Is the character realistic?

3. **Patriarchs:** Examine one of Faulkner's patriarchs, looking at both his positive and negative qualities.

   The incredibly powerful men of Faulkner's creation are driven by many things, but they all seem to want to leave behind their names and their progeny. What are some of their other motives? Do they strike you as good people? What are their flaws?

4. **Mothers:** How does Faulkner portray motherhood?

   Faulkner's mothers are an unconventional lot. You might find that the real work of mothering falls to someone else: a slave or a servant, or, in the case of the Compson family, a sister. In *As I Lay Dying*, two mothers occupy the novel's central focus. One is dead and loved, truly, by only one of her five children. One is pregnant and desperately seeks an abortion. Examine a mother or mothers in the works you are writing on. You might also give consideration to the vast number of women who have very little place in Faulkner's stories, because they perished in childbirth.

History and Context

As a young man, Faulkner thought of himself as a poet. His early attempts at fiction focused on war and the experience of soldiers returning from war. When he created Yoknapatawpha County, a fictionalization of his own Lafayette County, Mississippi, he found a setting that was inexhaustible for him in his lifetime. The city of Oxford becomes Jefferson in Faulkner's work. He peoples this landscape with the subjects of his writing, creating an imaginary rendering of his home that is more alive to most readers of Faulkner than Oxford is.

In some ways, Faulkner's setting is his subject, since so many of his works address life in the South after the Civil War. The North rarely intrudes. When a northerner moves to or visits the South, as Homer Barron does in "A Rose for Emily," trouble ensues. When a southerner moves North, as when Quentin Compson goes to Harvard University, the results are equally negative.

In *Absalom, Absalom!* the Civil War is an integral event in the lives of the novel's characters. Even when the war is not in the foreground, though, it is important. Faulkner was fascinated with military history as it affected his own family, and he was also fascinated by the two world wars of the early 20th century. One of Faulkner's chief subjects is how the Civil War changed the South. Not only the people of the South were changed, but everything: the economy, the society, the landscape, and much more.

Again in *Absalom, Absalom!* (as well as in *The Sound and the Fury*) there is a character, Quentin Compson, who is haunted by Civil War–era ghosts, though he was born well after the conflict ended. Faulkner makes it clear that it is not only the war that troubles Quentin; he is troubled by the entirety of the past. This is true of other characters as well, like Joanna Burden and Isaac McCaslin and many, many others. They labor under the shadow of the past and, in some cases, it is as if they never establish a life beyond what happened before they were born. As Gavin Stevens says in *Requiem for a Nun*: "The past is never dead. It's not even past" (act 1, scene III).

Sample Topics:

1. **Yoknapatawpha:** How is Yoknapatawpha County akin to a character in Faulkner's work?

An essay on this topic would argue for the primacy of setting in Faulkner. His work in general is replete with descriptions of roads, paths, woods, and streams, the physical characteristics of a land drawn in such detail that it is hard to regard it as fictionalized. Try to envision Faulkner's work without this landscape. How would it suffer?

2. **The South:** What makes Faulkner's characters particularly southern?

One way to approach this question would be to consider the northern characters in Faulkner, if you have encountered any in your reading. Another would be to look at "outsiders" or those who travel outside the South. How does the setting shape the characters and their behavior?

3. **The Civil War:** What is the importance of the Civil War in Faulkner's work?

This is an appropriate question to ask of any Faulkner story or novel. In a story such as "A Rose for Emily," the war utterly changes the possibilities of Emily Grierson, making her a woman with few opportunities for change or renewal, basically trapped in an old way of being without time or the wherewithal to learn a new mode of being. An essay on this topic might argue that the Civil War is the central shaping event of Faulkner's fiction.

4. **The past:** How important is the past to the work of William Faulkner?

When you begin to think about Faulkner's characters that are trapped in the past or stories of the past, the list is long. What kind of life can a person have when he or she is always looking back, mired in a personal or historical legacy? This is a central theme of Faulkner's. The past seems ever present and inescapable; nowhere does Faulkner seem to suggest that the past should be forgotten. In the stories or novels you have read, does it seem there is a middle ground that involves remembering the past without being oppressed or overcome by it?

Philosophy and Ideas

There are several key ideas that Faulkner returns to throughout the body of his work. As is true of many writers, religion is a subject that concerned Faulkner. His novel *The Fable* is a retelling of the Gospels. In *Light in August* and *The Sound and the Fury*, there are characters that are recognizable as Christlike figures or surrogates. Does religion help or hurt Faulkner's characters? Depending on the works you are examining, there may be a variety of answers, but religion informs and influences all of Faulkner's work, even if it is less than explicitly integrated or the characters involved are not overtly or at all religious.

There has been a great deal of critical work on the subject of Faulkner and time. As you read Faulkner, you may want to keep in mind that time in all its permutations is an important motif. Quentin Compson's section of *The Sound and the Fury* contains the most obsessive musings on the nature of time. In that section, repeated references to clocks, watches, the sun, and the seasons predominate. In "A Rose for Emily," Emily Grierson attempts to arrest time. Interest in the past might be considered a part of this. Do any of Faulkner's characters consider the future? Readers of Faulkner frequently find themselves asking where they are in time because Faulkner tends to rapidly move through time in his prose.

The lawyer Gavin Stevens is one of Faulkner's recurring characters, with a large role in *Sanctuary*, Faulkner's "potboiler" as he called it, which concludes with a courtroom scene. Other notable courtroom scenes are featured in "Barn Burning" and "Spotted Horses." There are also numerous instances in Faulkner of rough justice, like the slights and injustices suffered by the protagonist of *Light in August*. There are also shocking crimes committed that go unpunished. Emily Grierson kills Homer Barron, but the consequences she suffers are not punishment in the usual sense. Charles Sutpen kills Henry Bon and disappears, seemingly not at all held accountable for the murder. Readers might ask if there is any justice in Faulkner and, if so, what form it takes.

One possible answer to such a query is that justice is sometimes meted out over a long period of time, with basically the sons (and daughters) inheriting the sins of their fathers. When you consider the families that Faulkner follows through the generations, the family and its fortunes generally diminish over the years, with each succeeding generation less powerful, sane, or strong than the last. Often the decline of a clan is made explicit, as in the case of Thomas Sutpen, whose misguided way of starting the family that was to be his legacy potentially doomed the undertaking from the beginning. Sutpen is punished, but so is everyone who comes into contact with him. Is this justice? Or, like the lawsuits brought by the women in "Spotted Horses," is there the sense that the innocent cannot receive justice when facing those who have no moral code?

An inheritance could be good or bad. Sometimes people inherit sin, such as the sin of slavery, which stains many of Faulkner's characters. Sometimes people inherit an idea. Quentin Compson inherits his grandfather's watch and the obsession with time that goes with it. *Go Down, Moses* contains many stories of inheritances. There is the money that McCaslin leaves to the illegitimate, biracial children. There is the inheritance given to Isaac from his uncle Hubert Beauchamp that proves worthless and the inheritance from the McCaslin family that he rejects. There is the horn Isaac gives to the illegitimate son of Roth Edmonds, and there is the less tangible inheritance of the land that Sam Fathers seems to bequeath to Isaac. Sometimes the inheritance is more abstract or philosophical in nature. Many of Faulkner's characters are studies of the nature of sanity, how an individual becomes who he or she is, the nature of free will, and much more.

Sample Topics:

1. **Religion:** What is the importance of religion in Faulkner's work?

What is expressed about religion in the work you are writing about? Are there any explicitly religious characters? Is religion a more subtle presence? Is it something that oppresses the characters, like another ancestral story from the distant past? One possible thesis might be that it is a mistake to forget religion in Faulkner. In *Absalom, Absalom!* Thomas Sutpen lives as if there is no God, as his children reenact a biblical tragedy.

2. Time: What is the significance of time?

An essay on this topic might argue that time is fluid in Faulkner, and the most successful characters are the ones that can move through time with the least worry or resistance, like Lena Grove. But there are not many characters like that in Faulkner's fiction. More often time has bested them in some way, and they are enslaved or entombed by it, like Rosa Coldfield.

3. Justice: Is there any justice to be had in Faulkner?

One possible thesis on this subject is that justice comes slowly. Another is that the courtroom is not necessarily an arena where true justice can be found. Addressing this question might involve considering the community. Is the community the best agent of justice, or is it the only true agent of justice? The community in "A Rose for Emily," for instance, suspects that a dead body is in Miss Emily's closed-off room but fails to investigate out of deference to her.

4. Inheritance: What is the importance of inheritance?

Another way to consider inheritance in Faulkner is to ask whether it is a good or bad influence to have an inheritance in his work. One possible thesis is that it is impossible, in Faulkner, to be born without an inheritance. This coincides with the importance Faulkner places on family, names, and the land—the things we are born to. Even *Light in August*'s Joe Christmas, who is deprived of all of these, cannot escape their looming absence.

Language, Symbols, and Imagery

John T. Irwin's book, *Doubling and Incest/Repetition and Revenge*, is a fascinating discussion of these notable aspects of Faulkner's work. There are numerous instances in Faulkner in which characters are doubles of one another. Henry Sutpen and Charles Bon are not only half brothers, they are in some instances twins or arguably the same person because they are so closely intertwined. Quentin and Caddy Compson have a similarly odd relationship. In those novels in which they appear, the doubling is writ large; in others, it is less obvious. For instance, Boon Hogganbeck and Sam Fathers are nearly opposite in every way, but there is a relationship and resemblance between them that acknowledges that Boon is the person who should end Sam Fathers's life.

Another motif in Faulkner is family. Faulkner spends a great deal of time developing the stories of some of his families: the Compsons, the Sutpens, the Bundrens, the McCaslins, and the Snopeses, to name a few. He worked out intricate family trees for his families. Other authors move from subject to subject, but Faulkner stayed with these families throughout his career, allowing them to grow and change. We can infer that he found something fascinating about the interrelationships in families and extended clans. One of the recurring themes in his books is the way the generations before us affect our lives now.

Like the families they cannot escape, people in Faulkner could also be said to be trapped by their communities. In *As I Lay Dying*, the community judges the Bundrens, but it also tries to help them. In *Go Down, Moses*, the community works to bring home the body of Samuel Worsham Beauchamp, seemingly out of respect for Miss Molly. But at other times, as in *Light in August*, the community is an executioner. In "A Rose for Emily," the community (or a voice that seems to speak for or collectively represent it) is the narrator. In "Barn Burning," the Snopeses are itinerant farmers; they never truly belong to a community and function outside its bounds. In whatever works by William Faulkner you are reading, consider how the community shapes the characters and their behavior.

Similarly, the people in Faulkner's works are tied to the land, or should be. In "Barn Burning," the family has failed to make this connection. In other works, such as *The Sound and the Fury* and "The Bear," Faulkner portrays the selling of these tremendous holdings of land as tragic. The land bears the name of the families who own or owned it, and so it becomes a part of these families and their histories.

Sample Topics:

1. **Doubles:** What is the importance of doubles in Faulkner's work?

Is there an explicit or implicit set of doubles in the works you are concentrating on? Are any characters intertwined, so much so perhaps that they speak in one voice or finish one anothers' thoughts? If there are doubles, does one kill the other? A possible thesis might explore the fact that when two characters are strongly bound together, one suffers.

2. Family: What is the importance of family?

This is a large question and can be answered in a number of ways. Families in Faulkner affect individuals in both positive and negative ways. It is rare to have a character in Faulkner who is not portrayed as part of a family (Byron Bunch is one notable exception—is he better adjusted than other Faulkner characters?). One possible thesis is that family is the curse that everyone is born into in Faulkner.

3. Community: How does the community shape the individual?

Another way to look at this topic would be to consider how the community treats outsiders. How does the community regard someone from outside, such as a Homer Barron or V. K. Ratliff? It is likely that in any one work there will be examples of the community acting both positively and negatively.

4. The land: What is the importance of land in William Faulkner's stories and novels?

What happens to the characters without land of their own? Is owning land a burden or a privilege? Consider that the slaves could not possess their own land and how important it is to a character like Fonsiba's husband that he does own his land. Isaac McCaslin argues that no man can own the land. Yet another way to consider this topic is to think about how closely the characters identify themselves with the landscapes they are in. For instance, in *The Sound and the Fury*, Quentin becomes closely identified with the Charles River.

Bibliography and Online Resources

Backman, Melvin. *Faulkner: The Major Years: A Critical Study.* Bloomington: Indiana UP, 1966.

Bassett, John E. *Vision and Revisions: Essays on Faulkner.* West Cornwall, CT: Locust Hill, 1989.

Bleikasten, Andre. *The Ink of Melancholy.* Bloomington: Indiana UP, 1990.

Bloom, Harold, ed. *William Faulkner.* Modern Critical Views Series. New York: Chelsea House, 1986.

Blotner, Joseph. *Faulkner: A Biography.* New York: Random House, 1984.

Brodsky, Louis Daniel. *William Faulkner: Life Glimpses.* Austin: U of Texas P, 1990.

Brooks, Cleanth. *William Faulkner: First Encounters.* New Haven, CT: Yale UP, 1983.

———. *William Faulkner: Toward Yoknapatawpha and Beyond.* Baton Rouge: Louisiana State UP, 1978, 1990.

———. *William Faulkner: The Yoknapatawpha Country.* New Haven, CT: Yale UP, 1963.

Carey, Glenn O., ed. *Faulkner, the Unappeased Imagination: A Collection of Critical Essays.* Troy, NY: Whitston, 1980.

Carothers, James B. *William Faulkner's Short Stories.* Ann Arbor, MI: UMI Research Press, 1985.

Chabrier, Gwendolyn. *Faulkner's Families: A Southern Saga.* New York: Gordian, 1993.

Clarke, Deborah. *Robbing the Mother: Women in Faulkner.* Jackson: UP of Mississippi, 1994.

Coffee, James M. *Faulkner's Un-Christlike Christians: Biblical Allusions in the Novels.* Ann Arbor, MI: UMI Research Press, 1983.

Davis, Thadious M. *Faulkner's "Negro": Art and the Southern Context.* Baton Rouge: Louisiana State UP, 1983.

Dowling, David. *William Faulkner.* New York: Palgrave MacMillan, 1989.

Faulkner, William. *Faulkner in the University.* Eds. Frederick L. Gwynn and Joseph L. Blotner. Charlottesville: UP of Virginia, 1959.

———. Nobel Acceptance Speech. Accessed July 29, 2008. URL: http://www.rjgeib.com/thoughts/faulkner/faulkner.html.

The Faulkner Journal. Accessed July 29, 2008. URL: http://www.english.ucf.edu/faulkner/index.php?URL=FJmain.

Fowler, Doreen. *Faulkner's Changing Vision: From Outrage to Affirmation.* Ann Arbor, MI: UMI Research Press, 1983.

Fowler, Doreen, and Ann J. Abadie, eds. *"A Cosmos of My Own."* Faulkner and Yoknapatawpha Conference, 1980. Jackson: UP of Mississippi, 1981.

———. *Faulkner and Humor.* Faulkner and Yoknapatawpha Conference, 1984. Jackson: UP of Mississippi, 1986.

———. *Faulkner and Popular Culture.* Faulkner and Yoknapatawpha Conference, 1988. Jackson: UP of Mississippi, 1990.

———. *Faulkner and Race.* Faulkner and Yoknapatawpha Conference, 1986. Jackson: UP of Mississippi, 1987.

———. *Faulkner and Religion.* Faulkner and Yoknapatawpha Conference, 1989. Jackson: UP of Mississippi, 1991.

———. *Faulkner and the Craft of Fiction.* Faulkner and Yoknapatawpha Conference, 1987. Jackson: UP of Mississippi, 1989.

———. *Faulkner and the Southern Renaissance.* Faulkner and Yoknapatawpha Conference, 1981. Jackson: UP of Mississippi, 1982.

———. *Faulkner and Women.* Faulkner and Yoknapatawpha Conference, 1985. Jackson: UP of Mississippi, 1986.

———. *Faulkner: International Perspectives.* Faulkner and Yoknapatawpha Conference, 1982. Jackson: UP of Mississippi, 1984.

———. *Fifty Years of Yoknapatawpha.* Faulkner and Yoknapatawpha Conference, 1979. Jackson: UP of Mississippi, 1980.

———. *New Directions in Faulkner Studies.* Faulkner and Yoknapatawpha Conference, 1983. Jackson: UP of Mississippi, 1984.

Gray, Richard J. *The Life of William Faulkner: A Critical Biography.* Oxford; Cambridge, MA: Blackwell P, 1994.

Gwynn, Frederick L., and Joseph L. Blotner, eds. *Faulkner in the University: Class Conferences at the University of Virginia 1957–1958.* Charlottesville: U of Virginia P, 1959.

Harrington, Evans, and Ann J. Abadie, eds. *Faulkner and the Short Story.* Faulkner and Yoknapatawpha Conference, 1990. Jackson: UP of Mississippi, 1992.

———. *Faulkner, Modernism, and Film.* Faulkner and Yoknapatawpha Conference, 1978. Jackson: UP of Mississippi, 1979.

———. *The Maker and the Myth.* Faulkner and Yoknapatawpha Conference, 1977. Jackson: UP of Mississippi, 1978.

———. *The South and Faulkner's Yoknapatawpha: The Actual and the Apocryphal.* Faulkner and Yoknapatawpha Conference, 1976. Jackson: UP of Mississippi, 1977.

Hoffman, Frederick. *William Faulkner.* New York: Twayne, 1961.

Hoffman, Frederick, and Olga Vickery, eds. *William Faulkner: Three Decades of Criticism.* East Lansing: Michigan State UP, 1960.

Howe, Irving. *William Faulkner: A Critical Study.* 3d ed. Chicago: U of Chicago P, 1975.

Irwin, John T. *Doubling and Incest/Repetition and Revenge: A Speculative Reading of Faulkner.* 1975. Expanded ed. Baltimore: Johns Hopkins UP, 1996.

Karl, Frederick R. *William Faulkner: American Writer.* New York: Weidenfeld & Nicolson, 1989.

Kartiganer, Donald M. *The Fragile Thread: The Meaning of Form in Faulkner's Novels.* Amherst: U of Massachusetts P, 1979.

Kartiganer, Donald M., and Ann J. Abadie, eds. *Faulkner and Gender.* Faulkner and Yoknapatawpha Conference, 1994. Jackson: UP of Mississippi, 1996.

———. *Faulkner and Ideology.* Jackson: UP of Mississippi, 1995.

———. *Faulkner and Psychology.* Jackson: UP of Mississippi, 1994.

———. *Faulkner and the Artist.* Faulkner and Yoknapatawpha Conference, 1993. Jackson: UP of Mississippi, 1996.

———. *Faulkner and the Natural World.* Faulkner and Yoknapatawpha Conference. Jackson: UP of Mississippi, 1999.

Kinney, Arthur F., ed. *Critical Essays on William Faulkner: The Compson Family.* Boston: G. K. Hall, 1982.

———. *Critical Essays on William Faulkner: The Sartoris Family.* Boston: G. K. Hall, 1985.

Malin, Irving. *William Faulkner: An Interpretation.* Stanford, CA: Stanford UP, 1957.

Meriwether, James B., and Michael Millgate, eds. *Lion in the Garden: Interviews with William Faulkner: 1926–1962.* Lincoln: U of Nebraska P, 1968.

Millgate, Michael. *The Achievement of William Faulkner.* New York: Random House, 1966.

———. *William Faulkner.* New York: Grove Press, 1961.

Minter, David L. *A Cultural History of the American Novel: Henry James to William Faulkner.* Cambridge: Cambridge UP, 1994.

———. *William Faulkner: The Writing of a Life.* Baltimore: Johns Hopkins UP, 1980.

Moreland, Richard C. *Faulkner and Modernism: Rereading and Rewriting.* Madison: U of Wisconsin P, 1990.

Mortimer, Gail L. *Faulkner's Rhetoric of Loss: A Study in Perception and Meaning.* Austin: U of Texas P, 1983.

Oates, Stephen B. *William Faulkner: The Man and the Artist.* New York: Harper & Row, 1987.

Padgett, John B. *William Faulkner on the Web.* 17 Aug. 2006. Ed. John B. Padgett. U of Mississippi. 19 Dec. 2007. URL: http://www.mcsr.olemiss.edu/~egjbp/faulkner/faulkner.html.

Parker, Robert Dale. *Faulkner and the Novelistic Imagination.* Urbana: U of Illinois P, 1985.

Polk, Noel. *Children of the Dark House: Text and Context in Faulkner.* Jackson: UP of Mississippi, 1996.

Reuben, P. "Chapter 7: William Faulkner." *PAL: Perspectives in Literature—A Research and Reference Guide.* 20 Mar. 2008. URL: http://web.csustan.edu/english/reuben/pal/chap7/faulkner.html.

Roberts, Diane. *Faulkner and Southern Womanhood.* Athens: U of Georgia P, 1994.

Ruppersburg, Hugh M. *Voice and Eye in Faulkner's Fiction.* Athens: U of Georgia P, 1983.

Stegner, Wallace, ed. *The American Novel from James Fennimore Cooper to William Faulkner.* New York: Basic, 1965.

Sundquist, Eric J. *Faulkner: The House Divided.* Baltimore: Johns Hopkins UP, 1985.

Swiggart, Peter. *The Art of Faulkner's Novels.* Austin: U of Texas P, 1962.

Swisher, Clarice, ed. *Readings on William Faulkner.* San Diego, CA: Greenhaven Press: 1998.

Taylor, Walter. *Faulkner's Search for a South.* Urbana: U of Illinois P, 1983.

Thompson, Lawrence. *William Faulkner: An Introduction and Interpretation.* New York: Barnes and Noble, 1963.

Vickery, Olga W. *The Novels of William Faulkner: A Critical Interpretation.* Baton Rouge: Louisiana State UP, 1964.

Visser, Irene. *Compassion in Faulkner's Fiction.* Lewiston, NY: Edwin Mellen, 1996.

Wadlington, Warwick. *Reading Faulknerian Tragedy.* Ithaca: Cornell UP, 1987.

Warren, Robert Penn, ed. *Faulkner: A Collection of Critical Essays.* Englewood Cliffs, NJ: Prentice Hall, 1966.

Wasson, Ben. *Count No 'Count: Flashbacks to Faulkner.* Jackson: UP of Mississippi, 1983.

Weinstein, Phillip, ed. *The Cambridge Companion to William Faulkner.* New York: Cambridge UP, 1995.

Williams, David. *Faulkner's Women: The Myth and the Muse.* Montreal: McGill-Queen's UP, 1977.

Williamson, Joel. *William Faulkner and Southern History.* New York: Oxford UP, 1993.

Wittenberg, Judith Bryant. *Faulkner: The Transfiguration of Biography.* Lincoln: U of Nebraska P, 1979.

Zender, Karl F. *The Crossing of the Ways: William Faulkner, the South, and the Modern World.* New Brunswick, NJ: Rutgers UP, 1989.

THE SOUND
AND THE FURY

READING TO WRITE

THE SOUND AND THE FURY takes its title from Shakespeare's *Macbeth*, and Macbeth's soliloquy provides tremendous insight into the novel:

> Tomorrow, and tomorrow, and tomorrow
> Creeps in this petty pace from day to day
> To the last syllable of recorded time,
> And all our yesterdays have lighted fools
> The way to dusty death. Out, out, brief candle.
> Life's but a walking shadow, a poor player
> That struts and frets his hour upon the stage,
> And then is heard no more; it is a tale
> Told by an idiot, full of sound and fury,
> Signifying nothing.
>
> (Act V, scene 5, 12–21)

Perhaps the novel's greatest difficulty is that its first section is quite literally told by a developmentally disabled individual. Benjy Compson is mentally challenged and of limited abilities, and it is the workings of his mind that the reader attempts to follow in the story's opening. Having Benjy narrate the opening of the novel was a bold move for a novelist whose career had met with little success. Faulkner seems to have decided to write a novel without consideration for the ease of the reader. *The Sound and the Fury* tells its story from four different perspectives; it is not uncommon that, as you read Benjy's section, you are at times uncertain about what has happened. By the novel's end, those same events will be revisited by the other narrators.

Benjy's memories begin when he is three years old. Most of those memories have to do with his sister, Caddy. Caddy has been gone from the Compson home for many years, but her early presence in his life has left its mark on him. She was the most sympathetic family member to Benjy when they were children and was both a sister and a mother to him.

The Sound and the Fury was first published in 1929. Its experimental form attempts to tell, from several perspectives, the story of the Compsons, of Caddy, and the American southern family. *The Sound and the Fury* does not have a straightforward, chronological narrative; this is not a novel that can be summarized in terms of a listing of plot points and events. Instead, it is like looking at family "snapshots," in which the snapshots are narratives of one day in the life of the Compson brothers and Dilsey, the family's servant. Quentin's section recounts the last day of his life in June 1910. The other three sections are set on Easter weekend, April 1928. There is some overlap in the important memories or events recounted in each of these four sections, so that the reader often sees the same event from different viewpoints. As you read, you will be assembling, from those different views, a version of those events that you believe is the truest and most complete. Sometimes you might find a narrator to be untrustworthy, and you will want to take that perception into account.

As you read you might ask: Why is this family failing, and why are they failing in such a complete and spectacular fashion? You might wish to provide yourself with some background on the Compson family by reading the history that Faulkner wrote for them after the novel had been published; it can be found in *The Portable Faulkner* or the Norton Critical Edition.

The second section of *The Sound and the Fury* is told from the perspective of Quentin Compson. On June 2, 1910, Quentin is a student at Harvard University, and one difference of this section, apart from the fact that it occurs 18 years earlier than the novel's other sections, is that it is set in the North. But you will find that although Quentin is physically in Massachusetts, his thoughts are consumed by the South. Quentin is also, in contrast to Benjy, an intellectual. His thoughts might be fragmentary and not always coherent, but his concerns are at a different level than either of his brothers'. His concerns are with ideals and abstractions, like time, honor, duty, family, and death. There are particular motifs in Quentin's section that are important to the novel as a whole: time, water, and what it means to have a sister.

The third section of the novel belongs to Jason Compson and is set on Good Friday. Jason's section stands in contrast to those of his brothers. Benjy is concerned with the senses, what he can see, touch, and smell. Quentin is concerned with ideals. Jason is concerned with himself and with money. Jason is perhaps less obsessed with Caddy than the other two, or at least it might first seem that way. In reality, Jason is dependent on Caddy financially and wishes to control and punish her via her daughter, Miss Quentin. Miss Quentin is sexually promiscuous in a way that seems more coarse and reckless than her mother. That she is named for the uncle who committed suicide before she was born may suggest to the reader that she is likely to be unhappy or come to a tragic end herself.

The novel's final section is focused on Dilsey but also contains the account of Jason's pursuit of Miss Quentin, who has run off with a circus performer, taking approximately $7,000 from Jason's room with her. Jason is alone in pursuing her, because local law enforcement knows, as the reader does, that this money is actually Miss Quentin's. In a somewhat complex scheme, Jason has been receiving checks from Caddy that are meant for her daughter. He takes those checks to his mother and watches her burn them, since they have decided that they want nothing to do with Caddy or her money. But in truth, Jason only gives his mother copies to burn; he actually cashes Caddy's checks and keeps the money for himself. So Jason spends Easter Sunday in pursuit of what he has stolen. Dilsey and Benjy attend the Easter service, and Benjy and Luster attempt to visit the cemetery.

Faulkner many times referred to this novel as his "most splendid failure," his attempt four times to tell Caddy's story. Most literary critics consider it a success. If Caddy remains elusive at the novel's end, the four other principals, Benjy, Quentin, Jason, and Dilsey, have been made real and complete. Along with their stories, Faulkner tells the story of a family, a time, a place, and its people.

TOPICS AND STRATEGIES
Themes

One notable feature of *The Sound and the Fury* is that the novel comprises four separate narratives and that each of these four sections is told on a different date, which is that section's heading or title. The first section, told by Benjy, happens on April 7, 1928. The difficulty of this section is compounded by Benjy's unusual relationship to time. For Benjy, all time is the same. He cannot distinguish between the past and the present, and so the past is continually intruding on the present. The future seems beyond his comprehension. Images of clocks, watches, or even the shadows that mark the passage of time through the day are important symbols in *The Sound and the Fury,* particularly in Quentin's section, titled June 2, 1910. Quentin's troubles include a desire to escape from time and all that its passage demands. The section begins:

> When the shadow of the sash appeared on the curtains it was between seven and eight o'clock and then I was in time again, hearing the watch. It was Grandfather's and when Father gave it to me he said I give you the mausoleum of all hope and desire; it's rather excruciatingly apt that you will use it to gain the reducto absurdum of all human experience which can fit your individual needs no better than it fitted his or his father's. I give it to you not that you may remember time, but that you might forget it now and then for a moment and not spend all your breath trying to conquer it. (76)

Love or its absence is another central theme of *The Sound and the Fury.* Mrs. Compson is unable to provide her children with the love one would expect from a mother. Mr. Compson is affectionate with the children but does not adequately provide them with a loving environment. Dilsey's presence provides some stability, but she is a servant and not a Compson. Jason seems utterly devoid of any feeling. The strongest examples of love appear to be the emotion felt for Caddy by Benjy and by Quentin. In both cases, their love is tremendously flawed. Quentin's love for Caddy is an obsession less for the girl than for the image of southern womanhood she embodies to him. His difficulty in accepting Caddy's promiscuity contributes to his decision to take his life. His unresolved feelings for his sister lead him to claim that they have committed incest. Benjy's love for Caddy is far more innocent, but he is also incapable of loving Caddy as she is. For him, Caddy is a maternal figure, and he invests her with every positive quality of innocence and youth. When she fails to behave as she did when they were small children, Benjy is disappointed. In his mind, she is always a schoolgirl who is on her way home to him. Benjy's discomfort with Caddy's sexuality seems quite natural when one looks at *The Sound and the Fury* as a whole. There is no example of a healthy sexual relationship in the novel.

The Sound and the Fury tells the story of the death of the Compson family and the ideals that family might once have embodied. The three brothers will not have children. Benjy is castrated, Quentin commits suicide; and Jason is unwilling or unable to have a relationship that would produce children. Miss Quentin cannot carry the family name: She is female, illegitimate, and, at the novel's end, has run off with a traveling performer. She wants nothing to do with the Compsons. Along with the diminishment of the family is the suggestion that the southern ideals that plague Quentin are also dying. Honor, loyalty, chastity, and pride are no longer synonymous with the Compsons. It is possible to wonder if these values were ever possessed by them, or if these qualities are part of the family myth. Death seems almost to be a character in Quentin's section of the novel, doggedly accompanying him like a shadow. Likewise, Quentin's death casts a shadow over the novel as a whole and shapes what happens to the Compsons in the other three sections.

Those three sections take place on the weekend of Easter 1928 (Jason's section relates the events of April 6; Benjy's narrates the events of April 7; and Dilsey's section covers the events of Sunday, April 8). As in the biblical story, the Compson family has moved from death and mourning into the hope of resurrection. And yet, it is not a Compson who has this hope, it is Dilsey. Her values are the same ones that Quentin could not live without: loyalty, strength, maternal love, and faith.

Sample Topics:

1. Time: How do the four separate narrators of the novel experience time?

A writer working on this topic could choose to look at the novel as a whole, discussing each of the four narrators. A writer could also choose one of the sections to discuss in depth. One could examine the only section of the novel that is not set in 1928, Quentin's portion. Another way to approach this essay would be to consider the Easter weekend of 1928. Why does Faulkner allow Benjy to narrate the Saturday of that weekend, while Jason narrates the Friday, and Faulkner tells the story from Dilsey's perspective on Sunday? Is there any significant link between these three and the days that belong to them?

2. **Love:** What does *The Sound and the Fury* have to say about love?

An essay on this topic could discuss the way love is perverted in the novel. Incest, promiscuity, adultery, and prostitution are some of the deviant behaviors in the novel. Is there any admirable example of love? Who loves best? One possible thesis for an essay on this topic might be that *The Sound and the Fury* shows what the lack of love can do to a family. You might focus on the absence of maternal love, or think about what happens to Benjy without Caddy. You might want to consider the varying forms that love can take. For example, would you say that Dilsey loves the Compson children, or is her relationship with them one of duty and loyalty?

3. **Death:** How does death affect the characters of *The Sound and the Fury*?

Quentin's section would be a reliable place to begin thinking about this question. From his chapter's beginning and the date that precedes Benjy's section by 18 years, Quentin's death seems to be a certainty. As you read that section, you may find yourself growing resigned to it, with only the question of when and how he will kill himself to be answered by the end. The presence of another Quentin in Benjy's section, Miss Quentin, also points to Quentin Compson's absence. But his absence does not take him out of the narrative.

4. Resurrection: Is there any hope for resurrection for the Compson family?

Perhaps not for the family, but Dilsey's section, which concludes the novel, is set on Easter Sunday. Why is this significant? What are the connotations, or associations, of the Easter celebration? To write on this topic you might look carefully at the words of the sermon at the service Dilsey and Benjy attend. You could also look at the three sections set on the Easter weekend as a whole and discuss how they reflect or fail to reflect the Christian beliefs and practices in respect to those days. Does Faulkner offer a prescription for the South to flourish again?

Character

Benjy is a remarkable literary achievement. One of the difficulties of *The Sound and the Fury* is that the novel begins with Benjy, and Faulkner has attempted to tell the Compson story from Benjy's viewpoint, even though he cannot comprehend the significance of the events he relates. Benjy's section is set on April 6, 1928, the day before his 33rd birthday. As he wanders about the Compson lands with Luster, who is searching for a lost quarter, Benjy hears the golfers in the distance shouting "caddie." This is a bit of perverse humor on the part of the author. Benjy's pasture, as it was called, has been sold to pay for Quentin's year at Harvard, and it is now a golf course. As the golfers play, Benjy is reminded of the absence of his sister, Caddy, whose name is otherwise never spoken among the Compsons because Mrs. Compson feels she has disgraced the family by giving birth to the illegitimate Miss Quentin. Caddy is no longer considered part of the family. But the repetition of her name by the golfers suggests the impossibility of completely banishing any family member. She is still there. Similarly, Miss Quentin's presence is a reminder of the absence of both Caddy and Quentin. It is difficult to think of any of these characters apart from their roles in the family.

If you were to focus on Benjy as a character, you might ask yourself, first, is he a believable presence? Until you have read beyond his section, it might be difficult to decide. Much of what Benjy says is unclear until those other viewpoints are also absorbed and considered. For instance, Benjy's castration provides another joke in this first section, as he and Luster look for the lost balls of the golfers. Only when you understand that he has been castrated will the joke become clear. Benjy is about to turn 33, a significant age in the Bible, as it is the age of Christ at his crucifixion. Yet, in this first section, it is difficult to know how old Benjy is. Many of the thoughts that are present with him at 33 are the same as those he had as a child. His memories are not really memories to him because everything he has experienced is still as vivid as if it had only just happened. And so, even though Caddy has not come home for many years, Benjy waits at the fence for her, believing her still to be the age of the young girls that pass by. When he chased and attempted to speak to one of the girls, some thought he was attempting to sexually assault the child, and this led to the decision to castrate him. The reader knows that sexual violence was not his motive, having been informed by Benjy himself the real reason he is interested in these girls. Benjy is without sexual sin. This is one reason the evidence of Caddy's sexuality upsets him.

The characters of the Compson children are revealed in the pivotal early scene of their grandmother Damuddy's funeral. Caddy is the only child of the four who is brave and adventurous enough to climb the tree to look in the window and find out what is happening. Her ability to confront the death of their grandmother somewhat foreshadows the way Caddy will look unreservedly at life. The muddy underpants she reveals to the children on the ground below foreshadow her precocious sexuality and how all the brothers will witness and be ashamed of it. Caddy's sexuality is an obsession for Quentin as it is for Benjy. When Quentin learns that Caddy is no longer a virgin, and learns that he can do nothing to oppose Dalton Ames or the other men she might involve herself with, he suggests that they both commit incest or kill themselves. These might seem to the reader untenable and unlikely solutions to what might strike most as a less than serious problem. But his suggestions show that to Quentin Caddy's chastity is important; it is a question of life or death.

Jason Compson, though he bears his father's name, is perhaps, as his mother says, more like her family, the Bascombs, than the Compsons. If his section of the book presents any difficultly, it is the difficulty of spending time in the company of a narrator so thoroughly objectionable. You will notice that Mrs. Compson spends much of her time bemoaning the difficulties of her life and placing the blame for those difficulties on others. Although her brother Maury is a minor character in the novel, you see the same irresponsibility in him that allows him to live off the Compsons and to commit adultery with the local wives. Jason blames his family, which has given him all he has in life, for their failure to give him more. He specifically blames Caddy for giving birth to an illegitimate daughter, which subsequently caused the dissolution of her marriage and with it his chances at a bank job with Caddy's husband. Jason's dislike of Miss Quentin is in part rooted in that disappointment.

One distinctive element about Faulkner's approach as a novelist is that even though the stories he tells might seem overwhelmingly dark and devoid of hope, there are always the comic and uplifting elements that attempt to redeem the whole. Dilsey's character is the source of the more positive aspects of *The Sound and the Fury*. A range of admirable qualities is associated with her. Dilsey's family is a consistent and reliable presence for the Compsons. Dilsey is the most maternal figure in the book, caring for the Compson children and, later, Miss Quentin, protecting every member of the family, and, as is revealed in the final section, taking responsibility for the celebration of Benjy's birthday, something that would normally be a parent's task.

Since the first three sections of the novel are narrated by each Compson brother in turn, it might seem odd that Dilsey's section focuses on her, but she is not the narrator. Faulkner is the narrator. It is Easter Sunday, and Dilsey takes Benjy to the service at the black church to see the visiting reverend. She does not care that Benjy is white or that he is an "idiot"; she believes that the church welcomes all. Dilsey's family stands in strong contrast to the Compsons. Dilsey's husband, Roskus, is not significantly involved in the events of *The Sound and the Fury*, but every reported statement he makes is full of meaning. For instance, he is the one to say specifically that the names of the Compson children are ill-omened. Benjy was named for Mrs. Compson's brother Maury, but the child's name was changed when it became clear that he was disabled. Caddy's name is not spoken in the family after she gives birth to her daughter.

If you were to write on a character in *The Sound and the Fury*, one of these four major characters, the brothers or Dilsey, would make an obvious choice. Less obvious, perhaps, would be to focus on a character such as Roskus; his small but significant role could also be richly discussed in an essay. The Compson parents are significant characters, and a number of essays could be written focusing on them and their effect on their children.

Perhaps the most significant character in the novel is Caddy. If you were to ask yourself how all three brothers are similar, you might say that what they share is a nearly obsessive interest in their sister. For Faulkner, Caddy was the novel's protagonist and its unknowable center. Why do you think Caddy is not given a section of her own? The fact that the reader knows Caddy only through the memories of others gives her a certain mystery. In effect, you are allowed to form your own view of Caddy after assembling all the other views available. She is a dynamic character who does not, perhaps because she is female, become trapped in the Compson name or homestead. But she does give them her daughter.

Sample Topics:

1. **Benjy:** How does Benjy's narration illuminate the events of the novel?

An essay on this subject might argue that Benjy's section, while at first seeming to be the most difficult, is actually the most revealing of the novel. Benjy, because of his limitations, experiences the events and then narrates them without censor. The thoughts that come to Benjy on that Friday in April are on the page as they occur to him.

2. **Quentin:** Why does Quentin drown himself?

This is one of those questions meant to provoke your thinking because the expectation is not that there is a right or wrong answer. Rather, you would be expected to argue for the reason you think he drowns himself. Some of the possible explanations you can pursue are that his values are not reflective of and are incongruous with the time in which he lives, so that he cannot accept the mores of those around him. This answer alludes to time as a factor, and the argument can be made that time is somehow Quentin's enemy. Or perhaps he bears unresolved feelings for his sister; there is evidence of this in his relationship with Caddy and also in the final scenes with the lost girl. An argument could be made that he is overly sensitive and that this trait has been with him since he was a child. Perhaps Quentin suffers from mental illness as well, albeit in a less obvious way than his brother Benjy.

3. **Jason:** Jason's section of the novel is straightforward, particularly when compared to his two brothers. How would you describe his character as differing from theirs?

How are the three brothers the same? How are they different? If Benjy experiences all time as the present, and Quentin is trapped in the past (remember his chapter is set 18 years before his brothers'), then how does Jason experience time? How does he spend the Saturday of the Easter weekend? How does he spend the Friday or the Sunday? Can you trace the darker elements of his character to any event, or is he consistently portrayed even from the earliest descriptions of him? Is there anything redeeming about him? An interesting essay could also be written discussing the way Jason relates to women.

4. **Dilsey:** Why is Dilsey's the final voice in the novel?

You might imaginatively play with the idea of a rearrangement of the novel's chapters. How did Faulkner decide the arrangement and order of the four sections? What is the significance of an African-American voice being the most sympathetic of the novel? To write an essay on Dilsey, you might want to focus on the service she attends on Easter Sunday. Why does it affect her as it does? Dilsey has a faith that the Compsons lack. What is Faulkner saying about the importance of faith?

History and Context

The Sound and the Fury is set against a backdrop of a corrupted South. Caddy can be seen as the antithesis of the southern belle, as could her daughter. The myth of the southern belle encompasses a view that southern womanhood is refined and chaste, that a woman should be the model of decorum and stand for all that is good. To the extent that a woman possesses these virtues, she is revered. One presumed role of the southern man was to protect these women, even to the point of death. Quentin Compson still believes in these ideals, but it seems irrational to be willing to fight for a woman's honor in the 20th century, particularly if the woman herself does not find these values worth defending or fighting for. It may seem ironic that these values are more present in Dilsey's family than in the Compsons. You might ask yourself if these values, identified as "southern," are just as prevalent in northern society. You might also consider whether these values are tenable in the 20th century of the book's setting.

Yoknapatawpha County stands in for Faulkner's Lafayette County, Mississippi, so it is possible that some of the events or circumstances in the novels mirror ones that actually occurred in Lafayette County. The scene of Damuddy's funeral, for instance, is taken from Faulkner's memory of his grandmother's funeral when he was a child. Issues of class and race in Mississippi are also reflected in the novel. The word *nigger* is often used in *The Sound and the Fury*, by black and white characters alike. So although a racist society is depicted, not far removed from the practice of slavery, it seems highly possible that Dilsey's family will endure while the Compsons will not. The Gibsons embody the values that the Compsons, if they ever held them, have lost.

Three generations of Gibsons care for Benjy in the course of the novel. The Gibson family provides him with consistency and stability. The Gibsons are accepting of one another, and Dilsey is not ashamed of Benjy. She takes him to the black church with her, believing, it seems, that churchgoing is important, no matter what a person's racial background or level of understanding might be.

Caddy has a set of values that might not seem so unusual to a modern reader but that nonetheless set her far apart from a woman of the antebellum South. Faulkner said that his story started with Caddy. In childhood, she seems to embody a number of positive traits. She is courageous and spirited, and also compassionate and loving. Benjy in his innocence responds most to Caddy, and he never forgets her, even as he grows into a man and she has been long absent. However, as she matures and becomes sexually adventurous, her behavior begins to run counter to the standards of the time. In the appendix to the novel, "Compson 1699–1945," her adventurous nature has led her ever farther away from her family and from Mississippi. Faulkner notes her presence at important cultural and historical sites and moments—Hollywood, Mexico, and then France under the German occupation.

Sample Topics:

1. **Southern values:** How are the Compsons affected by the values of the South?

   The Compsons, particularly Quentin, seem to be adversely affected by the values they have been told they should adopt. An essay on this topic could chose a trait, such as the chastity of women, and analyze how it works in the novel. Is chastity practiced by the women, or is it like a myth or a fairy tale? Some other possible values that are espoused but not, perhaps, lived are honesty, forgiveness, industry, and loyalty.

2. **Race:** What relationship exists between the white and black races in *The Sound and the Fury*?

   An essay on this subject might have a thesis that argues that although race relations had not advanced far in the South depicted in the novel, Faulkner suggests that black characters have more reason to be hopeful about their futures. You might want to write about the obvious racism in the novel and how it functions and develops. One might predict that the futures of the Gibson children would be less promising than those of the children they serve, but they seem to be able to move into productive adult lives, while the Compsons cannot.

3. **Family:** What meaning does family have in the novel?

   This novel is focused on family, how it influences and molds us, how it changes us, how people often cannot escape the family fold. Two families are portrayed, the Compsons and the Gibsons, and their lives are so entwined that they almost function as one family. For the Compson children, the Gibsons provide the order and support the Compson siblings do not get at home. But the Gibsons and their influence cannot change the trajectory the Compsons have assumed. An essay on this subject could be approached in a number of ways, but one possible thesis is that the fates of the Compson children are bound up with that of their forebears.

4. **Women:** Does Caddy seem representative of 20th-century women?

There are various ways to consider this question. One might start by asking why Caddy marries Herbert Head while two months pregnant with another man's child. It is a match that makes her mother happy and a pairing that seems utterly traditional. But Quentin detests Herbert, and it seems likely that Caddy's feelings about the match are closer to her brother's than her mother's. After she gives birth to Miss Quentin, the ruse of the marriage is ended, although one might ask how Herbert discovers the child is not his. Then Caddy turns her child over to the family that had inflicted so much emotional damage on her already, never to be a mother to her daughter. In Faulkner's appendix, the reader learns that Caddy becomes a wealthy woman. She marries a Hollywood tycoon. She divorces. She travels. Faulkner last places her with a German officer in France.

Philosophy and Ideas

It is hard to imagine this novel having a title other than *The Sound and the Fury*, which seems to encapsulate what it is about. But Faulkner's working title was *Twilight*, and it is not hard to imagine why he at one time called the novel that before arriving at the final title. Names were important to Faulkner, and this is reflected in the names of the characters in *The Sound and the Fury*. The names become inseparable from the characters and in some cases perhaps gesture to the course of their personal destiny. When Benjy's name is changed from Maury, Dilsey tells Caddy:

"My name been Dilsey since fore I could remember and it be Dilsey when they's long forgot me."

"How will they know it's Dilsey, when it's long forgot, Dilsey," Caddy said.

"It'll be in the Book, honey," Dilsey said. "Writ out."

"Can you read it," Caddy said.

"Won't have to," Dilsey said. "They'll read it for me. All I got to do is say Ise here." (58)

Benjy's name is changed when his diminished capacity becomes clear. Does this change anything about Benjy's life? Dilsey seems to suggest that God identifies us in some way with our names. After Quentin commits suicide, Caddy gives his name to her daughter. When she comes to live with the Compsons, she is a walking, breathing reminder of the son and daughter the family has lost. It seems ill-omened to name a child after her uncle who committed suicide. Think about Macbeth's words that life is "a tale told by an idiot, signifying nothing." What does a name signify?

The novel also explores ideas about the nature of time. Quentin's father gives him the watch once owned by the boy's grandfather. The destruction of this watch and the desire to move out of or beyond time are central to Quentin's section of *The Sound and the Fury* and his decision to commit suicide. Benjy's mind does not grasp time, so to him all events are experienced as the present. Caddy seems thoroughly of her time and making. Jason perhaps represents the future. Whatever their individual relationships to time, the four siblings are still defined by the family, era, and place they are born into.

Some of the troubles of the Compson family seem to stem from a resistance to or rebellion against reality. Caddy makes choices that will clearly put her in opposition to the community. Quentin is unable or unwilling to accept that he cannot control Caddy, or time, or the people around him. Jason rejects his family and his community. Benjy is perhaps not given a choice, as evidenced in his fits and tantrums when his environment does not meet his expectations. These struggles, which are real to them, may seem futile to the reader. Returning to the passage from Macbeth, you might consider whether their struggles and lives finally signify "nothing."

The novel ends on Easter Sunday, 1928, a choice that was surely meant to signal to the reader Christian undertones of resurrection and sin. For Dilsey, faith is important. The other members of the family, with the exception of Benjy, who is taken to the church service by Dilsey, are not marking this holy day. Dilsey repeatedly speaks of seeing the beginning and the end, seeming to allude to the end of the Compson family.

Sample Topics:

1. **Identity and naming:** Does the novel suggest there is a significant relationship between identity and one's given name?

   Some of the initial confusion a reader of *The Sound and the Fury* might experience is due to the presence of two Quentins. Faulkner's appendix states that Caddy planned to name her child Quentin whether it was a boy or a girl. Does Miss Quentin represent a continuation of Quentin Compson's story or a transformation or reinvention of it? Is her presence a way of saying that the former Quentin is still a part of the family narrative, even though he has attempted to extricate himself from it?

2. **Time:** Does Faulkner's novel offer an alternative definition of time?

   The Sound and the Fury tells the Compsons' story from four different perspectives and on four different days. The reader becomes responsible for assembling the chronology of the story. Does the chronology matter? An essay on this topic might focus on Quentin's section and attempt to analyze what Quentin believes about time and his relationship to the previous generations of Compsons.

3. **Significance:** Do the struggles of the characters in *The Sound and the Fury* have any lasting significance?

   While it is possible to argue that the problems of the Compsons are isolated ones, is that the conclusion you reach after reading *The Sound and the Fury*? It might be possible to argue, for instance, that the questions that plague Quentin are questions that all human beings have to resolve for themselves. Quentin is concerned with sin and mortality, as all people are, though he thinks of these as honor and time. Benjy's thoughts are consumed by questions of physical and emotional comfort, considerations that are important to all of us. You might ask yourself if you think Faulkner wanted his readers to see these lives as significant or not.

4. **Belief:** Is the lack of religious belief a factor in the downfall of the Compson family?

The novel's final section concentrates on the Easter sermon given by Reverend Shegog. Benjy attends the service with Dilsey, Frony, and Luster. Would religious belief have saved the Compsons? You might argue that the hope for resurrection, which Dilsey possesses, frees her mind from dwelling on the temporal conditions and realities of the present. The world is a problem for each of the Compson children. If there is a sense of hope at the end of the novel, it seems likely that the hope is not for the living but for the dead.

Form and Genre

In *The Sound and the Fury*, Faulkner uses the narrative technique of stream of consciousness, conveying the thoughts, feelings, and sensations experienced by the narrators as their minds perceive them. The reader is allowed to follow each narrator's thoughts, so that nothing is hidden or censored. Curiously, the reader is given this insight into the thoughts of Benjy, Quentin, and Jason, but not Dilsey. The great advantage of this technique is that it allows full access to the characters' minds. One challenging aspect of the approach Faulkner chooses to adopt is that no mind is absolutely coherent. Thoughts intrude, ideas come and go without explanation, and memories arise without respect to chronology. Particularly in Benjy's section, the flights of his mind are difficult to follow; yet, there would be no other way for Benjy to communicate the depth of his story.

It is difficult to say what, succinctly, *The Sound and the Fury* is about. It does not have a conventional plot. The important events have mostly occurred in the past. There is no sense of a story building to its crisis with a denouement followed by a movement toward resolution.

Faulkner rather famously called this novel his "most splendid failure." Often he seemed to be referring to his inability to fully capture the character and story of Caddy Compson. So perhaps the core story of *The Sound and the Fury* centers on the failures of communication. The three chapters of the Compson brothers are told in stream-of-consciousness narration. It is impossible to imagine them otherwise. The thoughts that the reader has access to are completely hidden from the other characters in the novel. Think of how rarely Benjy makes himself understood to others. It seems that only Caddy and Dilsey understand him, and then only at times. The word *caddie* has an entirely different meaning to the golfers than it does to Benjy. His interest in the schoolgirls is also tragically misinterpreted. But Quentin and Jason are no better understood, and although Dilsey might provide the most overarching view of what is happening in the Compson family, her race and position in their household ensure that no one in the novel will look to her as the key to their story.

In terms of genre, the novel is a tragedy. In most cases, a tragedy tells the story of one heroic character who is brought to ruin by a fatal flaw. In this case, it is a family, once perhaps noble and great, that is brought to its end by a number of failings. It is also possible to argue that one of the characters is the tragic hero, particularly Benjy or Caddy. *The Sound and the Fury* might also be called a southern gothic novel. The story has elements of the gothic: the great house and family, insanity, illness, incest, and suicide.

Sample Topics:

1. **Stream of consciousness:** Considering Faulkner's heavy reliance on the technique of stream of consciousness, could you argue that Benjy is the most important of the narrators?

Although it might not be clear until you have finished the novel, Benjy's section touches on every aspect of the novel's story. In the later chapters, Benjy's scrambled thoughts are elaborated on, and the events of his memory are explained more clearly. An essay on this topic could argue that Benjy is the most important narrator because every significant event for the Compsons is experienced by Benjy as the present moment. Further, he is the brother who has the best understanding of Caddy, though his perceptions are sensory and intuitive.

2. **Plot:** What would you argue is the climactic or most important event that occurs in *The Sound and the Fury*?

This is an open-ended question that could be successfully answered in a number of ways as long as the answer was well supported with evidence. One possible thesis is that Quentin's suicide is the novel's central event. Quentin's narration, occurring 18 years before the rest of the novel, could be cited as evidence. Another possible argument is that Caddy's loss of innocence is the most significant event. All four narrators speak of this event and the introduction of Miss Quentin into the family. An argument could also be made that the Easter service attended by Benjy and the Gibson family is the novel's climax.

3. **Failures of language:** How does language fail in *The Sound and the Fury*?

An essay on this topic might focus on one instance or on the novel as a whole. Benjy, for instance, often thinks that "Caddy smelled like trees," but he is unable to put into words this thought or its conclusion, that when she no longer has that particular odor, it is because she is maturing and indulging in sexual behaviors. Quentin wants to say that he and Caddy committed incest because that would damn them both and negate the presence of Caddy's other romantic and sexual partners. This topic could also touch on the subject of names. Quentin wants Caddy to say the name "Dalton Ames," so that he will know if she loved him and if he was Miss Quentin's father. What does a person's name signify in this novel?

4. Tragedy: What is the fatal flaw of the Compson family?

An essay could argue that one particular character is the tragic hero of this novel. But if you accept that the tragedy belongs to the Compson family as a whole, then what would you say is their tragic flaw? A case could be made for self-delusion. The absence of maternal love can also be asserted as damning to the Compson children. This would allow you to focus on Mrs. Compson, who has likely been the subject of fewer essays than her children.

Language, Symbols, and Imagery

Water, representing innocence and purity, is perhaps the most prevalent symbol in *The Sound and the Fury*. Benjy remembers pulling Caddy away from one of her young men in this passage:

Caddy and I ran. We ran up the kitchen steps, onto the porch, and Caddy knelt down in the dark and held me. I could hear her and feel her chest. "I wont." she said. "I wont anymore, ever. Benjy. Benjy." Then she was crying, and I cried, and we held each other. "Hush." She said. "Hush. I wont anymore." So I hushed and Caddy got up and we went into the kitchen and turned the light on and Caddy took the kitchen soap and washed her mouth at the sink, hard. Caddy smelled like trees. (48)

Benjy is unhappy any time Caddy does not smell like a little girl, even if she is only wearing perfume, and so she washes the scent of the young man away. In one of Benjy's earliest memories, Caddy has mud on her exposed underpants and is unashamed by it. After she loses her virginity, she lays near the water with Quentin. Quentin's section is perhaps the most symbolic of the novel and is also the part that features water most prominently. Tellingly, Quentin commits suicide in the Charles River.

As he contemplates suicide, Quentin watches his shadow, another important symbol in the novel:

The shadow of the bridge, the tiers of railing, my shadow leaning flat upon the water, so easily had I tricked it that would not quit me. At least fifty feet it was, and if I only had something to blot it into the water, holding it until it was drowned, the shadow of the package like two shoes wrapped up lying on the water. Niggers say a drowned man's shadow was watching for him in the water all the time. It twinkled and glinted, like breathing, the float slow like breathing too, and debris half submerged, healing out to the sea and the caverns and the grottoes of the sea. The displacement of water is equal to the something of something. Reducto absurdum of all human experience, and two six-pound flat-irons weigh more than one tailor's goose. What a sinful waste Dilsey would say. (90)

Shadows are important, particularly in Benjy and Quentin's sections, because they mark the passing of time. Quentin would like to escape or "trick" his shadow, as he could thus escape from it and from time. One of Quentin's difficulties is that he feels trapped, or overshadowed, by the history of the South and the Compson family. The passage from *Macbeth* provides yet another possible meaning of "shadow." Shakespeare wrote: "Life's but a walking shadow, a poor player / That struts and frets his hour upon the stage."

Macbeth's speech seems to supply much of the imagery of *The Sound and the Fury*. In the play, time is symbolically limited to the duration of a performance. In *The Sound and the Fury,* all references to time are magnified and of heightened importance. The three brothers experience time differently. Benjy lives in an eternal present. Quentin, burdened by the past, seeks a release from the controlling strictures of time. In Jason's section, time is money, and his section moves hour by hour. Though Quentin's section of the novel is filled with references to time, clocks, and shadows, Quentin's watch is a particularly important symbol. Quentin's father gives him the watch, passed down from Quentin's grandfather, as a reminder not to attach so much importance to time. But to Quentin, it achieves the opposite, as the gift is a constant reminder. He tries to stop the watch by breaking its face and twisting the hands off, but the clock continues to tick. Quentin continues to hear this ticking throughout his final day.

Another concrete object that takes on symbolic importance, like Quentin's watch, is Caddy's body. Caddy's body has significance for her brothers beyond what it should. In early childhood on the day of Damuddy's funeral, Caddy slips out of her dress. She lacks the shame Quentin feels she should have. She gets mud on her undergarments, which is symbolic of her later sexual exploits. To Benjy, her body means comfort, love, and protection, and he experiences Caddy through his sense of smell. Jason views Caddy with the disgust that he seems to feel for all women, except that Caddy's sexuality brings money and shame to the Compsons, both of which he would use to his own ends. For Quentin, Caddy embodies meanings so complex that he cannot resolve them well enough to live in this world.

Sample Topics:

1. **Water:** Explain the significance of water in *The Sound and the Fury*.

   To write an essay on this topic, you would look at the instances when water appears in the novel. Water is most closely associated with Quentin and Caddy and with conceptions of sex and death. In Christian tradition, water has the property of cleansing, as in a baptism. You might argue that Quentin and Caddy wish for water to have this capability, but that it fails them. They do not emerge from the water clean; instead, they come out muddied.

2. **Shadow:** What meanings does the shadow take on in the novel beyond its use to mark time?

   The shadow as a symbol is particularly important in Benjy's and Quentin's sections. Benjy is always shadowed by one of the Gibson boys. At times, as in the previously cited passage when Quentin looks over the water, thoughts of shadows lead to thoughts about the black characters in the novel. It might be possible to argue that one shadow that haunts Quentin is the "shadow" family of the Gibsons, and one sin that follows him North is the curse of slavery. Another possibility is that the shadow is simply a dark version of the self. Passages that describe how Benjy goes to sleep might yield other possible interpretations.

3. **Quentin's watch:** What is the significance of Quentin's watch?

   Quentin's section begins with the breaking of his watch and ends after he places the watch in Shreve's drawer. What do you believe is the significance of Quentin's watch, which ticks on even after the face and hands are broken? One possible thesis is that Quentin believes that death can stop time, but the watch proves him wrong. Another is that the watch represents everything that Quentin is fleeing from, particularly the accumulated past of his family.

4. **Caddy's body:** Examine the importance of Caddy's body to any one of her brothers.

The suggestion above would be one possible way to write an essay on the symbolism of Caddy's body. Depending on which brother you choose, the essay could take on a variety of forms. If you were to write on the importance of her body to Benjy, you might discuss the scene of the dirty underpants. You would also likely include instances of the maternal care she provides Benjy, such as carrying him even when he is five years old. Benjy recognizes the transformations that are happening as Caddy matures by the changing way she smells. Like her other brothers, his love for her is mixed with the question of what she physically means to him.

Compare and Contrast Essays

A number of compare and contrast essays could be written by pairing the characters in *The Sound and the Fury*. For instance, on Quentin's final day alive, he is followed by a small girl he addresses as "sister." How does this child compare to Caddy? One notable difference in Quentin's mind is that the girl's brother comes to her defense, even though Quentin has done no harm to the child. Shreve and Quentin are yet another interesting pair. There are obvious homoerotic overtones to their friendship, but Shreve is also at times compared by Quentin to his father. Shreve is Canadian, and he urges Quentin to tell him about the South, thus the two could be seen as embodying a contrast between the North and the South. Unlike Quentin, Shreve is unburdened by history.

Benjy and Quentin could be compared as the two brothers most affected by Caddy's absence. Caddy could be seen in contrast to all of her brothers. She has a spirit the others lack. This is revealed when she climbs the tree to look into the parlor at the funeral. She is not afraid, as the others are.

Included in this section are two topics that prompt you to compare or contrast the novel's characters. The first asks that you compare or contrast Dilsey with Mrs. Compson. An obvious point to make is that Dilsey moves into the maternal role abandoned by Mrs. Compson. Less obvious, but important, is how Dilsey fails to be a mother to the children. She has her own family and cannot, no matter how she works at it, take the place of their mother.

One possible essay could contrast any of the children with his or her siblings, but one strong possibility would be to contrast Jason with the other Compson children. His mother insists he is the best of her children; readers sense how wrong she is in her assessment. An essay about him might discuss such things as his attitude toward women and people of other racial backgrounds. You might want to discuss his attitude toward work and money, both foreshadowed early in the novel when Benjy remembers him always with his hands in his pockets. It is Jason who is the end of the Compson family line, as the last surviving male who could have children but who chooses not to. He also sells the remainder of the family land and the home and puts Benjy in an institution. Jason fails to care about the fate of his sister or her child.

The characters in *The Sound and the Fury* appear in other works by Faulkner. It is an interesting fact that in his Yoknapatawpha County any of its residents might appear in any of his stories. It can be thrilling or unexpected to encounter these characters again in different surrounding. Each time they are seen again, we learn more about them and gain a new perspective on the character.

The Compson family appears in Faulkner's short story "That Evening Sun." The story involves a young black woman who sometimes works for the Compsons. She is pregnant with the child of a white man who has forced himself on her. She is terrified that her estranged husband, named Jesus, is going to kill her. She seeks protection from the Compsons and particularly tries to keep the children with her, believing she will not be killed if she can keep someone white nearby. The Compsons are portrayed much the same as they are in *The Sound and the Fury*, but the story's focus on the children while they are still young gives an even greater glimpse into their inner workings and past influences. Quentin Compson narrates the story.

Quentin is also a major character in Faulkner's novel *Absalom, Absalom!* He is chosen by Rosa Coldfield to hear the story of her family and that of Thomas Sutpen. Quentin in turn tells the story to Shreve. The Sutpen family has several things in common with the Compsons, including an extraordinarily close relationship between the brother and sister that borders on incest. But Henry Sutpen kills Judith's suitor, Bon, revealing the Sutpens to be far more corrupt (or more honorable) than the Compsons. As is likely the case in *The Sound and the Fury*, the last surviving member of the family is not in possession of his full mental faculties. Reading *Absalom, Absalom!* or "That Evening Sun" will give you greater insight into Quentin's character—why he is so burdened by his memories of the South and perhaps why he eventually commits suicide.

Sample Topics:

1. **Dilsey and Mrs. Compson:** Compare or contrast these two characters.

   An essay on this topic might look closely at those scenes when Mrs. Compson and Dilsey interact. There is ample evidence of Dilsey nurturing the Compson children. There is equally ample evidence of Mrs. Compson failing to do so. As he moves toward suicide, Quentin repeats, "if I'd just had a mother so I could say Mother Mother" (172). What does it mean to be unable to say "Mother"?

2. **Jason and the other children:** Compare Jason to the other Compson children.

   Mrs. Compson is always saying that Jason is more Bascomb than Compson. Do you see any evidence that supports her thinking, or is this another example of her delusions? How does Jason differ from Caddy, Benjy, and Quentin? Why do you think Faulkner gave Jason the same name as his father? You know that Benjy began his life with the name Maury. Would this name be more suitable for Jason Jr.?

3. **"That Evening Sun" and *The Sound and the Fury*:** Compare the Compson children of "That Evening Sun" to those of *The Sound and the Fury*.

In "That Evening Sun," the Compson children are shown facing a tragedy beyond their understanding. Caddy seems aware of Nancy's terror, but with a limited, child's understanding. Nancy looks to the children to protect her from her approaching death. It is ironic, since they are so small, but it shows that a white child held more power at the time than a mature black woman. An essay could be written exploring the thesis that the short story forecasts the problems that the Compson children will face as they mature.

4. **Quentin in this novel and Quentin in *Absalom, Absalom!*:** Does Quentin hate the South?

Absalom, Absalom! ends rather famously with Quentin protesting that he does not hate the South. Why does Shreve, who knows him so well, believe that he does? What is his evidence? Why is Quentin the narrator in two Faulkner novels? Why did Rosa Coldfield choose him to hear her story? What does Henry Sutpen mean to Quentin? In reading these two novels together, do you come to any better understanding of Quentin's decision to take his own life? You might consider whether it is significant that Quentin tells his story in the North, at Harvard, and to a Canadian.

Bibliography and Online Resources for *The Sound and the Fury*

Backman, Melvin. *Faulkner: The Major Years: A Critical Study*. Bloomington: Indiana UP, 1966.

Bassett, John E. *Vision and Revisions: Essays on Faulkner*. West Cornwall, CT: Locust Hill, 1989.

Bleikasten, Andre. *The Most Splendid Failure: Faulkner's The Sound and the Fury*. Bloomington: Indiana UP, 1976.

Bloom, Harold, ed. *Caddy Compson*. New York: Chelsea House, 1990.

———. *William Faulkner's The Sound and the Fury*. New York: Chelsea House, 1988.

Brooks, Cleanth. "Faulkner's Vision of Good and Evil." *Massachusetts Review* 3 (Summer 1962): 692–712.

Cowan, Michael H., ed. *Twentieth Century Interpretations of The Sound and the Fury*. Englewood Cliffs, NJ: Prentice, 1968.

Edel, Leon. "How to Read *The Sound and the Fury*." *Varieties of Literary Experience: Eighteen Essays in World Literature*. Ed. Stanley Burnshaw. New York: NYU Press, 1962. 241–57.

Faulkner, William. *Faulkner in the University*. Eds. Frederick L. Gwynn and Joseph L. Blotner. Charlottesville: UP of Virginia, 1959.

———. *The Sound and the Fury*. New York: Vintage International P, 1990.

Hahn, Stephen, and Arthur F. Kinney, eds. *Approaches to Teaching Faulkner's The Sound and the Fury*. New York: MLA, 1996.

Hoffman, Frederick. *William Faulkner*. New York: Twayne, 1961.

Hoffman, Frederick, and Olga Vickery, eds. *William Faulkner: Three Decades of Criticism*. East Lansing: Michigan State UP, 1960.

Howe, Irving. *William Faulkner: A Critical Study*. 3d ed. Chicago: UP of Chicago, 1975.

Irwin, John T. *Doubling and Incest/Repetition and Revenge: A Speculative Reading of Faulkner*. 1975. Expanded ed. Baltimore: Johns Hopkins UP, 1996.

Kinney, Arthur F. *Critical Essays on William Faulkner: The Compson Family*. Boston: G. K. Hall, 1982.

Matthews, John T. *The Sound and the Fury: Faulkner and the Lost Cause*. New York: Twayne, 1990.

Meriwether, James B., and Eileen Gregory. *Studies in The Sound and the Fury*. Columbus, OH: Charles E. Merrill, 1970.

Millgate, Michael. *William Faulkner*. New York: Grove Press, 1961.

Minter, David. "Faulkner, Childhood, and the Making of *The Sound and the Fury*." *American Literature* 51 (1979): 376–93.

———, ed. *The Sound and the Fury: A Norton Critical Edition*. New York: W. W. Norton, 1987.

Moser, Thomas C. "Faulkner's Muse: Speculations on the Genesis of *The Sound and the Fury*." *Critical Reconstructions: The Relationship of Fiction and Life*. Eds. Robert M. Polemus and Roger B. Henkle. Stanford, CA: Stanford UP, 1994. 187–211.

Novak, Phillip. "Meaning, Mourning, and the Form of Modern Narrative: The Inscription of Loss in Faulkner's *The Sound and the Fury*." *Faulkner Journal* 12.1 (Fall 1995–Spring 1996): 63–90.

Palumbo, Donald. "The Concept of God in Faulkner's 'Light in August', 'The Sound and the Fury', 'As I Lay Dying', and 'Absalom, Absalom!'" *South Central Bulletin* 34 (1979): 142–46.

Polk, Noel, ed. *New Essays on The Sound and the Fury*. Cambridge: Cambridge UP, 1993.

Ross, Stephen M. *Reading Faulkner: The Sound and the Fury*. Jackson: UP of Mississippi, 1996.

Stegner, Wallace, ed. *The American Novel from James Fennimore Cooper to William Faulkner*. New York: Basic, 1965.

Sundquist, Eric J. *Faulkner: The House Divided*. Baltimore: Johns Hopkins UP, 1983.

Swiggart, Peter. *The Art of Faulkner's Novels*. Austin: U of Texas P, 1962.

Swisher, Clarice, ed. *Readings on William Faulkner*. San Diego, CA: Greenhaven Press: 1998.

The Sound and the Fury: A Hypertext Edition. Eds. Stoicheff, Muri, Deshaye, et al. Updated March 2003. U. of Saskatchewan. Accessed November 10, 2007. URL: http://www.usask.ca/english/faulkner.

Thompson, Lawrence. *William Faulkner: An Introduction and Interpretation*. New York: Barnes and Noble, 1963.

Vickery, Olga W. *The Novels of William Faulkner: A Critical Interpretation*. Baton Rouge: Louisiana State UP, 1964.

Warren, Robert Penn, ed. *Faulkner: A Collection of Critical Essays*. Englewood Cliffs, NJ: Prentice Hall, 1966.

Weinstein, Philip M., ed. *William Faulkner's The Sound and the Fury: A Critical Casebook*. New York: Garland, 1982.

Wolff, Sally, and David Minter. "A 'Matchless Time': Faulkner and the Writing of *The Sound and the Fury*." *Writing the American Classics*. Eds. James Barbour and Tom Quirk. Chapel Hill: U of North Carolina P, 1990. 156–76.

"A ROSE FOR EMILY"

READING TO WRITE

"A ROSE FOR EMILY" was the first of Faulkner's stories to be published in a major magazine when it appeared in *Forum* on April 30, 1930. It remains one of Faulkner's most anthologized and widely read stories. The reader of Faulkner's novels will recognize that the story shares many elements with the larger works, while being eminently more accessible. In "A Rose for Emily," as in other Faulkner stories, Faulkner uses a recognizable setting and characters that are a part of his larger creation of Yoknapatawpha County. The story is short enough to read and then reread, as you will want to if you are going to write about "A Rose for Emily." One question to ask as you read is what genre does this story fit into? Is it a horror story, a gothic story, a love story, or something else altogether?

You will also want to identify the narrator. The narrator speaks in terms of "we," and he or she seems to represent the townspeople. Who is this individual? Do you take him to be, simply, "the town"? Is he an unnamed individual, and, if so, is he male or female? Is he young or old? You will have to come to the answer yourself, because Faulkner gives few clues. This unidentified voice also sets the tone of the story. As an observer, the narrator is at some distance from Emily Grierson's troubles, and yet he is quite knowledgeable about them. He recounts Emily's story from her youth until after her death and is present when her secret is brought to light.

This secret is the story's ending and the source of some amusement and shock for most readers. After having read the story once and learning Emily's secret of 40 years, read the story again. The second time it will be clear that Faulkner did provide the necessary details to lead the reader to the final revelation, though most readers cannot guess the ending at first or cannot imagine how twisted it really is.

TOPICS AND STRATEGIES
Themes

While it may be an unconventional one, "A Rose for Emily" is a love story. The revelation that Emily has slept beside Homer Barron's corpse for 40 years lets us know that his killing was motivated more by love than some other reason, such as pride or revenge. Emily takes care of Homer's corpse; she has a loyalty to him that lasts throughout her life.

Death is a theme in the story as well, and not only the death of Homer Barron. There are at least five deaths discussed in the course of the story; more than that, the tone of the story reminds the reader that death is ever present. Emily and her home are described in terms that remind one of death. The story begins with Emily's funeral and closes with the remains of Homer Barron.

The narrator's voice demonstrates another of the story's themes, which is the idea of community. The narrator seems to speak for the town. The town is "we," while Emily and Homer are outside that circle. While it is clear that Homer has reason to be, since he is a northerner and not from Jefferson, it is not immediately apparent why Emily is not embraced by the community. What the reader comes to realize is that Emily has set herself apart. This, in a sense, sets the tone for her life.

Isolation is another thematic concern. Emily is isolated from the community. Her isolation is so thorough that she does not or cannot have a suitor from Jefferson. Even her choice of lovers marks her as different. Her isolation eventually grows to resemble a living death in which her closest companion is a corpse.

Sample Topics:

1. Love: Can "A Rose for Emily" be considered a story of love?

A paper on this topic might illuminate the ways "A Rose for Emily" follows the conventions of a love story, or the way Emily's affair with Homer Barron follows the conventions of a love affair. Is

Emily a woman who has met her one true love, or is she a woman who has no idea how to love? How does "A Rose for Emily" reverse such traditional fairy tales as "Sleeping Beauty"?

2. **Death:** How strongly is death foretold in the story?

The ending of "A Rose for Emily" is intentionally shocking. But if you go back to the story's beginning and read it again, you will realize that death is a consistent undercurrent informing the story. If you were to write a paper on this topic, you might begin to illustrate the numerous instances that death is alluded to. How does Faulkner still manage to shock, when so many clues to the story's end are given throughout?

3. **Community:** What role does the community play in Homer Barron's death?

On your second reading, as you realize that Homer Barron's death was likely common knowledge in Jefferson, you may ask yourself if the community is complicit in his death. What did the narrator know, and when did he or she know it? Remember how the men of the town turn out to spread the lime in the night. Note also that the locked room in Emily's house is not opened until after the funeral.

4. **Isolation:** Why is Emily cut off from the community?

A paper discussing the theme of isolation could focus on Emily and her personality traits. Or it could veer into the realm of Emily's father and his attitudes. It could explore ideas of southern gentility. Why are there no appropriate suitors for Emily? Is it because of an inborn haughtiness or because the men who would have been eligible to marry her were killed in the Civil War?

Character

An essay on character might focus on any individual presence in the story. Emily Grierson is an obvious choice, and she is such a multifaceted character that she could bear extensive scrutiny. Why is she able to operate outside the law? How is she a product of her environment? An essay could consider Emily's personality and how it led to her crime. Emily seems to be a representative of the old South, and for this she is admired and condemned. One possible topic could lead to an analysis of Emily in terms of her physical description. Her appearance reflects the events of the story.

Homer Barron is at the center of "A Rose for Emily," but he receives little attention from the narrator. This invites the reader to imagine attributes that may or may not be a part of his character. For instance, when the narrator remarks that Barron "liked men" (126), some modern readers have taken this to mean that Barron was homosexual and thus had no interest in becoming Emily's romantic partner. But the remark must be taken in the context and time of the story, and here it probably means simply that Barron was a "man's man," a carouser and a drinker.

Emily's only companion after Homer disappears is her servant, Tobe. He provides one comical flourish in the story, when he opens the front door for the town's ladies and then walks directly out the back door never to be seen again. He knows what the townspeople will soon find in the house. Most of the time he is referred to as "the Negro." This indicates aspects of the racial climate of the period. Tobe's quick disappearance perhaps indicates what could happen to a black man found residing in a house that contains the corpse of a dead white man.

"A Rose for Emily" is a story with few characters, and as such it might be easy to overlook one of the most important, the town. The narrator seems to speak for the town. Whether this is the case or not, the entire story hinges on the town's relationship to Emily Grierson. One important question to ask might be to what extent the town is implicated in the killing of Homer Barron.

Sample Topics:

1. **Emily Grierson:** What do the physical descriptions of Emily Grierson tell us about her character?

    For instance, when Emily appears in public after her father's death, she is radically changed. When she appears after Homer's disappearance, she is changed once again. From these physical descriptions, the reader must surmise the interior of Emily Grierson's experience, because the narrator has no access to her actual thoughts and feelings.

2. **Homer Barron:** What is the nature of Homer Barron's character?

One potentially fruitful approach to an essay on character is to explore the connotations and implications of the character's name. What does Homer Barron's name suggest about him? Is he some sort of "robber baron" from the North, hoping to exploit the South for his personal profit? Is his death less important to the townspeople because he is a northerner? Is he meant to suggest the comforts of "home" or the wanderings of a character out of Homer's *Iliad* or *Odyssey*?

3. **Tobe:** What role does Tobe play in the story? Why is his presence important?

An essay on this topic might discuss racial relations in the time of "A Rose for Emily." Tobe has a small role but an important one. For one thing, he demonstrates the loyalty a house servant might have, one who goes so far as to remain silent about his knowledge of a murder.

4. **The town:** Discuss the importance of the town as a character in "A Rose for Emily."

It could be argued that the town is the central character of the story. The unnamed narrator has been taken by many critics to be the collective voice of the townspeople. An essay on this topic could discuss the town's treatment of Emily Grierson through the years. It might consider, too, the question of whether the town knew that they would find evidence of Homer Barron's murder in Miss Emily's house.

History and Context

"A Rose for Emily" takes in some of the changes that occurred in the South after the Civil War, in the period of Reconstruction, a time when the status of many aristocratic southern families like the Griersons diminished. Northerners like Homer Barron are still considered "Yankees," but in spite of that difference he is able to form an intimate relationship with a southerner.

One relationship in the story is between the deaths Emily experiences and the death of the South. Emily cannot accept death as a natural progression, and she represents numerous southerners who could not accept that the South as they knew it was no more or soon on its way out.

The narrator describes Emily as a "fallen monument" (119). As a southern woman, in the past she would have been afforded special treatment due to her status as a lady. Her fall, when it comes, is on several levels. She is fallen because the economic privilege of her family is lost. The class distinctions that set her apart from the townspeople no longer hold the importance they once did. She is also compromised in the sense that she has violated the codes of those class differences in her relations with Homer Barron. She is fallen in the conventional sense of a woman who is no longer innocent and also in that the status she might have enjoyed as a woman of a certain class no longer exists at all.

Sample Topics:

1. **Reconstruction:** How does the story highlight the problems of the South during Reconstruction?

   Perhaps one of the reasons Homer Barron's death goes unmarked by the people of Jefferson is because he is a northerner. The town is moving forward, but not without resistance. Emily Grierson's stronger refusal to accept change is viewed by some with admiration and thus worth protecting with the town's collective silence.

2. **Southern gothic:** If Emily is representative of the South, then what is Faulkner saying about the South?

Reread the story with the consideration that Emily Grierson is a symbol for the South. What conclusions might be drawn? Is the South unmoored? Has it become cut off from reality? Would it rather hold fast to a corpse, an outmoded way of life, than move into the future?

3. **Southern women:** How can Emily Grierson be considered representative of southern women?

What does the story have to tell us about the position of southern women after the Civil War? Discuss Emily's portrayal as a woman. What do you learn about other women from the story? How is Emily like others? Is she capable of things others are not?

4. **Class:** How can "A Rose for Emily" be said to be about class in the South?

It is possible to argue that Emily gets away with her crime because of her class. Consider how she is dismissive of those she perceives as beneath her, like the druggist or the authorities who come to collect the tax.

Philosophy and Ideas

Like many Faulkner characters, Emily Grierson has her own problem with time. Time is one of the central themes in "A Rose for Emily." The title character may be seen as attempting to stop time, or she could be seen as being in denial about time's progression. She might also not be alone in her difficulties. If you were to write about the problem of time in the story, you will want to pay attention to the passage in which Faulkner discusses the men who attend Emily's funeral. He writes that they have confused "time with its mathematical progression, as the old do, [and] to whom all the past is not a diminishing road but, instead, a huge meadow which no winter ever quite touches, divided from them now by the narrow bottle-neck of the most recent decade of years" (129).

Emily's problem with time might be synonymous with or directly linked to her problem with accepting death. The story recounts how she is unwilling to let her father's body be taken from her home, a fore-shadowing of the later relationship with Homer Barron's body. Still, an argument could be made that her denial of the realities of death is a more vexing problem than her denial of the passing of time. Her embrace of the decaying bodies of both Homer and her father show an unwillingness to accept this most certain eventuality.

The town views Emily's relationship with Homer Barron as a scandal and Emily as a woman who has been cast off by her lover. When the marriage that would legitimize their relationship fails to take place, Emily is pitied. But since there is little indication of how Emily herself felt, it is possible to imagine that her feelings about Homer Barron were not pitiable. There is a difference between Emily as the narrator sees her and the way Emily herself behaves. Her obstinacy might be less a sign of delusion than a sign of strength. Perhaps Emily Grierson was a budding feminist: sure of herself, able to live alone, untouched by public opinion, and able to get her way, even if it required murder.

A reader of "A Rose for Emily" might be moved to question Emily's sanity. It would be easy to read the last episode of the story and conclude that Emily was insane. But since Faulkner gives no access to Emily's thoughts, it might be possible to imagine that she was in full possession of her mental faculties. The narrator relates incidences that seem to be evidence of her imbalance (the confrontation over the taxes, the smell from her house, and her unusual withdrawal from her neighbors). Has she lost touch with reality, or is there another explanation?

Sample Topics:

1. **The problem of time:** How does the narrator make us aware of the problem of time?

> There are many ways to discuss how time functions in the story. Time is often symbolized by something else, like the marks of decay or a watch. The chronology of the story is fractured and disjointed, so that time does not proceed in a linear fashion. One argument to make on this topic is that Emily's attempts to stop time fail.

2. **The problem of death:** Why is death a "problem" in "A Rose for Emily"?

Is death a problem for Emily? In a sense, it saves her relationship with Homer, preserving it just as it was. In death, he is unable to leave her. Her father's death, however, is clearly difficult for her to accept. But after her mourning is over, she appears reborn. One possible thesis on this subject would be that Emily attempts to manage the problem of death by refusing to face its reality.

3. **Feminism:** Defend Emily Grierson as a feminist heroine.

A common interpretation of the story is that Emily is placed at a disadvantage in her surroundings because she is a woman. Yet, there are many instances in "A Rose for Emily" in which being female works to her advantage. An essay on this topic could enlarge on those instances and discuss how, in nearly every instance, Emily gets her way.

4. **Sanity:** Can it be argued that Emily Grierson is sane?

This would make a potentially more compelling essay than one that argued for her insanity because it would be harder to prove. One way to approach such a topic would be to consider the possibility that the narrator is less reliable than he or she may at first appear. Although we trust that Emily did all that the narrator recounts, her motives and thoughts may not be just those he or she ascribes to her.

Form and Genre

One of the great pleasures of "A Rose for Emily" is the shock of the ending, its violation of expectation. It is the rare reader who sees the final outcome of the story before arriving at its actual conclusion. But after reading it, it might be worth asking if the resolution is foreshadowed and how it was. If the ending could not be anticipated, Faulkner has still taken steps to ensure that it is plausible. For instance, Emily did not want to part with the body of her father nor admit that he had died. Faulkner also describes Emily and her house in terms of decay.

The conclusion of "A Rose for Emily" might have been less surprising had Faulkner not violated chronological order in telling the story. A useful exercise before writing about "A Rose for Emily" would be to reorder the individual sections or events chronologically and see how that affects the overall story. What logic does Faulkner bring to his organization?

One of the other aspects of this story that is often noted is the narrator. The narrator plays such a significant role, yet he or she is never identified. The narrator brings knowledge, humor, and a unique voice and viewpoint to the story.

If you were to try to characterize "A Rose for Emily" as belonging to a genre other than the short story, you might employ such terms as southern gothic. It might also be useful to think of "A Rose for Emily" as a horror story. It both violates and conforms to our expectations for that genre.

Sample Topics:

1. **Foreshadowing:** How does Faulkner foreshadow the ending of "A Rose for Emily" without overtly telegraphing it?

   An essay on this topic might argue that the story contains obvious clues that Homer Barron has been murdered. Careful reading combined with a discussion would bolster the argument. An exploration of the chronology of "A Rose for Emily" and the significance of a nonlinear approach would also enrich such a discussion.

2. **Chronology:** How does Faulkner's arrangement of "A Rose for Emily" build to the story's final effect?

   Faulkner does not tell "A Rose for Emily" chronologically. An essay on this topic might argue that it is Faulkner's arrangement, outside of chronological order, that ensures the story's ending will be a surprise. Such a paper could also possibly address the other ways an element of surprise is kept alive throughout the story, because readers do not see Emily Grierson's life as one of uninterrupted decline.

3. **Narrator:** Who is the narrator? What is his or her contribution to the story?

An essay on this topic would open up plenty of room for speculation, as these questions could be answered in a number of ways, as long as there is evidence given in support of your conclusion. It would be difficult to discount the narrator's importance. Additional topics that present themselves would be to define the characteristics of the narrator. For instance, what sort of person is he or she: profane, reliable, fair?

4. **Horror:** Is "A Rose for Emily" a horror story?

An essay on this topic could be addressed in a number of ways. A writer might argue that the story belongs to some other genre altogether. Greater familiarity with the conventions of the horror story could bolster an argument either for or against the story belonging to that subgenre. A writer could also compare this story with another horror story, perhaps one by Edgar Allan Poe.

Language, Symbols, and Imagery

The language, symbols, and imagery of "A Rose for Emily" build to a memorable conclusion. But throughout the story the sense of something being amiss is ever present, sustained by the very same elements. This could be identified as the story's tone. What feelings does the story inspire in you? Can you identify the overall tone, or say what it is that gives the story this feeling?

One way a particular tone is achieved is through the use of imagery and language that has meaning beyond itself. Someone who wanted to write about the symbols in "A Rose for Emily" could easily turn to a number of objects that have both practical meaning and larger, symbolic import beyond their mere physical presence in the story. For instance, there is the toiletry set Emily buys for Homer Barron, even though she clearly knows he will have little use for it. There is also the rose of the title, or Emily's steel gray hair. Another image of interest is her father's portrait. An essay writer might want to consider every portrayal of Emily's father in the story. He seems to preside over the house like a god, even after his death.

What does Emily's pocket watch suggest? She carries it with her always. Does it bear a relation to the body upstairs? Emily's house is described as decaying. Its contents are "tarnished," and there is a thick cover of dust on everything. If her house is meant to be a tomb or coffin, then what has happened to time inside this structure?

Sample Topics:

1. **Tone:** Identify and analyze the tone of "A Rose for Emily."

There are many possible ways to describe the story's tone. After arriving at an answer for yourself, consider how Faulkner builds and sustains this tone throughout. Careful attention to details and word choice will facilitate exploring such a topic. An argument could be formed that, because of the tone, the reader becomes aware, even in the first paragraph, that something is amiss in Emily's world.

2. **The portrait:** What does Emily's father's portrait seem to suggest about him?

Consider each appearance of Emily's father in "A Rose for Emily," both when he actually appears and when he is referred to or represented. Why does Emily keep the portrait of her father displayed? How much influence has he exerted over his daughter?

3. **Emily's watch:** Analyze Emily's watch as a symbol.

Does Emily use the watch as a means to control time? Does time always haunt or dog her? When the reader first encounters the watch, how does Faulkner signify its importance?

4. The house: Analyze Emily's house as a symbol.

How is the reader to understand Emily's house? Look carefully at how Faulkner describes it. Is it Emily's tomb? Why is her funeral held there? Why do the townspeople wait until she is buried to open the room upstairs?

Bibliography and Online Resources for "A Rose for Emily"

Allen, Dennis W. "Horror and Perverse Delight: Faulkner's 'A Rose for Emily'." *Modern Fiction Studies* 30 (Winter 1984): 685–96.

Blythe, Hal. "Faulkner's 'A Rose for Emily'." *Explicator* 47.2 (Winter 1989): 49–50.

Brooks, Cleanth. "The Sense of Community in Yoknapatawpha Fiction." *University of Mississippi Studies in English* 15 (1978): 3–18.

Burduck, Michael L. "Another View of Faulkner's Narrator in 'A Rose for Emily'." *University of Mississippi Studies in English* 8 (1990): 209–11.

Davis, William V. "Another Flower for Faulkner's Bouquet: Theme and Structure in 'A Rose for Emily'." *Notes on Mississippi Writers* 7 (1974): 34–38.

Faulkner, William. *Collected Stories of William Faulkner.* New York: Vintage, 1995.

Hays, Peter L. "Who Is Faulkner's Emily?" *Studies in American Fiction* 16 (Spring 1988): 105–110.

Inge, M. Thomas. *William Faulkner: "A Rose for Emily."* Columbus, OH: Merrill, 1970.

Jacobs, John T. "Ironic Allusions in 'A Rose for Emily'." *Notes on Mississippi Writers* 14 (1982): 77–79.

Kobler, J. F. "Faulkner's 'A Rose for Emily'." *Explicator* 32 (1974): 65.

Kurtz, Elizabeth Carney. "Faulkner's 'A Rose for Emily'." *Explicator* 44 (Winter 1986): 40.

Moore, Gene M. "Of Time and Its Mathematical Progression: Problems of Chronology in Faulkner's 'A Rose for Emily'." *Studies in Short Fiction* 29. 2 (Spring 1992): 195–204.

Muller, Gil. "Faulkner's 'A Rose for Emily'." *Explicator* 33 (1975): 79.

Petry, Alice Hall. "Faulkner's 'A Rose for Emily'." *Explicator* 44 (Spring 1986): 52–54.

Rodgers, Lawrence R. "We All Said, 'She Will Kill Herself': The Narrator/Detective in William Faulkner's 'A Rose for Emily'." *Clues: A Journal of Detection* 16.1 (1995): 117–29.

Schwab, Milinda. "A Watch for Emily." *Studies in Short Fiction* 28.2 (Spring 1991): 215–17.

Skinner, John L. "'A Rose for Emily': Against Interpretation." *Journal of Narrative Technique* 15 (Winter 1985): 42–51.

Sullivan, Ruth. "The Narrator in 'A Rose for Emily'." *Journal of Narrative Technique* 1 (1971): 159–78.

Wallace, James M. "Faulkner's 'A Rose for Emily'." *Explicator* 50 (Winter 1992): 105–07.

Weaks, Mary Louise. "The Meaning of Miss Emily's Rose." *Notes of Contemporary Literature* 11.5 (1981): 11–12.

West, Ray B., Jr. "Atmosphere and Theme in 'A Rose for Emily'." *Readings on William Faulkner.* Ed. Clarice Swisher. San Diego, CA: Greenhaven, 1998. 65–73.

AS I LAY DYING

READING TO WRITE

As *I Lay Dying*, a novel that William Faulkner reportedly wrote in six weeks while working nights in a power plant, was first published in 1930. It is Faulkner's fifth novel and is marked by the same originality of form as his others. The novel is told in short chapters, each named for the character whose thoughts are related in the form of an interior monologue. Although Faulkner also uses the interior monologue in *The Sound and the Fury*, in *As I Lay Dying* the voices belong to a number of characters, even the dead Addie Bundren.

The plot of the novel is straightforward: The Bundren family travels to Jefferson to bury Addie. But the story surrounding this journey is far more complex. While the Bundrens attempt to fulfill their promise to Addie, they are also beset with their own troubles and concerns. Anse, the father, wants to acquire a new set of teeth, and perhaps, as we find out later, to find a replacement for Addie. Dewey Dell is seeking a way to end her pregnancy. Cash hopes to buy a gramophone, and Vardaman wants to see a toy train. Jewell and Darl want to see their mother buried, but the difficulties they encounter trying to accomplish this prove too much for them to bear.

Addie is eventually buried in Jefferson, and, to some extent, Anse and Cash get what they came for, but the Bundren family is irrevocably altered along the way. As you read the novel, you might consider what the Bundren family carries with them when they set out for Jefferson. In addition to the coffin carrying Addie's body, each family member bears the personal weight of his or her relationship with her. The characters carry a number of psychological burdens (and the way the family name, Bundren, echoes the word *burden* is probably not an accident). For Addie's children, many of these burdens were passed to them even before their births, given to them during the pregnancies when Addie decided what she felt for them.

As you read and come to know the various characters in the novel, you will want to decide which voice is most compelling and which voice, if any, is to be trusted. The interior monologue allows readers to "hear" the characters' thoughts, but does that mean that we truly know them in a more direct, unfiltered, or uncensored way? One theme in *As I Lay Dying* is the inability of knowing one another. Even within a family, mother and child or husband and wife, true communication seems limited if not impossible. The Bundren children do not know their mother; Anse knows her even less. Darl is believed to have the most insight into the rest of his family, and his insight fuels their mistrust of him. They do not want to be known. None of the family knows the true reason Addie wished to be buried in Jefferson.

How does this diverse group, its members with their own distinct thoughts and desires, often at odds with one another, form a family? Is there anything admirable in them or their mission? What do they accomplish? As you read, think about the obstacles the Bundrens encounter on their journey. Which of those obstacles come from outside the family, such as the weather, and which come from within? Which ones prove insurmountable?

TOPICS AND STRATEGIES
Themes

Addie says of Anse, "He had a word, too. Love, he called it. But I had been used to words for a long time. I knew that that word was like the others: just a shape to fill a lack; that when the right time came, you wouldn't need a word for that anymore than for pride or fear" (172). The question of what words are and what they do or do not mean is one of the chief themes of *As I Lay Dying*. Addie is particularly eloquent on the subject of words and their lack of meaning. The unique structure of the novel, in which the characters each speak in turn, highlights how a person can be revealed or concealed by his or her own words. Examining the novel's sequence of monologues, the reader might also wonder about the adequacy of words. For instance, can any one character convey the entire story, or are we dependent on all the characters to get some semblance of a collective narrative? Darl and Vardaman talk about what "is" and "was." Vardaman asks him, "What is your ma, Darl?" And he answers, "I haven't got ere one. . . . Because if I had one, it is *was*. And if it is was, it cant be *is*. Can it?" (101). Darl's words argue him out of existence.

Words in all their power cannot negate the physical body, and the body is another important theme of the novel. Addie's body is the reason for their journey, and her body cannot be forgotten at any point in the novel. The body smells as it rots in the sun; it is heavy; it attracts buzzards. While it seems that any corpse should be treated with respect, the journey reveals how difficult it can be. In spite of the family's efforts, Addie's corpse is repugnant and the source of much of the novel's humor. It is a classic Faulknerian irony that it was Addie's body that also produced the Bundren children. Her family is intimately connected to her body. Dewey Dell believes her body has betrayed her by becoming pregnant, and she spends the trip attempting to hide and abort her pregnancy. Her feelings about motherhood are not unlike her mother's. For both women, conception is a type of violation of their physical selves, an unwanted intimacy. Cash's body, which is broken and abused in the journey, is another instance in which the physical is portrayed as repulsive and the flesh is revealed to be vulnerable and easily hurt.

The idea of the journey is a powerful theme in this novel, as it is in many other works of literature. Most commonly, the journey symbolically represents the notion that all people are set on a path at birth that ends only at death. The entire Bundren family is undertaking this particular journey, which begins with the death of Addie Bundren. The novel's title, *As I Lay Dying*, seems to suggest other deaths in addition to Addie's; since Addie is already dead, who can be said to be dying? It might be the Bundren family, but there are other possibilities as well. Their journey is marked by almost epical trials and tribulations, and, even with the addition of a new Mrs. Bundren, they return with one less family member after the loss of Darl.

It is impossible not to mention death as a theme in *As I Lay Dying*. We are accustomed to the idea of the dead being somehow revered and respected. What happens to Addie's corpse provides some comedy perhaps, but it also shows death as an ugly, inescapable, physical fact. The idea that death is about repose and a rest from the responsibilities of life is undone in Faulkner's visceral treatment. Addie's death prompts this journey, which involves real labor and physical effort.

Sample Topics:

1. **Words:** To what extent does *As I Lay Dying* suggest that a person is the actual words he or she speaks?

Addie has a strong distrust of words. Darl seems to know about the interior lives of people without any need for words. If you were to write an essay on this subject, there are many ways to approach it. You could focus on the words used by any one character. Since the novel is told by its characters in their own sections, reading only the sections belonging, say, to Vardaman, might lead to a thesis on Vardaman's words. Another possibility is to focus on what Addie has to say on this subject. Why is her distrust and hatred of words so strong?

2. **The body:** To what extent does *As I Lay Dying* suggest that a person is his or her body?

Addie's body is central to the novel, even before her death. She is the matriarch of the clan, and it is her body, after all, that produced nearly all the novel's main characters. You might want to consider, after thinking about what Addie says about pregnancy and Dewey Dell's strong reaction to her own pregnancy, the importance of the female body. Does the novel suggest that women have a stronger investment in their bodies, or that more is demanded of their bodies as evidenced in the transformations prompted by pregnancy? How related are they to their pregnancies? It seems Addie only had maternal feelings for one of her children. This may cause the reader to question many of the attitudes we expect mothers to hold for their offspring, as well as the idea that a mother is invested in her child bodily.

3. The journey: How is this journey different from the use of the journey in other novels?

So often the journey is cast in literature as a process of growth. Perhaps a character is set on a given course from cradle to grave, or a child embarks on a journey that will take him or her to adulthood. The journey has various landmarks and challenges, but the final result is arrival at the path's end, a better, stronger, or wiser person. Is there any growth for the Bundren family after their journey has ended? What effect does it have on the reader that Addie's journey is all about her burial?

4. Death: Does *As I Lay Dying* show a different version of death than you are accustomed to seeing?

This novel is atypical because the journey the characters take is about death instead of life. In most works of literature, death is about absence. A character will die and perhaps funeral proceedings will be recounted, but for the most part the death represents the end of that character. Addie dies as the novel begins, and one could argue that she is even more present and more a force within her family after her death. An essay on this topic might discuss how death is customarily thought of as an end, a cessation, but *As I Lay Dying* portrays it as a continuation of life. Addie's life after death is as fraught with difficulties and disrespect as her life before was.

Character

Addie is a richly interesting character. Her section of the novel, approximately six pages long, reveals much about the Bundren family and Addie herself. Quite possibly, up until the time she speaks, the reader has imbued Addie with whatever traits he or she associates with the idea of "mother." But Addie does not fit any conventional idea of a woman in that role. She is bitter and angry. She holds an unusual preoccupation with death, one that looks at all of life as a prelude to it. The dislike she felt for her students is transferred to Anse after their marriage, although it is possible that Anse affects her more than her students did. Her relations to her children are defined by what she felt for them during her pregnancies. These feelings seem to be a reflection of how their conceptions changed Addie's life. The birth of her first child, Cash, altered her conception of herself and placed her in the undesired position of no longer being in a solitary state. Each successive child altered her aloneness that much more.

Addie's vision of maternity is different from how it is commonly portrayed. The reader is not made privy to her relationships with her children as they grow (other than the occasional glimpse, for instance, of how troubled she is that Jewell has worn himself out to buy a horse). She also does not reflect conventional notions of a schoolteacher. Her illicit relationship with the pastor Whitfield further complicates her. She successfully keeps the secret of her adultery and Jewell's true parentage her entire life. The reader learns of both after Addie's death, and again, notably, from her corpse. It is impossible to forget that Addie speaks only after she is dead. When she does speak, she gives voice to her ideas about the nature of words and deeds, the nature of life and death, and love and sin. As her corpse is a weighty burden on the Bundren family, her monologue adds weight to the novel as a whole. What she adds complicates our view of the journey and the family undertaking it.

If Addie adds to the tragedy of the proceedings, then Anse adds to the comedy. It is difficult to imagine the marriage between these two. Anse is pathetically lazy and ridiculous in his excuses and desires; one would not wish to have him as a father. He sends Jewell and Darl off to work for three dollars, knowing that their mother is close to death. His attempts at tenderness, such as smoothing the quilt over his dead wife, are inept. The solemnity is entirely disrupted with what he says next: "God's will be done. . . . Now I can get them teeth" (52).

Jewell is Addie's third and favorite child, and he is shown to be a strong and capable man. His father, as revealed in Addie's narration, is the preacher Whitfield. Although Darl and Jewell both seem aware that Anse is not Jewell's father, there is nothing to indicate that either suspects the preacher. But there are other things that set Jewell apart from the rest of his family. We learn very little about his interior life. In that way, he most resembles Addie. Mirroring her interest in what worth words have when set against actions, Jewell is a man of action. His grief is expressed in his actions, and in his actions he reveals his depth of feeling for Addie. This characteristic is among his more admirable traits. It cannot be doubted that he has a passionate attachment to his mother, his horse, and himself. But he isolates himself from other people, just as Addie did. He independently earns his horse, doing the work for it secretly and alone.

Darl is Addie's second son. She felt Cash's birth violated her and her sense of being alone and beholden to no one. Darl has this effect on everyone, as if he possesses some ability to read their hearts and minds. He knows, intuitively it seems, that Jewell is not his father's biological son. He knows of Dewey Dell's pregnancy, and she resents the fact. Faulkner gave this sort of awareness and perception to Benjy in *The Sound and the Fury*. For Benjy, his knowledge of people's secret feelings and acts seems a recompense for his lack of understanding. But Darl is a character of tremendous intelligence. He is the most frequent narrator of *As I Lay Dying* (19 of the novel's 59 chapters are related by Darl), and his sections of the book are characterized by his eloquence and his philosophical leanings. Introspection and philosophy have no place in the Bundren family, and Darl is considered odd, an outsider.

Some of Darl's perceptions and insights border on the eerie, as when he knows that Addie is dead even though he and Jewell are far from home. He sometimes has an awareness or a vision of a scene that seems uncannily accurate, again, even though he is not present. Since these scenes are only related to the reader through him, there is a temptation to accept that he knows the details of what happened. Darl is the only one of the Bundren children to have left home; he fought in World War I. His attempt to end the journey by setting fire to the barn where Addie's coffin is provides the reason his family has him committed to a mental institution. But when we last see Darl, he is in fact mentally compromised in some way.

These four individuals represent the main characters of *As I Lay Dying*, but it is possible to imagine whole essays written on the lesser of even the minor characters in the novel. Whitfield, the preacher who knows himself to be Jewell's father but fails to take responsibility for the young man, could become the focus of an insightful essay. He speaks in only one chapter, as he makes his way, slowly, to confess his and Addie's sin. He is a marvel of self-delusion. His section illustrates beautifully the quarrel Addie has with words as opposed to deeds. Addie vowed to him she would never reveal their adulterous relationship. Yet, he believes she will make a deathbed confession. She does not, of course, and he takes her death as a sign that God has forgiven him. Now there is no need for him to confess, even though he has a grown son who will never know who his actual father is.

Cash Bundren is the eldest of the Bundren family. Like the other Bundren children, and unlike Anse, Cash is a capable person. His character is conveyed in his relationship with his tools and with his skill as a carpenter. The novel begins with Cash building Addie's coffin just outside the bedroom where she is dying. Though at first this might seem odd or macabre, it seems to be something that Addie wants. His feelings for his mother are expressed in his concern for the coffin.

Dewey Dell is the only Bundren daughter. Even in her naming, she represents something soft and alluring. In the novel, she is aligned or associated with spring and the fecundity of that season, for we learn early on that Dewey Dell is expecting a child and the reason she has to make the trip to Jefferson is to obtain an abortion. This is noteworthy in part because her mother equated childbearing with an unwanted disruption of her relationship with herself. Dewey Dell feels similarly violated by the "seed" planted within her. The father of her child has given her 10 dollars to obtain a prescription that would allow her to abort, and he has since disappeared.

Vardaman is the youngest of the Bundren children, and his chapters are curious for the psychological insight they offer into the child's mind in a state of ineffable grief and for the possible symbolic meaning they have. He does not accept the reality of his mother's death, instead equating her with the fish he caught. One of the strangest, most troubling, and comic moments in the book occurs when Vardaman, attempting to drill holes into the coffin so that his mother can breathe, actually drills holes in Addie's face.

Sample Topics:

1. **Addie:** What significance does Addie's monologue have to the book as a whole?

   One possible approach to an essay on this subject would be to discuss Addie's conception of the difference between words and deeds. How is her interest in this expressed throughout the novel? (For example, her son Cash looks at everything through the model of carpentry and a job, or action, properly done—words are, to him, no substitute for this.) Another possibility would be to look at sexuality as it is expressed in Addie's section. A paper on this topic might focus on such images and motifs as blood, violations, space, and lack. Further, the entire chapter is an expression of Addie's views on motherhood. Some of these views carry over to Dewey Dell. Addie's section is also an extended rumination on death.

2. **Anse:** Anse is responsible for a good deal of the book's humor; to what extent is Anse a comic character?

This topic might reflect your final feeling about the novel, whether it is a comedy or a tragedy. Anse is undeniably funny, though he does not know it or intentionally try to inject humor into the narrative. As a father, he is less than admirable. Why do his children stand by him? A paper on this topic might become a discussion of the tragedy of their fidelity to him.

3. **Jewell:** Why does Jewell wish for Darl to be committed?

What happens to Darl is shocking, not only his overall removal from the family but also how it is enacted, particularly the anger and violence that Jewell and Dewey Dell bring to the scene. An essay that attempted to explain Jewell's behavior might focus on the rivalry between the two sons. Who loves his mother more, Jewell or Darl? How do they each express that love? How can it be said that love set them in opposition? A paper on this topic might also focus on the scenes of near-destruction to the coffin, the fire and water that Addie knew Jewell would save her from.

4. **Darl:** Why is Darl committed to an asylum by his family?

An alternative question to ask might be why Darl finally goes insane. Does the novel prepare you for either of these eventualities? A paper on this topic would have to discuss more than the obvious reason he is committed: He has burned down the barn, and the family will be asked to make restitution unless they commit Darl as a way out of their legal troubles. But, like the ulterior motives the family has for the trip to Jefferson, there are other, secret reasons some members of the family have for wanting Darl incarcerated.

History and Context

The South is always a part of the context of Faulkner's work. In *As I Lay Dying,* Faulkner looks at the South between World War I and World War II, a time of economic downturn. Yet, the Bundrens have never known prosperity, and so there is not a sense of looking back, as there is in other Faulkner novels, to a time of antebellum grace and ease. There is, instead, an unrelenting sense of despair, and in this novel Faulkner presents a very different look at the South. The difficulties of this family can be seen as mirroring the condition of the South that serves as the novel's setting. Of those elements that are dead or dying, one is the community and its focus on agriculture. The novel carefully distinguishes between the Bundrens and the townspeople. We cannot forget that Addie is from the town of Jefferson; the book's premise is that she wants to be taken back there when she dies. For Vardaman, having been born in the country is a cruel accident. He believes his life would have been different had he been born in town, and he is likely right. Certainly his experience would have been altered if he had different parents. There is a sense of corruption in the Bundrens that could be extrapolated as belonging to the South as a whole.

As I Lay Dying should also be seen in the context of the roles and rights of women in the early 20th century in the rural American South. Remember, at this time women had just earned the right to vote, a controversial development at the time. There was a general attitude that politics was not a suitable interest for women. An unmarried woman would have had a difficult road ahead of her, particularly if she were without means and family. In another time and place, Addie might not have married. She decides to marry Anse before she has even met him, because marriage is an expectation of her society and the only way she can be financially provided for without having to continue teaching school.

Once married, a divorce would have been unthinkable and nearly impossible to come by. *As I Lay Dying* portrays a number of longstanding marriages, the Bundrens, the Armstids, the Samsons, and the Tulls. You might consider the dynamics of these various unions. In every case, it is the man who deals directly with the business of life, who makes decisions for the family. The women, however, wield considerable influence, usually from the kitchen.

This does not necessarily point to a more innocent time, for the book has no shortage of sexuality. Addie's monologue refers a number of times to Anse's rights as her husband, making it clear that he has a right to her body, even if she feels violated by him. She does not feel that her marriage vow keeps her from giving her body to another, because she engages in the affair with Whitfield for as long as she can hold the minister's attention. Throughout the novel, Dewey Dell attempts to abort her unwanted child, also conceived furtively in the woods. Although she is young and naive in many ways, she is still a sexual being. Yet she does not understand her body well enough to avoid being tricked by the pharmacy clerk. The novel also portrays the difficulties Dewey Dell has in discussing her troubles, since abortion is illegal.

In all of Faulkner's works, there is not a poorer family portrayed than the Bundrens. Their poverty is perhaps the chief obstacle they face when trying to carry out Addie's last wishes. Is their poverty the result of Anse's poor work ethic or is it their heritage? That is, did someone living in rural Mississippi at this time have the means of escaping what is basically a subsistence life? Faulkner depicts an environment without much hope. The Bundren children are not educated. They are accustomed to hard labor. Dewey Dell has been given the role of the "woman" of the house, which means cooking and cleaning and minding Vardaman in addition to planting and harvesting. The Bundrens' desires are for small things: teeth, a gramophone, a toy. Small amounts of money, like the three dollars Jewell and Darl earn while their mother dies, or the 10 dollars Dewey Dell has to pay for her abortion, are of great importance to them. Notably absent from the novel are the aristocratic class of southerners who are often the focus of Faulkner's works.

Class is such an important aspect of *As I Lay Dying* that it could be identified as yet another of the book's themes. As you read the novel, be aware that the South in which it is set still maintained a hierarchy of social classes. The Bundrens are easily identifiable as belonging to the class of poor, rural whites who were not prepared to change with the times. They are lacking in education, and the rural, agriculturally based existence they rely on is dying. Yet, Faulkner does not make these individuals into caricatures. The reader hopes they will succeed in reaching Jefferson and somehow move beyond the strictures of their lives, even though there is little reason to believe they will.

Sample Topics:

1. **The South:** How does this novel represent a South that is on the decline?

A paper on this topic might consider other representations of the South. How is this novel distinctively southern? How does it differ from other depictions of the South? Does it depict recognizable southern "types" in the Bundrens? Have people like the Bundrens, even in the 21st century, become the stereotype of a certain type of white southerner?

2. **Women:** Is there a sense that the women in this novel are repressed?

One possible thesis concerning women in this novel is that their passions are inexpressible in the societies in which they live. Addie experienced true passion with Whitfield, and her love for Jewell reflects this, but it seems to have no other outlet. Dewey Dell does what is expected of her in her family, yet she is also sexualized. The other wives also do what is expected, but they seem to seethe with anger and resentment. Even the new "Mrs. Bundren" has eyes that flash with anger.

3. **Poverty:** How is poverty the main obstacle the Bundrens face on their journey?

The novel certainly emphasizes money, what it can do, and the Bundrens' lack of it. When Anse takes Dewey Dell's money in order to get his teeth and woo the woman who will become his wife, the reader knows that Dewey Dell will never have her abortion and will instead soon become an unwed mother. To Dewey Dell and Anse, that 10 dollars is life changing. There are few troubles in the family that money would not ease. Possibly, money and the opportunity it represents would have kept Darl from the mental institution.

4. **Class:** How do class issues factor into the treatment the Bundrens receive throughout the novel?

The Bundrens seem a hopeless lot, and their patriarch, Anse, is a feckless character. Yet, a number of people reach out to help them throughout the novel. Why is that help so often refused? An essay on class divisions could discuss the Bundrens' attitudes and how those attitudes ensure that they will remain in the underclass. A writer might choose to discuss what each member of the Bundren family desires from the trip to Jefferson and the relative smallness of their ambitions.

Philosophy and Ideas

Religion may not seem central to *As I Lay Dying*, but it is actually an important part of the novel. The characters call on God, they pray and consider his influence, and they wonder what is beyond death. Addie's affair with Whitfield is shocking because he is a minister. It is more shocking when Addie's dialogue reveals that the sexual excitement she felt when she was with Whitfield was in part based on her knowledge that the sin they were committing was a grave one. In Whitfield's section of the novel, he shows himself to be a shallow hypocrite. He reveals no tenderness for Addie. His main concern is that his secret not be told. She keeps her word to him; he seems to have held no faith with her. He knows that Jewell is his child, but he does not recognize his responsibility to him. Whitfield's section is also notable for its blasphemy and the belief that God takes such an interest in him that he would hide his sin and allow Addie to go to the grave unforgiven for her own.

Cora Tull often talks to Addie about the importance of having the right relationship with God. But Cora's pieties seem empty; she shows little understanding of the depth that Addie has already thought about God and sin. Cora is completely deluded about Whitfield, holding him up to Addie as an example of a godly man. In Cora's eyes, Addie commits a grave blasphemy when she says, "He is my cross and he will be my salvation. He will save me from the water and from the fire. Even though I have laid down my life, he will save me" (168). It sounds as if Addie is talking about God, but to her horror Cora realizes that Addie is really talking about Jewell:

> Then I realized that she did not mean God. I realised that out of the vanity of her heart she had spoken sacrilege. And I went down on my knees right there. I begged her to kneel and open her heart and cast from it the devil of vanity and cast herself upon the mercy of the Lord. But she wouldn't. She just sat there, lost in her vanity and her pride, that had closed her heart to God and set that selfish mortal boy in His place. (168)

In the course of the novel, Jewell will save Addie from the water and the fire. Addie's trust in Jewell is not misplaced.

Related to religious faith is the belief in an existence after death. Although the novel's characters speak of this belief, the physical realities Faulkner depicts make it seem less certain. Dr. Peabody muses on death as he makes his journey to Addie, thinking, "I can remember how when I was young I believed death to be a phenomenon of the body; now I know it to be merely a function of the mind—and that of the minds of the ones who suffer the bereavement. The nihilists say it is the end; the fundamentalists, the beginning; when in reality it is no more than a single tenant or family moving out of a tenement or town" (43–44). There is evidence in *As I Lay Dying* to argue that it depicts a Christian life after death or that death is only a physical change. Remember that Addie only speaks her monologue after she has died.

The novel is also concerned with ideas about identity and existence. Nearly every character muses on the question of who he is, Darl most often of all. Darl speaks to Vardaman at length about the nature of "was" and "is" (101). To his thinking, if something "was" then it cannot be "is." Therefore, their mother, who "was," cannot have existed. If this assertion is true, then none of the Bundren children exists either. His logic can be hard to follow, but basically he is reasoning himself out of existence. By the end of the novel, when Darl has been committed to a mental institution, he thinks of himself as someone he is watching and talking to. He is outside himself, and the only answer Darl can muster is the word *yes* (254).

Also toward the novel's end, Cash begins to refer to Mrs. Bundren's house. Since they are still in possession of Addie Bundren's corpse, his references to her house are confusing. When Anse, the morning after burying Addie, introduces the children to Mrs. Bundren, the confusion is cleared up. In the time it has taken to bury Addie in Jefferson, Anse has procured a new wife. The name, which technically belongs to Addie, has been transferred to another. This displacement brings up questions of what it means to be "Mrs. Bundren," or if a name has any meaning at all. In one of the shortest chapters in the history of the novel, Vardaman states: "My mother is a fish" (84). Darl says that Jewell's mother is a horse. Addie's death throws everything into question for the family, including their roles in the family and their personal identities.

Another question wrestled with in the novel is what defines family. The Bundrens are fully drawn individuals; what unites them? Obviously, there are blood ties uniting them, despite the fact that Jewell is not Anse's biological son. By the novel's end, the family that began the journey to Jefferson has changed. There is some sense of loyalty among the family members, but there are also terrible betrayals. The intimacy of family is a problem because the Bundren children seem to share, perhaps as a family trait, a desire to be alone and to hold to their own secrets.

Sample Topics:

1. **Religion:** Examine any character in the novel in terms of his or her religious belief.

   Any number of essays could focus on religion in *As I Lay Dying*. One place to start thinking about religion would be to consider any one character in terms of his or her belief system. What is interesting about this exercise is that none of the characters thinks about religion in absolutely clear or simplistic ways. Addie longs for death and is sacrilegious in her love for Jewell, but she also believes in sin and punishment. Cora holds some of the more typical Christian beliefs, but she is also often wrong in her perceptions and has little ability to understand or to empathize. Whitfield or Peabody would also be interesting characters to discuss in these terms.

2. **Death:** Does the novel betray any belief in life after death?

This question could be answered with either a yes or a no, depending on the evidence that is brought to support the argument. The graphic depiction of Addie's rotting body and the indignities her corpse is exposed to emphasize the physical realities of death. But is Addie more than her body?

3. **Identity:** What does *As I Lay Dying* suggest about the problem of identity?

The musings on identity in this novel are very sophisticated at times, at other times, with Vardaman particularly, they are funny. If identity is fluid and changes with the circumstance, if two separate women in the novel can rightfully be called Mrs. Bundren, then how can one ever define a self? This problem becomes critical with Darl, and Vardaman will struggle with identity issues as well. What defines the self? While it may be easy to get another Mrs. Bundren, it is hard to forget Addie.

4. **Family:** What does it mean to be a family in the context of *As I Lay Dying*?

How does the novel define family? Do the Bundrens at all fit this definition? It seems that Cora Tull, for instance, has a different definition. Addie's dying wish is to be taken back to her family. You might argue that the novel takes a pessimistic view of family. A possible thesis would be that *As I Lay Dying* is a depiction of a dying family.

Form and Genre

This novel, like many of Faulkner's works, has an unusual and inventive structure. It is composed of short chapters that are the interior monologues of the novel's characters. Since these chapters are generally short, the reader can spend the necessary time to work out what is happening and what the individual speakers are like. Since the monologues originate in the minds of the characters, the writing takes the form of stream of consciousness. This type of writing requires the reader to follow the sometimes random and sometimes deluded thoughts of the characters. This approach, as a narrative strategy, can prove challenging. The plot is clear enough: The Bundrens must take Addie's body to Jefferson, but it takes a while to understand fully why this journey is under way. It takes the accumulation of voices to construct the narrative. No one voice can tell the story in whole. Further, the story is not in strict chronological order because the characters are sometimes thinking of the past and sometimes of the future.

There are 59 chapters in *As I Lay Dying*, divided among 15 different speakers. There is no omniscient narrator, so there is no one to view or explain the story from the outside. The reader must rely on the characters for the story they tell. The stream-of-consciousness monologues allow the reader unique insight into the psychology of the characters. Their thoughts reveal more about them than they would choose to reveal. You might notice that the chapters of the Bundrens are usually in the present tense, while the chapters of others are usually in past tense. This puts some distance between the events related by the Bundrens and those related by the other characters.

To write *As I Lay Dying*, Faulkner had to give each of his 15 speakers distinct voices. Their speech needed to reflect their place and time, as well as their level of education, and then it had to capture each character's personal concerns. For instance, the speech of Cora Tull is riddled with Bible verses and stories and bits of sermons. Most of the characters speak in an idiom that places them in rural Mississippi at a time when formal education was not a requirement. Addie's education sets her somewhat apart from her family and the community surrounding her, while Darl speaks with an eloquence that sets him apart from the rest of his family. Also, his concerns are loftier. It is tempting to think of Darl as a sort of narrator and to imagine that he possesses the voice closest to Faulkner's own. Like Quentin in *The Sound and the Fury*, his eloquence is likely a sign that his mind is troubled.

The title of the work you are planning to write about is always an appropriate place to begin generating ideas for an essay. *As I Lay Dying* takes its title from a passage in Homer's *Odyssey*. There, Agamemnon says to Odysseus: "As I lay dying, the woman with the dog's eyes would not close my eyes as I descended into Hades." The reader's first reaction to the title is that the "I" of the title is Addie Bundren. Yet, she is only dying in the first few chapters. In the majority of the book, she is dead, not in the process of dying. Thus, it is possible that the title does not refer to Addie alone and that the book is about something more than the passing of this one woman.

Sample Topics:

1. **Structure:** What is the effect of the novel's structure?

> An essay on this topic might argue that by writing his novel in this form, Faulkner makes the reader particularly aware of each character's individual voice. The essay might also make note of the fact that, by the novel's end, there is a disjunction between the monologues and real time; the chronology becomes even more disrupted than it was in the rest of the book. You might want to argue that this story could not be told by a sole narrator.

2. **The interior monologue:** Which is the most important monologue in the novel?

> Choose any one chapter (one monologue) and discuss its importance to the book as a whole. Is it possible that one character's voice encapsulates the experience, plot, or tone of *As I Lay Dying*? This could be a productive way to approach a paper about this novel. There are the obvious choices you might cite, such as Vardaman's: "My mother is a fish" (84) or Addie's monologue. But it would also be helpful to choose a less likely chapter and see what it has to reveal about the book as a whole.

3. **Idiom:** How does the language of the novel add to the reader's enjoyment?

Analyze any character's speech for its particular idiom. What does the character's speech reveal about him or her? Is it appropriate for the character's place and time? Does it help you to envision the character? What is Faulkner telling you about this character by way of the words the character chooses? In the absence of a consistent single narrator, the reader is dependent on these monologues to draw meaning from the work.

4. **The title:** What significance does the novel's title have to the book as a whole?

One way to approach this topic would be to ask who the "I" of the title is. Perhaps the "I" refers to the Bundren family, or the South, or to all people. Another approach would be to read the passage in *The Odyssey* and attempt to discover why Faulkner chose this title. Is the action in *The Odyssey* anything like the action in *As I Lay Dying*? What is the significance of the woman not closing Agamemnon's eyes? Does *As I Lay Dying* have anything in common with *The Odyssey*?

Language, Symbols, and Imagery

As I Lay Dying seems deceptively straightforward, but the novel contains numerous symbols that enlarge on its meaning. As the novel opens, Cash is building Addie's coffin. The coffin has tremendous symbolic import. On the journey to Jefferson, the coffin is a literal manifestation of the burden the Bundrens carry. While it should be a resting place, Addie's coffin is dynamic and mobile. It not only travels the 40 miles of the journey, it also complicates the trip at every turn. It is clear that Cash has brought all of his skill as a carpenter to bear in making the coffin. One of Cash's chapters is a list of reasons he made the coffin on the bevel (82–83). His careful work does not spare Addie any indignities, however. Vardaman drills holes in the coffin (and his mother's face) to ensure she is able to breathe while inside. The women who prepare the body put her head first in the box so that her dress will not be wrinkled.

During the trip to Jefferson, Addie's coffin is threatened with destruction twice. First, Addie's coffin is nearly swept away in the flooded river as the Bundrens attempt to cross. Later, the coffin is almost burned in the fire in the barn. Earlier, Addie told Cora that Jewell would save her "from the water and from the fire" (168), and he does both. Tull describes the flooded river as cold; he says, "It was thick, like slush ice. Only it kind of lived. One part of you knowed it was just water, the same thing that had been running under this same bridge for a long time, yet when them logs would come spewing up outen it, you were not surprised, like they was a part of water, of the waiting and the threat" (138). Water is sometimes aligned with life, but when Tull says that the water "lived," it seems menacing. Sometimes death is referred to as a crossing over, and in the Greek myths the body must travel over water after death. In the Christian tradition, water is identified with new life and the act of baptism. Fire and water also represent traditional ways of disposing of a body. Cora Tull believes that it would have been better had Addie's body been lost in the river. Perhaps Darl had hoped for the same. When Darl sets fire to the barn, he is deliberately trying to incinerate Addie's body and end the Bundrens' journey.

Vardaman fixates on the idea that his mother is a fish. For him, her near escape into the river is yet another example of her behaving as a fish would. There is other animal imagery attached to Addie. Darl tells Jewell that his mother is a horse. Vardaman's fish is cooked and eaten—it has changed from a living thing into something different, devoid of blood and bones. But he seems to believe his mother is alive: He drills holes into the coffin so that she may breathe. Although he always refers to the body in the coffin as "her," he also believes that his mother the fish escaped back into the water through the holes he made in the coffin. The thought seems to console him, the idea that the body they carry is not his actual mother.

Anse's inability to work, or his avoidance of work (if you believe his story that work would be fatal to him), is the source of many of the Bundren problems. Work is an important measure of character in the novel. Cash is identified with his tools and his labor as a carpenter. He takes pride in his craftsmanship. When the story begins, he is recovering from a broken leg that was the result of a fall from the roof he was working on. He builds Addie's coffin, working through the night and in the rain. He plans to return to a job after the trip to Jefferson, and the whole family recognizes the importance that his tools have for him, and they know that losing them would be devastating. Jewell purchases his horse by working through the nights, alone, clearing farmland. That he alone worked to earn it fuels the pride he takes in the horse. When Anse later sells the horse, he is stealing from Jewell his most important possession. He likewise deprives Cash of the gramophone he wishes to buy when he takes Cash's money.

Sample Topics:

1. **The coffin:** What symbolic value does Addie's coffin hold?

A writer might begin thinking about this in terms of Cash and his work. To Cash, the coffin represents his skill employed in service to his mother. To the others, is it a box, a burden, a final resting place? What does the box signify to those outside the family, especially as time passes? The coffin has an odd importance to Addie. She wants to see it completed, but why?

2. **Fire and water:** Why are fire and water the two trials the coffin has to survive?

It is curious that Addie predicts that Jewell will save her from the fire and the water. An essay on this topic would carefully analyze the scenes of the flood and the fire. If Addie's journey is also representative of her life, then she survives the extremes of heat and cold. What sort of connotations do fire and water hold?

3. **The fish:** Why does Vardaman equate his mother with the fish?

The fish, too, is a Christian symbol. While the reader might understand the leaps Vardaman's mind takes from catching the fish to his mother's death, an essay on this topic could discuss the symbolic meaning of the mother/fish throughout the novel. The fish is caught, cleaned, and eaten. Addie dies, but her story continues. How does the dead fish allow Vardaman to keep his mother alive?

4. Work: What is the significance of work in *As I Lay Dying*?

An essay on this topic might choose to focus on work in relation to one character. For instance, Cash's relationship to his
trade is an obvious choice, as is Anse in his avoidance of work.
An essay could be written on the subject of Cora's cakes and
the work of women.

Compare and Contrast Essays

Various ideas in *As I Lay Dying* can be considered for an essay that com-
pares or contrasts elements of the novel. One of these is the relationship
between childbearing and death. *As I Lay Dying* depicts a time when
childbirth was more likely to result in the mother's death, and that fact
might help readers to understand something of Addie and Dewey Dell's
attitude toward childbearing. An expectant mother in the Bundren
household would still be responsible for her usual tasks. Labor would be
undertaken without the comforts of modern medicine, perhaps without
the help of a doctor at all. But those difficulties are not mentioned anywhere in Addie or Dewey's Dell's monologues; to them, childbirth also
represents a metaphorical death of the person they were before. Addie
has the exact amount of children she feels she owes Anse. Dewey Dell
desperately wants an abortion. Mother and daughter's feelings about
pregnancy are remarkably similar and can be contrasted with those of
Cora Tull, who sees children as God's blessing.

An important theme throughout the book is the gulf between words
and actions. Many of the characters express some belief about words and
actions, but Addie's monologue demonstrates how difficult she finds it to
reconcile the two. There is another dichotomy at work in the novel; the
novel is made up of monologues, and yet there is very little dialogue. The
reader is allowed access to the thoughts of the characters. If the reader
had to rely on the dialogue that passes between characters, this would
have been a very different story.

As I Lay Dying balances comic elements with the tragic. It would be
difficult to imagine a sadder plot than the story of an impoverished and
injured family trying to take their mother's corpse to its final resting
place. Yet, there are moments that are undeniably funny. The novel seems
to pull the reader in both directions. It is funny that Vardaman drills

holes into his mother's face, but it is also horrific. The "cure" adminis-tered to Dewey Dell is also as funny as it is horrible. Is the ending happy or sad? Or does it contain elements that are both?

At the end of *As I Lay Dying*, Darl is placed in an asylum for the insane. When the reader last sees him, he would seem to be insane by anyone's definition, but was he insane before his family betrayed him? Are there any other characters in the novel whom you would judge to be insane? When Cash considers the difference between insanity and sanity, he thinks, "Sometimes I aint so sho who's got ere a right to say when a man is crazy and when he aint. Sometimes I think it aint none of us pure crazy and aint none of us pure sane until the balance of us talks him that-a-way. It's like it aint so much what a fellow does, but it's the way the majority of folks is looking at him when he does it" (223). Darl is the only one of the Bundrens to have left home. Does his military service change him?

Sample Topics:

1. **Childbearing and death:** Compare Addie and Dewey Dell's feelings about maternity.

   Addie views her children as something she owes to Anse. Dewey Dell wants badly to terminate her pregnancy. But the way each woman feels about her growing child is very similar. An essay on this topic might attempt to understand why each woman feels that pregnancy is intrusive. The essay could com-pare and contrast what each woman says about her pregnancy or pregnancies.

2. **Words and actions:** Choose any two characters and compare their views on the difference between words and action.

   It seems that every major character in the novel expresses a view about the difference between words and actions. Addie and Darl give deep consideration to this topic. How important are words to the novel? How important are actions?

3. **Comedy and tragedy:** Is *As I Lay Dying* a comic or a tragic novel?

Compare and contrast scenes in the novel for their comic and tragic elements. Depending on the length of your essay, you might choose one scene or several for analysis. Faulkner tends to mix the humorous elements with the tragic. On balance, what would you judge the scene, or the novel, to be?

4. Sanity and insanity: What in *As I Lay Dying* is the line between sanity and insanity?

Darl is termed insane by a number of the characters in the novel. To others, he is the sanest of the Bundrens. What constitutes insanity in *As I Lay Dying*? An essay on this topic could argue that another of the novel's characters is insane instead, citing that character's monologues as evidence.

Bibliography and Online Resources for *As I Lay Dying*

"*As I Lay Dying*: Bibliography." *William Faulkner on the Web.* 17 Aug. 2006. Ed. John B. Padgett. U of Mississippi. 15 Dec. 2007. URL: http://www.mcsr.olemiss.edu/~egjbp/faulkner/b_n_aild.html.

Blotner, Joseph. *Faulkner: A Biography.* New York: Vintage Books, 1991.

———. "How *As I Lay Dying* Came to Be." *Readings on William Faulkner.* Ed. Clarice Swisher. San Diego, CA: Greenhaven, 1998. 113–19.

Brooks, Cleanth. *William Faulkner: First Encounters.* New Haven, CT: Yale UP, 1983.

———. *William Faulkner: The Yoknapatawpha Country.* Baton Rouge: Louisiana State UP, 1963.

Faulkner, William. *As I Lay Dying.* New York: Random House, 1930.

Henninger, Katherine. "'It's an Outrage': Pregnancy and Abortion in Faulkner's Fiction of the Thirties." *Faulkner Journal* 12.1 (Fall 1996): 23–41.

Howe, Irving. *William Faulkner: A Critical Study.* Chicago: Elephant Paperbacks, 1951.

Hustis, Harriet. "The Tangled Webs We Weave: Faulkner Scholarship and the Significance of Addie Bundren's Monologue." *Faulkner Journal* 12.1 (Fall 1996): 3–21.

Luce, Dianne C. *Annotations to William Faulkner's As I Lay Dying.* New York: Garland, 1990.

Nielsen, Paul S. "What Does Addie Bundren Mean, and How Does She Mean It?" *Southern Literary Journal* 25.1 (Fall 1992): 33–39.

Rule, Philip C. "The Old Testament Themes in *As I Lay Dying.*" *Readings on William Faulkner.* Ed. Clarice Swisher. San Diego, CA: Greenhaven, 1998. 120–28.

Sass, Karen R. "At a Loss for Words: Addie and Language in *As I Lay Dying.*" *Faulkner Journal* 6.2 (Spring 1991): 9–21.

Tredell, Nicolas, ed. *William Faulkner: The Sound and the Fury and As I Lay Dying.* New York: Columbia UP, 1999.

Wadlington, Warwick. *As I Lay Dying: Stories out of Stories.* New York: Twayne, 1992.

"SPOTTED HORSES"

READING TO WRITE

"SPOTTED HORSES" was first published in *Scribner's Magazine* in June 1931. The story was later expanded and became a part of the novel *The Hamlet*, published in 1940. *The Hamlet* is a part of Faulkner's "Snopes Trilogy," which also includes *The Town* and *The Mansion.* In the expanded version, there is a courtroom scene wherein Mrs. Armstid sues Flem Snopes (if you think about the word *phlegm* when you hear his name, you are well on your way to understanding something about his character) and Mrs. Tull sues Eck Snopes. Neither woman wins her suit. The Snopes family is like some sort of force that cannot be bested. If not exactly evil, they are entirely unsavory. In a sense, they are a family without any moral qualms whatsoever. In this story, a traveling sewing machine salesman, V. K. Ratliff, who appears in other Faulkner stories, watches and narrates as Eck Snopes attempts to sell wild horses to the townspeople.

"Spotted Horses" highlights the comical side of Faulkner's work. Although questions of justice and morality are broached, the overall tone is light. The reader will condemn Snopes, but his victims are not much more sympathetic. As you read, notice whom has your sympathy. Notice, too, Faulkner's descriptions of the horses. Like the Snopes family, they are like a swirling force of nature. They can neither be captured nor reckoned with.

TOPICS AND STRATEGIES
Themes

One theme in "Spotted Horses" is the con. How can a person trick another for financial gain? Do people who allow themselves to be taken deserve what happens to them? Ratliff noticeably disdains the whole operation; moreover, he advises everyone around him not to take part in the horse auction. One reason Ratliff recognizes that the deal is a bad one is that Ratliff himself is something of a con artist. The traveling salesman was a stock figure of the time and usually portrayed as deceptive by trade.

The worst deal made during the auction is the one made with Henry Armstid. Even the Texan tries to back away from it. Mrs. Armstid is a particularly pathetic character. She is abused by her husband in front of the crowd and without intervention. He takes the money that she has made herself to buy their children shoes and uses it to buy a horse that he will never catch. It is their last five dollars.

As in "Barn Burning," Faulkner shows how poorly people lived in rural Mississippi. There are those like the Armstids, who do not have money for shoes for their children. Mrs. Armstid's appearance suggests that she does not have enough to eat. But even the other farmers who attend the auction are using their "seed-money" for bidding. "Barn Burning" shows how a farmer's livelihood could easily be destroyed by burning his barn. Here, the people are spending the money that they would use to buy seeds for next year's crops. They are setting themselves up for economic failure and possibly hunger.

Much is made of the "wildness" of the ponies. When they are first seen, it seems that no one would dare bid on them. Yet people do. But the ponies do not lose any of their wildness.

Sample Topics:

1. **The con:** What is the difference between Ratliff, Flem Snopes, and the Texan?

   One possible thesis for an essay on this topic would be that the story makes a distinction between conning strangers and conning your neighbors. As is mentioned several times, Flem would not hesitate to con his own family if money were to be made, and Eck Snopes comes out a little bit worse than the other men who purchase the horses. But if all three are con men, what makes one con different from another?

2. **Men and women:** How would you characterize the women of "Spotted Horses"?

Mrs. Armstid is more central to the action of "Spotted Horses" than Mrs. Tull or Mrs. Littlejohn, but all three women make a strong impression. An essay could be written that analyzes the role or roles these women play. How are they different from the men? (None of the women buy any horses.) The two lawsuits are brought by women, but neither suit is won. An essay could also be written about any one of these three.

3. **Work:** What separates the con from the worker?

"Spotted Horses" seems to implicitly set a value upon work versus earning money the way Flem and the Texan do. If you were to talk about work in the story, you might want to linger over the description of how Mrs. Armstid has earned the five dollars. Why are the Armstids so poor? Is her husband lazy? The other men have helped them to make their crops. What is Flem Snopes's profession? Notice that the candy he gives to Mrs. Armstid comes from Lump Snopes's store, and that there is no indication Flem has paid for it.

4. **Wildness:** How do the ponies resemble the Snopes family, or Flem Snopes in particular?

After all the ponies are sold, they break free and run loose over Frenchman's Bend, perhaps roaming 20 or 30 miles away. There is no sign that anyone will ever lay hold to them or that they can ever be broken. The Texan, Flem, and even Ratliff are travelers. They are not explicitly connected to the land. Frenchman's Bend is not their home. There might be parallels between the ponies and these three. But Faulkner might also be saying something about the Snopeses, who have come to Frenchman's Bend from somewhere else and, basically, infiltrated life there.

Character

V. K. Ratliff is the narrator of "Spotted Horses." It is important that he is also, as an itinerant salesman, something of a con man and that he is not a member of this community. Perhaps he is a little more sophisticated than the townspeople. That he is just passing through allows him to view the proceedings and the personalities involved with some detachment. But he does not claim any moral superiority. He does not dispute Flem Snopes's right to con his neighbors if he wishes, but he subtly conveys his disapproval.

The Texan is also an outsider. His only identity, "the Texan," is a statement of how much he is an outsider. He is not a product of Yoknapatawpha or even Mississippi. The implication is that he has come to a place, via Flem Snopes, that he would not come to otherwise and that he will not see again. In the time he spends in Frenchman's Bend, he upsets the natural order of the place. The community comes to a standstill on the day of the auction. When he leaves, he leaves behind the chaos he helped to introduce in Frenchman's Bend. But he is not without some sympathy. He refuses to sell a horse to Henry Armstid.

Flem is a character without any redeeming qualities in this story. The auction is essentially his production, but he denies any knowledge of it. As a member of the community, he should have some compunction against defrauding his neighbors (and his family members), but he does not. His introduction of the horses into the life and mythology of Frenchman's Bend is analogous to the unleashing of a destructive force. The horses divide people, as seen in the court cases and the fighting within the families involved. The only time the reader gets to hear from Flem Snopes is when Mrs. Armstid works up her courage to ask him for her money back. When Flem gives her instead some candy for her children, he seems purely evil. A few pieces of candy will not help Mrs. Armstid.

Mrs. Armstid is such a downtrodden woman. The five dollars she wanted to use to put shoes on her children for the winter is lost to Flem Snopes. The reader sees how she is abused by her husband. Even Mrs. Littlejohn is frustrated by her complacency. And the community, which should protect her and does sympathize with her and helps her from time to time make her crops, fails her completely. When the court fails to right the wrongs done to her, it is incredibly disappointing because she seems not to deserve her fate but can do nothing to change it.

Sample Topics:

1. The narrator: How would you characterize V. K. Ratliff?

How important is Ratliff to the events of the story? Ratliff and Mrs. Littlejohn seem to be the only people in Frenchman's Bend not buying horses. One possible thesis discussing the narrator would be to link these two. Why is it important that not everyone takes the bait in this con? How would the story change with Mrs. Littlejohn as a narrator?

2. The Texan: Why isn't "the Texan" named?

One possible thesis on this topic is that the most important quality of the Texan is where he comes from. It reinforces how foreign he is to this community; like the horses, he is somewhat exotic. Is the Texan another victim of Flem Snopes?

3. Flem Snopes: Is Flem Snopes a well-developed character?

Flem is offstage for most of the story. The reader comes to know Flem by reputation. When we finally meet Flem Snopes, we have a sense of the sort of person he is. Is his behavior in keeping with his reputation, or is it far more sinister?

4. Mrs. Armstid: What role does Mrs. Armstid play in "Spotted Horses"?

An essay on this topic might argue that Mrs. Armstid's interactions with Flem and the Texan allow the reader to see the true nature of these two characters. She represents the serious aspect of the auction. When the townspeople witness her husband's poor treatment of her and fail to interfere, does it implicate them in her maltreatment?

Philosophy and Ideas

The only way the Texan is able to get the bidding started is to give Eck a horse for free. He knows that greed will move the other men, the desire to prevent one of their neighbors getting something that they do not have. This works most effectively on Henry Armstid. Henry is willing to spend his family's last five dollars for one of these horses, rather than see Eck take two for two dollars. Greed is a powerful motivator throughout the story. Those who bid on the horses are hoping to get a valuable horse at a cheap price. To enrich themselves, the Texan and Eck Snopes are selling horses they believe, and who prove to be, worthless.

The question of morality is not explicitly broached, but it is implicitly a part of the proceedings. Everyone seems to know there is something wrong with the auction, but since all the participants are willing, it is a bit more difficult to condemn Eck and the Texan. It is easy to condemn Henry Armstid, who brutalizes his wife and takes her money. Yet, all the other men watch him do so and do not intervene. When Mrs. Armstid begs the Texan not to sell her husband a horse, she says that if he does "it'll be a curse onto you and yours during all the time of man" (29). Her language sounds biblical, and her curse directly indicts him morally.

The story may move the reader to wonder about the proper role of women in the proceedings. Compared to a modern woman, the women of "Spotted Horses" may seem inhibited. Mrs. Armstid is obviously cowed by her husband. Mrs. Littlejohn appears in contrast to her; even when faced with a wild beast, Mrs. Littlejohn acts decisively. Mrs. Tull is not afraid to stand up to the Snopeses either.

One source of humor in "Spotted Horses" is Ad Snopes. He continues to tempt fate by coming into contact with the horses, but the horses never touch him, even as they rage all about him. Ad defies his father's warnings repeatedly, and the only answer for his safety in the midst of the chaos is luck.

Sample Topics:

1. **Greed:** Does the author or the narrator condemn the men for their greed?

   Ratliff seems to recognize that it is the way of men to want something for nothing. Without this, it would be difficult to perpetuate a con. Does Faulkner believe the same? One possible thesis for an essay on this topic would be that the story shows that hard work is rewarded and Mrs. Littlejohn is an example of this. On the other hand, Mrs. Armstid seems to work hard only to lose everything.

2. **Morality:** What does "Spotted Horses" have to say about morality?

One could argue that "Spotted Horses" is primarily about moral choices. To what extent should a community behave morally, so that all members of that community are protected? Everyone seems to recognize that the horse auction is a con, but still the auction takes place. As in the maltreatment of Mrs. Armstid, people watch uncomfortably, but do nothing to intervene.

3. **Role of women:** Does the story have any message about the proper role of women?

Do you get the sense that the women in "Spotted Horses" are smarter than the men? Is there any other reason the women would be uninterested in the horses? One possible thesis is that the women are relatively powerless. Although all three assert themselves in various ways, they are not particularly successful. In the courtroom scene, we see that even the law seems to be against them, where morality would say both women were in the right.

4. **Luck:** What role does luck have in "Spotted Horses"?

The men say at one point that the Armstid family has no luck. Does the story evince a faith in luck as something that some people have, like Ad Snopes, while others do without? Is Flem Snopes untouchable because he is lucky?

Form and Genre

"Spotted Horses" shows Faulkner having some fun. It shows a community, as his work almost always does, but without the shadows that are characteristic of his novels. Although it seems the type of story to come out of the American West, it retains something of the American South as well. The character of the itinerant salesman sets the story at a time in American history when such people were an important source of contact between rural people and the larger world. The comedy is a unique blend of the fantastic (the horses) and the realistic (the women, the poverty) coming together in an exaggerated, violent way.

The story showcases the work of the con man. Even as people suspect that the horses are no bargain, they seem to get swept up in the excitement of the auction and the possibility of getting a horse, which could prove to be very valuable, at an unrealistically low price. For the reader, there is an interest in seeing who will fall for the con.

One characteristic of the tall tale is exaggeration. Much of the language is exaggerated and humorous. Some of the characters like Ad Snopes or Mrs. Tull are also larger than life and a source of humor. The horses are like no horses ever seen. The horses are like a force introduced into the community. It is impossible to see the horses as individual animals; they are a swirling mass of horseflesh. When they are unleashed from the corral, they become almost the stuff of legend. They are heard running about, and the people are aware that they are there, but no one is able to lay claim to one.

Sample Topics:

1. **Comedy:** Discuss what makes "Spotted Horses" comic.

There are a number of richly comic moments in "Spotted Horses." For instance, when the horse runs through Mrs. Littlejohn's boardinghouse it has something of the slapstick of a Marx Brothers movie. An essay on this topic might argue that "Spotted Horses" is largely a farce, and the comedy of it outweighs the moments of pathos.

2. **The tall tale:** How would this compare to a tall tale?

The tall tale is marked by exaggeration. An essay on "Spotted Horses" as a tall tale could focus on Flem Snopes and the way his character and exploits are enlarged upon by the townspeople. Alternatively, an essay on this topic might focus on the horses. These horses are like none seen in reality. How do the descriptions of the horses serve to make them seem wild beyond reason or imagination?

3. **The western:** How does this story compare to the western?

This story has many elements of the western, such as the stranger coming into town and upsetting the natural order. You have probably read or seen stories about horses that are hard to break. Some of the characters are standard as well, like the itinerant salesman or the hardened boardinghouse keeper or the eccentric doctor. Other elements are missing, like a hero or other person who maintains order.

4. Realism: How can "Spotted Horses" be said to be realistic?

A thesis for this essay could be that "Spotted Horses" partakes in some of the elements of the tall tale, but it is essentially a realistic story. Its outcome is not a satisfyingly happy ending for the reader, but more resembles the disappointments of real life. Poverty is depicted, as well as the closeness of small-town life.

Bibliography and Online Resources for "Spotted Horses"

Carothers, James B. *William Faulkner's Short Stories.* Ann Arbor: UMI Research Press, 1985.

———. "Faulkner's Short Stories: 'And Now What's to Do.'" *New Directions in Faulkner Studies.* Eds. Fowler and Abadie. Oxford: U of Mississippi P, 1984, 202–27.

Dowling, David. *William Faulkner.* New York: Palgrave MacMillan, 1989, 144–56.

Eddins, Dwight. "Metahumor in Faulkner's 'Spotted Horses'." *ARIEL* 13.1 (1982): 23–31.

Faulkner, William. *Three Famous Short Novels.* New York: Vintage International P, 1961.

Ferguson, James. *Faulkner's Short Fiction.* Knoxville: U of Tennessee P, 1991.

Greiner, Donald J. "Universal Snopesism: The Significance of 'Spotted Horses'." *The English Journal,* 57.8 (Nov. 1968): 1,133–37.

Jones, Diane Brown. *A Reader's Guide to the Short Stories of William Faulkner.* New York: G. K. Hall, 1994.

Padgett, John B. "'Spotted Horses': Commentary & Resources." *William Faulkner on the Web.* 17 Aug. 2006. 18 Dec. 2007. URL: http://www.mcsr. olemiss.edu/~egjbp/faulkner/r_ss_spottedhorses.html.

Ramsey, Allen. "'Spotted Horses' and Spotted Pups." *The Faulkner Journal* 5.2 (1990): 35–38.

Rankin, Elizabeth D. "Chasing Spotted Horses: The Quest for Human Dignity in Faulkner's Snopes Trilogy." *Faulkner: The Unappeased Imagination. A Collection of Essays.* Ed. Glenn O. Carey. Troy, NY: Whitston, 1980. 139–56.

Skei, Hans H. *Reading Faulkner's Best Short Stories.* Columbia: U of South Carolina P, 1999.

———. *William Faulkner: The Novelist as Short Story Writer.* New York: Columbia UP, 1985.

———. *William Faulkner, The Short Story Career: An Outline of Faulkner's Short Story Writing from 1919 to 1962.* New York: Columbia UP, 1981.

LIGHT IN AUGUST

READING TO WRITE

As you read William Faulkner's 1932 novel *Light in August,* you may consider the violence of racial conflict in the history of the American South. One message the novel seems to carry is that the memory of that conflict is carried within a people, and the past, then, cannot be forgotten. There are moments of horrific violence in *Light in August,* and these are shown in the bright light of day, in a detail that might cause the reader some discomfort. Although the events of the novel could have occurred in our nation's history, Faulkner's story seems to reach mythic importance. Joe Christmas is a martyr and Christ-figure, even if Christmas possesses few qualities that might actually be redeeming.

Faulkner's working title for his manuscript was *Dark House,* and you might consider why he settled on *Light in August* instead. What seems predominant in the novel, darkness or light? What are the connotations of each of these, or the connotations that come to mind when you hear these two titles? Faulkner's earliest ambition was to be a poet, and you might see in the novel the poet's concern with words and their nuances. Some readers dismiss Faulkner out of hand as difficult. If you read him knowing that there will be passages closer to poetry than to prose, that difficulty might fall away somewhat.

The novel has many passages that are examples of stream of consciousness. Faulkner seeks to reveal what is inside the character's mind. This narrative technique can result in a jumble of unedited, fragmented thoughts. But it also reveals more of the character than he or she might willingly reveal, allowing access to motivations and thoughts that the character would not willingly discuss and might not even admit to himself. There is a fluid nature to what Faulkner many times refers to as "memory" and "knowing."

This same fluidity characterizes the past and the present and other thematic concerns of the novel that you might consider clearly distinct, such as black and white. To write on this novel you might want to look at John Keats's "Ode on a Grecian Urn," because Faulkner's description of Lena Grove owes something to this work. It is also possible to imagine the poem germinating other ideas that are explored in the novel, such as the difference between motion and paralysis. Is life motion and the absence of motion death?

Light in August is a novel rich in symbols, imagery, and meaning. The difficulty in writing about it will be in choosing what aspect to address and deciding upon a thesis to argue. With no shortage of secondary materials about this book, there is plenty to be said. What strikes you as important in this novel? One place to begin could be with the title: What are the connotations of light? What associations does August hold?

TOPICS AND STRATEGIES
Themes

Perhaps the central theme in *Light in August* is race, particularly race in the American South. Certainly Joe Christmas's story, his very character, is shaped by concerns of race. The belief that he may have even a trace of black blood determines how the characters in *Light in August* relate to Christmas and his feelings about himself. In a world less concerned with racial identity, and less consumed by racial prejudice, a character like Christmas could not exist.

And yet, Joe Christmas's resemblance to Jesus Christ should not be overlooked, and with that the theme of Christianity or religious belief. When asked about the echoes of Christmas's story to the story of Christ, Faulkner was somewhat evasive, answering, "That Christ story is one of the best stories that man has invented, assuming that he did invent that story, and of course it will recur. Everyone that has had the story of Christ and the Passion as a part of his Christian background will in time draw from that. There was no deliberate intent to repeat it. That the people to me come first. The symbolism comes second" (Gwynn and Blotner 117). As you read *Light in August,* you should be aware of the parallels. First, there are the shared initials, J. C. There is the name Christmas, given when he is brought to the orphanage on Christmas day, to underscore the relationship. Christmas is persecuted. The description of his death has some echoes of the Crucifixion. The relationship between Lena Grove, her infant, and Byron Bunch resembles that of Mary, Jesus, and Joseph. McEachern uses religion to justify his violence and cruelty. Religion motivates Doc Hines. The Reverend Gail Hightower's life is also shaped by religion. Byron Bunch travels each Sunday to sing in a choir. Joanna Burden's admonishment to pray triggers Christmas's anger.

But it is equally true that each character is defined by his or her sexuality. Bobbie Allen, Lena Grove, Millie Hines, Miss Atkins, Hightower's wife, and Joanna Burden are all characters whose sexual behavior creates conflict in the novel. Joe Christmas's feelings of disgust at female sexuality propel much of the action. Lena Grove's pregnancy is the genesis of *Light in August.* Although she is judged by the community for carrying a child out of wedlock, her own attitude, unembarrassed and unashamed, mediates how she is treated. Lena's attitude could be contrasted with Christmas's. At the novel's conclusion, each is still sexualized and judged for his or her sexuality.

There are scenes of horrible violence in *Light in August.* The violence is not only physical, it is also psychological. Christmas is born into a world of violence. His father is murdered; his mother dies after his birth. As a small child, he experiences the violence of the orphanage, and the violence only grows as he gets older, culminating in the greatest violence of the novel, his murder. After Christmas has been hunted by a lynch mob, Percy Grimm shoots him five times and then castrates him while he is still alive.

The town of Jefferson becomes, in a sense, another character in *Light in August.* The idea of community becomes one of its themes. A number of characters can be considered in their relationships to Jefferson. Lena Grove travels into the community, as does Joe Christmas. They reside in Jefferson for a time, but they are never a part of that community. Joanna Burden and Reverend Hightower are marginalized by Jefferson. Byron isolates himself, forming his strongest connection, before Lena arrives, with Hightower.

Of a number of other thematic concerns in the novel, one is time. Each character relates differently to time. Reverend Hightower's great mistake is that he lives his life always thinking of the past. Lena seems to think only of the present; even the imminent birth of her child does not worry her when she sets off on her journey. Christmas never seems to escape the circumstances of his conception. It would be fair to ask if any of these characters has free will, or are their lives mapped out for them, even before their births? Do any of the characters change in the course of the novel?

Sample Topics:

1. **Race:** What does *Light in August* have to say about race, particularly in the American South of the early 20th century?

   Joanna Burden comes from a family of abolitionists. Are her family's ideas about race admirable, or is there something misguided about their attempts to change Jefferson? The reader can never know if Christmas in fact has "black blood." Doc Hines believes he does, but Doc Hines is not a reliable source. Christmas, particularly in his final flight from justice, moves between the worlds of black and white. Perhaps his inability to belong to either finally condemns him.

2. **Religion:** What does *Light in August* say about religion and religious belief?

   There are many possible ways to answer this question. While there is a great deal of religious symbolism in *Light in August,* is there a religious message? Many of the most overtly religious characters, like Doc Hines and Simon McEachern, are despicable characters. And Lena Grove, who shows no particular religiosity and whose pregnancy is evidence of what others would judge to be sinning, is admirably good. Do you think Faulkner is saying something negative about organized religion?

3. **Sexuality:** How is sexuality portrayed in *Light in August*?

   You might say that the only healthy example of sexuality in the book comes in the final chapter, when the furniture repairer tells his wife about Lena and Byron, seducing her in the process. Lena Grove might offer another model, but her encounter with Lucas Burch is hardly admirable. Hightower finds himself unable to sustain a happy marriage. Much could be said about Joe Christmas as a sexual being. He is not only self-loathing, but he is misogynistic and repulsed by the female body.

4. **Violence:** What does the novel tell us about violence?

Light in August is a novel with scenes of tremendous violence. One could write a paper that traced the violence of Christmas's life, arguing that in his beginning is his end. His life is never without violence. Christmas's death is so horrifying, you might believe that Faulkner is writing an indictment against the violence that human beings inflict upon one another.

5. **Community:** What role does the community play in *Light in August*?

When Percy Grimm executes Christmas, is he acting as the executioner for Jefferson, or is he acting alone? Could the events of the novel happen in a place other than Jefferson? Could they happen in the North, or now? If Jefferson were a different sort of place, if it embraced people who were different, like Joanna Burden or Gail Hightower, would this be a different sort of story? What role does gossip play in the unfolding of events?

Character

Light in August features some of Faulkner's most memorable characters, any of whom could bear analysis for the purposes of a paper. Lena is a pregnant teenager who has set out on foot to find her baby's father. Her last name, Grove, seems to identify her with the natural world. As you read *Light in August,* you might note the many references to wood or to trees. Her name is only the first. She seeks Lucas Burch at the planing mill where he worked under the name of Joe Brown. Although Faulkner uses bovine imagery to describe Lena, she also resembles an ancient fertility goddess. As Hightower muses, *"She will have to have others, more* remembering the young strong body from out whose travail even there shone something tranquil and unafraid. *More of them. Many more. That will be her life, her destiny. The good stock peopling in tranquil obedience to it the good earth; from these hearty loins without hurry or haste descending mother and daughter"* (406). She is also an echo of the Virgin Mary.

Light in August is also the story of Reverend Gail Hightower. He is drawn into Lena and Christmas's troubles through his friendship with Byron Bunch. Hightower's name offers a significant clue to how he lives. He is isolated from the community, but not apart or unmoved by it. He is like someone in a high tower who is buffeted by strong gale winds. Hightower has come to Jefferson because it was the site of his Confederate grandfather's death, but even this death, which haunts him, was shameful. His grandfather was killed not in the heat of battle but while stealing chickens. Hightower's preoccupation with that death and the war makes him an ineffective preacher. His wife's erratic behavior and infidelities, which culminate in her scandalous suicide, causes him to eventually lose his position in the church. Christmas dies in Hightower's home, where Hightower letters "Xmas" cards. Hightower assists in the delivery of Lena's baby, so he is the witness to the ending and beginning of those two lives. Although Lena and Christmas never meet, they are connected by Hightower.

Joe Christmas's name has tremendous significance. Byron recognizes this immediately upon hearing it: "And that was the first time Byron remembered that he had ever thought how a man's name, which is supposed to be just the sound for who he is, can be somehow an augur of what he will do, if other men can only read the meaning in time. It seemed to him that none of them had looked especially at the stranger until they heard his name. But as soon as they heard it, it was as though there was something in the sound of it that was trying to tell them what to expect; that he carried with him his own inescapable warning, like a flower its scent or a rattlesnake its rattle" (33). In many ways, Christmas's life parallels that of Jesus. It could also be noted that his first name links him to the biblical Joseph. This echo is reinforced by the confusion Mrs. Hines experiences when Lena's baby is born. She mistakes the newborn for her grandson Christmas, but she also, Lena thinks, believes at times that Joe Christmas is the child's father.

Byron Bunch is perhaps the most straightforward and uncomplicated character in *Light in August,* although even he is misidentified at first as possibly being the Lucas Burch whom Lena is seeking. Of course, while Lena has come searching for Burch, the man who impregnated her, she will find Bunch, who will become the child's father. Meanwhile, Burch, with his name that conjures up the image of a tree, is trying to sever his connection to Lena Grove, whose name suggests many trees. Burch is living in Jefferson under the name Joe Brown. This name connects him to Christmas in many ways—the initials J. C. versus J. B., the shared first name, the name Brown reminding us that Christmas is neither black nor white but exists somehow between the two. Also, his name echoes Joanna Burden's; they share the same initials, while her name is a feminine form of Joe.

Sample Topics:

1. **Lena Grove:** What sort of character is Lena Grove? Would you say she is a "round" (three-dimensional, fully developed, and capable of change) or "flat" (static, perhaps more symbolic than true-to-life, and unchanging) character?

   The question above represents one way to begin thinking about Lena as a character. Is she like anyone you know, or do you see her as playing a role Faulkner has placed her in—more fertility goddess or symbol of womanhood than real woman? Consider some of the descriptions of Lena. She seems relatively unmoved by the dramatic events occurring around her. Faulkner unflatteringly describes her as "sheeplike" (6) but also as beyond time and godlike: "She ha[d] traveled for four weeks with the untroubled unhaste of a change of season" (52).

2. **Gail Hightower:** How is Reverend Hightower changed by the events that take place in *Light in August*? Is he changed at all?

   Hightower has attempted to remove himself from the community of Jefferson. By the end of the novel, he has been the one character who connects the stories of Lena Grove and Joe

Christmas. What is it that happens to him as a result? Pay particular attention to his story as related in chapter 20.

3. **Joe Christmas:** Is Christmas a Christ figure or a character whose resemblance to Christ serves to point out the differences between them? Is there any redemption for Christmas? Do you feel any sympathy for him?

Christmas's life is marked by unrelenting violence. If you were to write about this character, you would want to consider what Faulkner is saying about the effect of violence upon an individual. Readers cannot be certain about the presence of "black blood," but the belief that Christmas carries it is enough to seal his fate. What is race to Christmas? What is family? How does he feel about women, food, home, or sexuality? There are a number of ways to approach an essay on this complex character, and a number of questions that could be asked in an attempt to understand him.

4. **Byron Bunch:** What motivates Byron Bunch? What do you make of his rapid involvement with Lena Grove and the Hines family?

Byron falls in love with Lena almost instantaneously. Like Hightower, he is someone who has lived quietly and separately from the community of Jefferson. When Lena arrives, he suddenly becomes central to the events of the novel, even trying to save Christmas and to reunite Lena with Lucas Burch. By the novel's end, he has assumed the role of husband and father, almost a figure of Joseph in the holy family. One possible thesis for an essay analyzing the character of Byron Bunch would be that he reacts to Lena more as if she were a type than an individual.

History and Context

At the heart of *Light in August* are issues of race. Race is not only central to the story of Joe Christmas; it is also a part of every character's experience. Questions posed in *Light in August* may be answerable only in light of the history and context of the novel. For instance, what is race? Is it "one drop" of black blood, as was sometimes said in the past? Readers know that if Christmas is "black," he is only so on his father's side. In current times, he would perhaps be considered biracial. His appearance does not immediately signal that he is of two races, so it is not a matter strictly of appearances. Is race only identification? That is, if Christmas decides he is black, then he is so. Or, if others identify him as black, then he is categorized as such. And this is equally true if he identified as white. There are characters in the novel, including Christmas himself, who equate "blackness" with the darker aspects of human behavior: evil, violence, and sexual deviance, for example. "Whiteness," then, carries more positive connotations and is ultimately "good." This is Christmas's view, and it is particular to his time and place. He is of questionable racial identity in the American South of the early 20th century.

It is southern racism that allows Doc Hines to kill the father of his daughter's child and go unpunished because the supposition is that his victim was black. Christmas is not punished simply for the murder of Joanna Burden, but because he is believed to be a black man who murdered a white woman and had also slept with her. His castration is punishment specifically for the sexual relationship, even though the relationship was consensual.

The actions in *Light in August* take place decades after the Emancipation Proclamation and the Civil War, but for the characters in the novel, the war is not over. There are two distinct ways that the war affects these characters. On the one hand, the South lost the war, and this fact is a source of shame. On the other hand, there is a longing for the glories of battle and for a time when men would take action to defend their beliefs, and there is the lingering desire to maintain honor, particularly the honor of the South in reference to ideals of womanhood. Curiously, the Reverend Gail Hightower and Joanna Burden are particularly in thrall to past, and neither is considered truly a part of Jefferson. Hightower has come to Jefferson to live at the site of his grandfather's death. According to family legend, Hightower's grandfather was a heroic member of the Confederacy, responsible for the deaths of many Yankees. But his death was inglorious, as he was shot while stealing chickens in Jefferson. Joanna Burden's family were abolitionists who moved to Jefferson from the North. Even though she herself was born in Jefferson, she cannot escape the past that saw her half brother and grandfather killed by Colonel Sartoris over the question of Negro voting rights. Her story echoes Hightower's as her life is shadowed by these Civil War–era ghosts, people killed before she was born. Her story also echoes Christmas's. Her half brother, Calvin, was dark-skinned; his mother, Juana, was Hispanic. His grave and that of his grandfather are hidden, because her father feared that their bodies might be desecrated by an angry mob.

One of the great achievements of Faulkner is his creation of Yoknapatawpha County. The Jefferson of *Light in August* is located in this fictional county and modeled on Faulkner's hometown of Oxford, Mississippi. The title *Light in August* refers to the quality of the light in the deep South in that month. The setting takes on an important role in the novel; it almost becomes a character in itself. The novel begins with Lena Grove's journey into town, and it ends with her journey away. Christmas's story is in part an exploration of the landscape of Jefferson, with its black and white sections of town that he seems compelled to travel through. There is the center of town and the road through it, and then there are the outlying sites, like the Burden house and Hightower's home. The slave cabin where Joe lives and where Lena's child is born becomes a place that is significant to both characters, though they never meet in the novel.

Sample Topics:

1. **Race:** What does *Light in August* tell readers about racism as it is experienced in this specific time and place?

   Light in August could be approached as a historical document. It depicts a lynching, not unlike those that might be found in accounts of southern history. However, the fictional account enlarges upon those stories, allowing readers to know Joe Christmas's story from its beginning to its end, and even to gain some insight into a character such as Percy Grimm. One question you might want to answer if you were to write on this topic is how closely Faulkner may have followed actual events or attitudes. You might ask whether the story would be dramatically altered if its setting were different. How would characters like these interact in another time or place?

2. **The South:** Is *Light in August* an indictment of the American South?

Is the South of *Light in August* without redemption? What does Lena's child represent, or Christmas's last moments? Certainly there are instances of unusual kindness and grace in the novel, such as the way the community seems to unite to care for Lena Grove, without, of course, explicitly accepting her. But the community also unites in another way in its condemnation of Christmas. Christmas dies in Jefferson; Lena keeps moving. Does Faulkner leave the impression that there is hope for the people who remain? Is there light amid the violence and darkness of the novel?

3. **The Civil War:** How does the Civil War continue to cast its shadow in *Light in August*?

The war affects Hightower and Joanna Burden to an unusual degree. Like Christmas, the two are enslaved to a past that should have been over before they were born. Another similarity that binds these two is that they were children born into families already on the decline, to parents who were beyond the usual age and who are depicted as ghostlike and removed from life, so that their children seem to be reared by ghosts. But it is hard not to view the two as wrongheaded in their lives. Why can't they cast off the past? Why can't they interact with the living in a more healthy way? You might argue that their childlessness is symptomatic of their preoccupation with the past. Does Joanna believe she is pregnant? That she is in menopause seems to signal the end of her life. When Hightower delivers Lena's child, he is for a moment drawn into the world of the living. And yet, while Lena is depicted as moving, these two are frozen, still fighting battles that are not even their own.

4. **Yoknapatawpha:** What role does place, and the county of Yoknapatawpha, play in the novel?

Consider the geography of *Light in August.* On the first page, we learn that Lena has "come from "Alabama—a fur piece." The novel is bookended by her entrance into Jefferson and her exit. Christmas travels throughout Jefferson. After he has killed Joanna, he wanders through the white and black sections of Jefferson. This last, aimless journey seems to echo a struggle that has taken place his entire life, as he has moved between the white and black communities. The community of Jefferson has collectively ostracized Reverend Hightower and Joanna Burden (who remains a "carpetbagger" and a Yankee in spite of being born in Jefferson). It also protects Lena Grove and her unborn child.

Philosophy and Ideas

As in other Faulkner novels, most notably *The Sound and the Fury, Light in August* has a complex structure. The reader will not have the sensation of a story that begins, builds, reaches a crisis, and then is resolved. On the first page of the novel, the reader meets Lena Grove, and her story, like her pregnancy, is rather far along. The novel could be said to take place over a handful of days, and yet the stories told within it reach back to the Civil War and decades before. The smoke from Miss Burden's house is visible in the first chapter, but we do not learn the details of her murder until very late in the book. The various stories are related in segments, so that we learn slowly and in a fragmented fashion what has happened. Most of the characters (Byron Bunch is a notable exception) are presented not simply as they are but as the products of the generations that preceded them. This might cause you to consider the question of free will. To what extent does anyone in the novel exercise free will; are they simply part of a machine that was set into motion before their births? And, if so, what is time? Is it escapable? Can anyone break free of the past, or is each birth part of a narrative that has already begun? And if the past is only revealed in a scattershot fashion, in unconnected bits of narrative, then how can it ever be truly known? Because certainly it comes to each character in a fragmented version and filtered through someone else's lens.

Light in August may cause you to reflect on the nature of justice. What is justice? Can justice be meted out by an imperfect society? There are many crimes portrayed in the novel, and the majority go unpunished. Child abuse, for instance, seems to be considered in the novel a private, family matter. Parents could manage their children by any means. In the story of Doc Hines's daughter Millie, Doc Hines punishes her by killing the father of her unborn child and perhaps allowing Millie to die of neglect of care after giving birth. And yet he is not punished. Christmas has committed many crimes before he murders Joanna Burden. He deserves punishment. And yet, what happens to Christmas is not just. You might imagine him in a trial situation. A good lawyer would cite his background, would argue that he was mentally unstable, would possibly talk about crimes of passion, and would certainly bring up the shot that Joanna fires at Christmas first and issues of self-defense. Even if a prosecutor dismissed all these factors, they would possibly mitigate his sentence. Can Percy Grimm be an agent of justice? Some might see his killing of Christmas as worse or no more justified than what happened to Joanna. As Hightower muses: "No man is, can be, justified in taking human life" (414).

One of the more curious points in the novel is when Faulkner relates Grimm's pursuit of Christmas in terms of a pawn being moved about on a "Board" by some unnamed "Player" (462). Is this player God or a devil or some other Supreme Being or principle? Is there an order at work? What sort of principle could move Percy Grimm in his actions? What role would God play in a scene like this? You might want to consider any resemblance this scene has to the Crucifixion. Can there be meaning or divine intervention in a scene of such cruelty and violence?

In *Light in August,* the psychology of the characters might be said to be of more interest than the plot. Psychology examines, for instance, the debate between nature and nurture. Which makes a man? This is an important question to ask in relation to Christmas, for although the opinion given by characters such as Gavin Stevens is that Christmas acts according to his nature, a modern reader might see Christmas as warped by the nurture, or lack of care, given to him as a child. This question could be asked of other characters as well, such as Gail Hightower. If you consider self-image, or identity, or other important psychological concepts, Christmas gains still greater interest. Christmas could be seen as someone who suffers from a lack of identity, which renders him unable to find his place in the world. If you have knowledge of Freudian psychology, you might find Christmas's behavior in relation to food curious. From the early scene of his consumption of the dietitian's toothpaste, Christmas's problems center on food, blood, vomit, and a disgust with the body that links all of these to sexuality.

Sample Topics:

1. **Time:** What is the nature of time in the novel? Is it linear or cyclical? And what does this tell you about the nature of time in *Light in August*?

   The story of *Light in August* is revealed to the reader almost as is it revealed to the characters; fragments are revealed in their own time, and the line of narrative has to be assembled in the mind of the reader. There is a circling back through time to the past. No one character holds the key to all. No one is fully aware of another's story. The ending bears some resemblance, however, to the beginning: Lena is still on the road. Do all stories repeat, or is each story an opportunity for a new start?

2. **Justice:** The reader knows rather early on that Christmas has committed murder. Why is there so little sense of justice at his death?

   A paper on this topic might consider the theme of justice as it is presented in *Light in August.* Does anyone ever pay for his or her sins, or is justice missing? Do some characters seem to be paying a debt for their ancestors or the sins of others? Faulkner introduces the idea that the white race will have to pay for what it has done to the black. Do you see evidence of this happening? Can a mob ever be the agent of justice? What about a character like Percy Grimm?

3. Religion: What role does religion play in *Light in August*?

A paper on this topic could focus on the final moments of Christmas's life and Faulkner's introduction of a "Player" and a "Board." Is this reminiscent of the image of Death playing chess, the movement between the black and white squares? Who or what moves these characters? Is there a god present in the novel? Why can Christmas not pray? You might consider how characters who regard themselves as true believers, like Doc Hines and McEachern, perpetrate some of the great cruelties related here. Why would a supreme being allow children to suffer as Christmas does as a child, or to die as he does? There are many passages that might be considered in an essay on this topic. When Byron brings Doc and Mrs. Hines to see Hightower and they relate the circumstances of Christmas's birth, Mrs. Hines says about it all: "And so sometime I would think how the devil had conquered God" (377).

4. Psychology: What are the psychological motivations of the characters in *Light in August*?

To write an essay on this topic you might choose a character to analyze from the perspective of psychology. Joe Christmas is an obvious choice. He has problems with identity, violence, food, the body, sexuality, religion, race, misogyny, and more. But nearly every major character, with the possible exception of Lena Grove, could be the subject of an interesting essay. Percy Grimm is not, in terms of word count, the strongest presence in *Light in August*, and yet Faulkner creates for him a complex psychological profile. Byron is not given tremendous depth, but there is room to consider why he behaves as he does. Joanna Burden is of tremendous interest. To some extent a product of her family, the turns her character takes after becoming Christmas's lover are startling. She continues to behave as an isolated spinster at day, becoming at night a woman in the "throes of nymphomania" (259), as he writes, "completely corrupted" (260). How can these changes be understood? And how do her final changes relate to her passing through menopause?

Form and Genre

Form and genre can cause some readers to be frustrated by Faulkner. Some will see his experiments as evidence of admirable control, while others will feel he is placing before them unnecessary obstacles. *Light in August* is a complex book in part because it tells (at least) three stories, those of Christmas, Hightower, and Lena Grove. The book begins and ends with Lena, but all that occurs between her entrance and departure from town moves forward and backward in time. As in life, important events may take place simultaneously or without witnesses. Readers learn of these sometime after they have occurred. Since the story is told from several perspectives, readers might have to decide for themselves what is the most complete and accurate account. Some of the narratives are not completely accurate; some are incredibly biased.

The novel begins in the present tense with Lena Grove. Until its final moments, Christmas's story is in the past tense. Hightower's story moves between the present and the past. Some of the most important events in the novel, such as the story of Joanna Burden, occur before Lena enters Jefferson. These shifts in tense may cause some initial confusion, as readers have to come to an understanding of the chronology. Is there a main character in this novel? Is there even a time or event that is central to the story?

It may be that there is no single voice that takes precedence. There is no unified tone as the novel ranges from comedy to tragedy. Sometimes characters are presented superficially; at other times, the awareness of those characters' subconscious thoughts and motivations are deeper than the characters' own self-knowledge. Faulkner combines storytelling techniques such as stream-of-consciousness narrative with dialogue, monologue, and regional dialect.

What we know of Lena Grove and Byron Bunch's future we have to surmise from the furniture dealer's talk with his wife, so we really do not know what will happen to them, or what their thoughts or feelings are at the novel's end. This can be frustrating because the novel lacks a true conclusion. Rather, their story continues. This ambiguity is present throughout. If you enjoy the novel, you may believe that this is an accurate portrayal of the way life happens. We sometimes see to the depths but more often see only the surface of things. We learn a story in pieces, and the whole is unknowable. We cannot see in our lifetimes how a story we are a part of ends. Major questions go unanswered. Readers do not know if Joe is part black or not. It is unclear whether Hightower dies (Faulkner later stated that he did not). Readers can only guess at the future of Byron and Lena.

Sample Topics:

1. **Three narratives:** Who is the novel's protagonist?

An essay could be written that argued for the centrality of one character. A possible thesis would be that Lena's presence at the beginning and end of the novel proves that *Light in August* is her story, or the story of her child. One could argue that it is Hightower's story, as he is the character who unites the other major characters of the novel. Certainly it could be argued that Christmas is the main character, and although it would not be as obvious, it could be interesting to argue that Byron Bunch is the protagonist.

2. **Tense:** Considering the changes in tense throughout the novel, would you say *Light in August* is a novel concerned mainly with the past, the present, or the future?

All three are options that could be successfully argued. One approach to an essay on this topic would be to say that *Light in August* demonstrates that the past carries through into the present and into the future. To write an essay on this topic, you might consider how much of the novel takes place in August, and how much takes place at other times.

3. **Structure:** What is the effect of beginning and ending the novel with Lena Grove?

Curiously, when Faulkner first planned *Light in August,* the novel began with Reverend Hightower. Did Faulkner make a good decision when he structured it differently? One possible thesis is that its current structure suffuses the novel with hope. Certainly it would be a different book that ended in Hightower's garden or with the death of Christmas. Another consideration is that Lena leads us into and then out of Jefferson.

4. **Ambiguity:** Why do you think Faulkner leaves some of the novel's major questions unanswered?

"If I'm not, damned if I haven't wasted a lot of time," Christmas says when Joanna asks him how he knows he is part black (254). That Christmas does not know is one of the major uncertainties of the novel. Try to answer one of these questions in an essay: Does the novel provide any evidence that Christmas has black blood? Can you argue that Hightower lives in the final scene? Is there any way to predict what the future might be for Lena and Bryon?

Language, Symbols, and Imagery

A common trope in literature is the idea of the journey and, more specifically, the journey as a metaphor for the life. In *Light in August,* this idea also recurs, although sometimes the reference will be to the street or the road. The first four words of the novel refer to Lena "sitting beside the road" (3). Shortly thereafter, Faulkner describes how Lena, as a young girl, would leave her father's wagon in order to walk into town. Christmas's father is an itinerant circus performer, and all of Christmas's life seems to relate to the road. Faulkner writes, "Knowing not grieving remembers a thousand savage and lonely streets" (220). When Christmas first sets out on his own, Faulkner says that he "entered the street which was to run for fifteen years" (223). The final segment of his journey is his wandering through the black and white sections of Jefferson.

Faulkner was very deliberate in his naming of characters. Sometimes the name's meaning may exist as an echo that hints at something else, as Lena Grove sounds young, sexual, and related to the natural world. Joanna Burden's family has taken on the "burden" of racial inequality. Hightower's name seems to suggest someone who is segregated from others, while "Gail" might cause one to think of strong winds, such as those that would disturb someone in a high tower and make complete isolation and security unattainable. Christmas's name at once reveals that he is without family. His name is a reminder of his birth and his abandonment at the orphanage. "Joe" is a name that implies anonymity. His initials, J. C., along with the name Christmas, relate him to Jesus Christ. Lucas Burch's name seems to tie him to Lena (Burch-Grove), but the name he takes, Joe Brown, links him to Christmas. And Burch's name is enough like Byron Bunch to lead Lena to Bunch when she is looking for Burch. The women tied to Christmas, Bobbie and Joanna, have names derived from male names. Joanna's name seems to relate her to Joe.

For some of the characters, their fates seem to be written on their bodies. Gail Hightower's body is a ruin described as "obese shapelessness" (362). Lena's body suggests to Hightower that she will be a mother to many children. Her pregnancy is a conspicuous reminder of her sexuality to all who meet her. But her body does not only represent her sin, it also represents life. Christmas is at war with his body, and this causes him to be in turn repulsed by all bodies. He is not comfortable with the body's reminders of life or of death, with food or with blood. He is sickened by the sexuality of women, and when Joanna ceases to menstruate, he is repelled again. Percy Grimm is not content to kill Christmas, but he must mutilate his body as well.

Blood, as a symbol and as an image, is significant in *Light in August.* There are the continuing references to Christmas's white or black blood, including the idea advanced by Gavin Stevens that the two types of blood are at war with each other. When Joe first learns that women menstruate, he finds it repugnant and impossible to accept. The following weekend he shoots a sheep and bathes his hands in its warm blood. The killing and the blood, like a ritual sacrifice, seem to wash away the disgust he feels, or to at least make him forget. In the final moments of Christmas's life, the men with Percy Grimm vomit when they see that Grimm is castrating Christmas. Faulkner writes, "Then his face, body, all seemed to collapse, to fall in upon itself, and from out of the slashed garments about his hips and loins the pent black blood seemed to rush like a released breath" (465). Blood is an important aspect of Christian belief, and Christmas's death echoes the Crucifixion in the triumph of that blood and in other ways. For instance, Christmas has five gunshot wounds, as Christ is believed to have suffered five wounds. Another important image that recurs throughout this novel is the wood that seems linked to the cross. Christmas dies helplessly behind Hightower's table, but there are many other instances that could be cited in which wood seems significant, such as the names Grove and Burch, or that the planing mill is the workplace for many of the principal characters. At one point, McEachern beats Christmas, and Faulkner writes, "The boy's body might have been wood or stone; a post or a tower upon which the sentient part of him mused like a hermit, contemplative and remote with ecstasy and selfcrucifixion" (159–160).

Sample Topics:

1. **The street:** How is the road, the street, or the journey significant for the characters in *Light in August*?

   An essay could be written that examined Joe Christmas's life in relation to his journey. His father is a person of the road; his mother is unable to escape her father's house. A close examination of his final journey, which could be read as a metaphor for his entire life, would make an interesting essay topic. Other possibilities are to discuss Lena in relation to the road, or Joanna or Hightower as people who cannot, metaphorically or physically, move on.

2. **Names:** Consider the importance of any one character's name in *Light in August*.

   When Christmas comes to work at the planing mill, we are told "that was the first time Bryon Bunch remembered that he had ever thought how a man's name, which is supposed to be just the sound for who he is, can be somehow an augur of what he will do, if other men can only read the meaning in time. It seemed to him that none of them had looked especially at the stranger until they heard his name. But as soon as they heard it, it was as though there was something in the sound of it that was trying to tell them what to expect; that he carried with him his own inescapable warning, like a flower its scent or a rattlesnake its rattle" (33). You might argue that this is the case with any other of the characters in the novel. Or you might look to see if the opposite is true by considering the case of Lena's infant, who is still unnamed at the novel's end.

3. **The body:** To what extent in *Light in August* is a person's fate written on his or her body?

Many of the novel's characters could be discussed in these terms. For instance, Joanna Burden at one time seems to believe she is pregnant, that she and Joe have created life. But her body betrays that hope. Instead, she is aging, and her body is no longer capable of bearing children. Joe accuses her of being "worn out" and "not any good anymore" (278). He mutilates her body as Percy Grimm will eventually mutilate his. This provides a moment of perverse humor when the man who finds her describes her corpse: "Her head was turned clean around like she was looking behind her. And [I] thought how if she could just have done that when she was alive, she might not have been doing it now" (92).

4. **Blood:** Choose one of the recurring images of the book, such as blood, and explain its significance.

An essay on this topic might take as its thesis a statement such as: In *Light in August,* blood has religious significance. A different paper could be written that discussed blood in terms of sexual significance. Another thesis might be that blood is neither black nor white but signifies only life. Christmas is not at peace until his blood is spilled. Other images that could be explored are the Crucifixion or the images and references to wood.

Compare and Contrast Essays

Perhaps you have heard the expression "traveling light" to describe someone who either literally or figuratively is relatively unencumbered. There is a great deal of traveling in *Light in August,* as well as characters who might be considered in terms of heaviness or lightness. Joanna Burden seems to carry the burden of her family's past. Hightower's weight might stand in for the memories that he carries of his family history. Lena Grove is comically heavy at the novel's beginning but becomes "light" when she gives birth. She is, however, always light if you think of her in terms of psychological burdens. Does Christmas become light when his blood is spilled? Is Christmas's body like the cross that Christ carried?

Readers might want to compare "day" and "night" in *Light in August*. Think about the events that transpire at night and those that happen in the light of day. Are people at night different than they are in the day? McEachern finds the suit Joe has purchased to wear to court Bobbie, and he recognizes right away that these are clothes to be worn at night. Joe describes Joanna as having two personalities, one for the day and one for night.

Joanna tells Christmas that as a child she dreamed "of all the children coming forever and ever into the world, white, with the black shadow already falling upon them before they drew breath. And I seemed to see the black shadow in the shape of a cross. And it seemed like the white babies were struggling, even before they drew breath, to escape from the shadow that was not only upon them but beneath them too, flung out like their arms were flung out, as if they were nailed to the cross" (253). This is one of the many startling images in *Light in August* of black and white. Here blackness becomes equated with original sin, a curse that must be borne. The connotations attached to black are filth, sin, sexuality, and death. For white, the opposite is often true. In Joanna's dream, black and white are inextricably linked. When Christmas is killed, does he die for the sins of the white race against the black?

Christmas is a misogynist, and his disgust with women often turns violent. The other major male characters in the novel, Lucas Burch, Byron Bunch, and Gail Hightower, avoid women. Is there an example of a healthy male-female relationship in the novel? It seems that the women are characterized to a large extent by their sexuality, which includes whether or not they are mothers. Percy Grimm castrates Christmas because he has had a sexual relationship with Joanna Burden, but the community had (since before her birth) isolated and failed to protect her.

Sample Topics:

1. **Light versus heavy:** Contrast the concepts of "light" and "heavy" in *Light in August.*

   An essay on this topic might begin with the novel's title. What are the possible reasons it is called *Light in August*? What does it mean to be "light"? Related to these might be images of raising or lowering.

2. **Night versus day:** Consider the novel's portrayal of night and day.

   One possible thesis is that *Light in August* shows that what occurs at night will be revealed in the day. The sins committed in the night by Lena, Joanna, Hightower's wife, and Joe, to name only a few, do not remain hidden. Maybe there should not be a strict divide between the two. Lena leaves her brother's home through the window at night, even though she knows there was nothing to stop her leaving by the door in the day; why does she do this?

3. **White versus black:** In a novel that takes race as such a central theme, is it odd to find no major characters who identify themselves, wholly, as black?

   This is one question that might provoke some thought about white and black in the novel. An essay could also be written that sought to explain one of the passages that moves between black and white, such as Joanna's dream or Christmas's murder. You could also attempt to look at some of the black characters in the novel; none are named. Instead, they are referred to as "negro" or by some other name that marks them as black without giving them any other identifying trait.

4. **Male versus female:** How does *Light in August* portray the relations between men and women?

Are there any admirable women in this novel? Any number of statements made about women in the novel could provide a place to begin thinking about this topic, such as when Hightower tells Byron, "No woman who has a child is ever betrayed; the husband of a mother, whether he be the father or not, is already a cuckold" (316). Are there any instances of women viewed as more than lovers, wives, or mothers? Are the relations between men and women always adversarial? Does the novel reveal a fundamental distrust of female sexuality?

Bibliography and Online Resources for *Light in August*

Banta, Martha. "The Razor, the Pistol, and the Ideology of Race Etiquette." *Faulkner and Ideology. Faulkner and Yoknapatawpha 1992.* Eds. Donald M. Kartiganer and Ann J. Abadie. Jackson: UP of Mississippi, 1995. 172–216.

Bercovitch, Sacvan. "Culture in a Faulknerian Context." *Faulkner in Cultural Context. Faulkner and Yoknapatawpha 1995.* Eds. Donald M. Kartiganer and Ann J. Abadie. Jackson: UP of Mississippi, 1997. 284–310.

Berland, Alwyn. *Light in August: A Study in Black and White.* New York: Twayne, 1992.

Bloom, Harold. *William Faulkner's Light in August.* New York: Chelsea, 1988.

Brooks, Cleanth. "The Community and the Pariah." *William Faulkner: The Yoknapatawpha Country.* Rpt. in Minter, *Twentieth Century Interpretations of Light in August* (1969): 55–70.

Chase, Richard. "The Three Narratives of Light in August." *Readings on William Faulkner.* Ed. Clarice Swisher. San Diego, CA: Greenhaven, 1998. 129–33.

Faulkner, William. *Light in August.* New York: Vintage International P, 1990.

Hays, Peter L. "Racial Predestination: The Elect and the Damned in *Light in August.*" *English Language Notes* 33.2 (December 1995): 62–69.

Hlavsa, Virginia V. "The Crucifixion in Light in August: Suspending the Rules at the Post." *Faulkner and Religion.* Eds. Doreen Fowler and Ann J. Abadie. Jackson: UP of Mississippi, 1991. 127–39.

Kartiganer, Donald M., and Ann J. Abadie, eds. *Faulkner and Psychology.* Jackson: UP of Mississippi, 1994.

———. *Faulkner and the Natural World: Faulkner and Yoknapatawpha.* Jackson: UP of Mississippi, 1999.

"Light in August: Bibliography." *William Faulkner on the Web.* 17 Aug. 2006. Ed. John B. Padgett. U of Mississippi. 17 Oct. 2007. URL: http://www.mcsr. olemiss.edu/~egjbp/faulkner/b_n_lia.html.

Millgate, Michael, ed. *New Essays on Light in August.* Cambridge: Cambridge UP, 1987.

Minter, David L., ed. *Twentieth Century Interpretations of Light in August: A Collection of Critical Essays.* Englewood Cliffs, NJ: Prentice, 1969.

Moreland, Richard C. "Faulkner and Modernism." *The Cambridge Companion to William Faulkner.* Ed. Philip Weinstein. New York: Cambridge UP, 1995. 17–30.

Pitavy, Francois, L., ed. *William Faulkner's Light in August: A Critical Casebook.* New York: Garland, 1982.

Ruppersburg, Hugh M. *Reading Faulkner: Light in August.* Jackson: UP of Mississippi, 1994.

Vickery, Olga W. "The Shadow and the Mirror: *Light in August.*" *The Novels of William Faulkner.* Rpt. in Minter, *Twentieth Century Interpretations of Light in August* (1969): 25–41.

Watkins, Ralph. "'It Was Like I Was the Woman and She Was the Man': Boundaries, Portals, and Pollution in Light in August." *Southern Literary Journal* 26.2 (Spring 1994): 11–24.

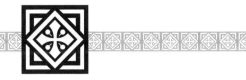

ABSALOM, ABSALOM!

READING TO WRITE

A<small>BSALOM, ABSALOM!</small> (1936) is considered by many to be Faulkner's masterpiece. As in other of Faulkner's works, the reader is plunged into the stories of the people who inhabit Yoknapatawpha County. Characters and stories belonging to other Faulkner novels and short stories are revisited and developed in this novel. And, as in other of Faulkner's works, the narrative's structure may pose some difficulties. The story of *Absalom, Absalom!* takes a number of narrators to tell. These narrators perhaps know only a fragment of the story. Throughout the novel, the tale is colored by the narrators, reflecting each one's individual perception of it. As the narrators tell the story of Thomas Sutpen, his story becomes a part of their experience. The reader has the experience of assembling Thomas Sutpen's story into one narrative, while also coming to understand the stories of its tellers, particularly Rosa Coldfield and Quentin Compson.

Thomas Sutpen arrives in Jefferson prepared to execute his "design," to distance himself from his origins as a poor white child born in West Virginia in 1807. As an adolescent, he learned that a complicated class structure existed in the American South, wherein poor whites were considered to have no better status than that of the black slaves. Upon being directed to the back door of a large mansion by the Negro butler, he comes to understand that the house servants of the wealthy planters actually enjoyed a status greater than his own. He says that it is at that moment he vowed to amass property, servants, and the prosperity that would guarantee his acceptance among the highest ranks of society.

But, in fact, his design, its execution, or the man himself contains a fatal flaw that will destroy all three. Sutpen's plan will sow seeds that will continue to affect those who learn of his story generations later, most notably Quentin Compson. The outline of Sutpen's story is evident in the early chapters of the novel. The details of his story will be slowly revealed through the later chapters. The novel eventually answers, or provides several possible answers, to the question of why Henry Sutpen murders his sister Judith's suitor, Charles Bon.

The story Quentin Compson tells to his roommate Shreve McCannon in their Harvard dorm room in 1910 is lurid and grotesque. In the tradition of the southern gothic, it features incest, miscegenation, sexual deviance, and a dark, mysterious house that seems to hold ghosts and the remnants of a cursed family. The story is also an allegory for the South in ruins after the Civil War.

The novel's title is taken from the lament of King David in 2 Samuel 13–18. The king's oldest son has had incestuous relations with his sister, Tamar. Their brother Absalom kills his eldest brother and then is killed himself. The Bible states that when he learned of this death, "The king was much moved, and went up to the chamber over the gate, and wept: and as he went, thus he said, O my son Absalom, my son, my son Absalom! would God I had died for thee, O Absalom, my son, my son!" (2 Sam 18: 33).

Helpfully, Faulkner includes in this novel a chronology, a genealogy, and a map of Yoknapatawpha County. The map shows the settings for many of the events he recounts in this and other stories and novels. As in other of his works, such as *Light in August,* this novel shows people still attempting to bear the burdens of having once enslaved another people. Truly, here, the sins of the fathers are revisited upon the sons. They cannot escape even in the North, even at Harvard, where Shreve remarks, "Jesus, the South is fine, isn't it. It's better than the theatre, isn't it. It's better than Ben Hur, isn't it. No wonder you have to come away now and then, isn't it" (176). As you read about the destruction of the Sutpen family, keep in mind that its destruction mirrors that of the American South. It is not an outside threat that brings about its destruction; rather, it destroys itself.

TOPICS AND STRATEGIES
Themes

The theme of race is important to *Absalom, Absalom!* The impact it has on the characters in the novel may seem unusual to the modern reader because here race is of more importance than incest or the presence of a mistress or shadow wife. Issues of race also divide families, creating brothers and sisters who live in privilege (the white family) and are served by their half brothers and sisters (the black, or shadow, family). During the war, Judith, Clytie, and Rosa survive by clinging to one another, eating, sleeping, and working side by side. In spite of this necessary closeness and the fact that they are family, Clytie is still treated as a slave. Is her last act, to shield Henry, motivated by familial love or does it demonstrate the loyalty of a slave to her master?

The ideal of racial purity moves Henry to kill Charles Bon. The novel leaves open the question of whether Bon actually was of mixed race or not. That question is of less importance than the suggestion that he is of mixed race. (This is similar to the situation of Joe Christmas in *Light in August*; he is believed to have "black blood," so he is treated as black.) This illustrates another theme of the novel, the importance of public perception. Bon appears to be a wealthy white man and is treated as such, but the suggestion of black blood is enough to alter how Henry perceives him. It also causes Sutpen to reject Bon as his son. Sutpen is perceived by the town to be a crook, and all that he builds and accumulates fails to alter this perception.

As Charles Bon says to Henry, "So it's the miscegenation, not the incest, which you cant bear" (285). It seems possible that Henry could have, as he says, gotten used to the idea of his brother and sister making an incestuous marriage, but after his father tells him that Bon is part black, Bon's death at Henry's hand seems certain. Miscegenation, or sexual relations between blacks and whites, was considered a tremendous threat to southern society. But, as *Absalom, Absalom!* shows, this taboo was consistently violated, particularly by white men having sexual relations with black women.

For the modern reader, the incestuous nature of Bon's relations with Judith will be more troubling. Particularly if you consider that Bon's black lineage is more rumor than proven fact, and that if he does possess "black blood," the amount is small, no more than one-quarter. In appearance he is *no* more black than Henry or Judith, and any child born to Judith and Bon would be no more than one-eighth black. That Bon is Judith's brother, however, is irrefutable.

The reader, pointedly, does not know what has occurred between Bon and Henry immediately before the shot at the gate. Why has Henry allowed Bon to come this far? He could have shot Bon at any point, particularly while they were at war together. Faulkner's novel hints at the incestuous feelings between the three siblings. Bon and Henry have more of a foundation for a relationship than Bon and Judith, and there does seem to be homoerotic overtones to their friendship. As Quentin imagines, it is a case of Henry "taking that virginity in the person of the brother-in-law, the man who would be if he could become, metamorphose into, the lover, the husband; by whom he would be despoiled, choose for despoiler, if he could become, metamorphose into the sister, the mistress, the bride" (77). Bon and Judith see so little of each other that it is hard to accept the depth of their love. It seems, instead, a feeling mediated by their feelings for Henry. And Bon's motives may have less to do with love than with taking revenge upon his father.

The challenge to interpreting what has happened to the Sutpen family is made greater by the distance that separates the reader from their story and that separates even Quentin from their story. This is, quite literally, a history, and it is reliant on memory. Each new narrator provides more of the story, but each also alters what has been said previously. What the narrators tell of the Sutpen story tells the reader as much about them as it does about Sutpen, in some cases more. Quentin, particularly, is haunted by the tale, though it began nearly 100 years before. Another theme is time and what time does to a person or a story. Does time make the story of the Sutpen family any less disturbing? Does the time that has passed alter the story? Or does the story alter time and continue to affect the future?

Sample Topics:

    1. Race: Why do none of the "black" characters tell their version of this tale?

        There are many ways to discuss race in *Absalom, Absalom!* One would be to discuss the way the "black" characters are silenced. To put the word *black* into quotation marks allows it to include those characters who are presumed to be black or racially mixed, such as Bon and his mother. Clytie is perhaps the most developed of these characters, but even so we know little about her. What motivates her to burn the house to the ground? She holds exactly the same genetic relationship to Judith and Henry as Bon does; she is their half sister. And yet, she seems to accept her role as a favored servant.

2. **Miscegenation:** What does Faulkner show about miscegenation in the South?

We learn that miscegenation was taboo; it was enough, Sutpen believed, to stand in the way of his plan to enter respectable society. And yet, miscegenation is everywhere in the novel. Only the nameless men who build Sutpen's house and Charles Etienne St. Valery Bon's wife seem to be wholly African. The novel reveals the practice of young men of means taking octoroon mistresses in the deep South. Having children of mixed race was not the problem faced by Thomas Sutpen in his first marriage; it was having legitimate children of mixed race. Clytie is not the threat to his plan that Bon is.

3. **Incest:** Does the novel imply that incest is the worst transgression?

The possibility of an incestuous marriage between Bon and Judith is shocking. Perhaps more shocking are Henry's ruminations about why it might be okay. After all, he thinks, it has occurred in other societies, particularly among noble families. If you have read *The Sound and the Fury,* you know to wonder about any statement Quentin Compson makes about incest. What he imagines went on between Bon and Henry is likely colored by his own feelings for his sister, Caddy. Was there ever any chance that Henry would have allowed Bon and Judith to marry?

4. **Time:** What does *Absalom, Absalom!* imply about time?

The stories told in *Absalom, Absalom!* span more than 100 years, from Sutpen's beginnings to Quentin's suicide or even, though it is only a mention in the appendix, the future of

Shreve McCannon. Is Quentin the final victim of Sutpen's design? How does Sutpen's story change through time? How does Sutpen himself change? Is time the great destroyer of these people and their plans?

Character

If you intend to write about a character or a number of characters from *Absalom, Absalom!* the best essay will likely focus on the character or characters most intriguing to you. One of the more obvious choices would be to write about Thomas Sutpen. He is seen through the eyes of many other characters in the novel. The reader is forced to view him through these other characters because much of the story is not from his perspective at all. Is he an innocent in some ways, still the small boy who is shocked to be shown to the back door of the grand house? Or is he the devil Rosa Coldfield believes him to be?

Just as the reader learns about Sutpen from the stories others tell about him, his son Charles Bon is even more a mystery. What the reader knows of him comes largely from the imaginings of Quentin and Shreve, in a dorm room at Harvard, 55 years after Bon had been killed. The reader does not truly know what motivates him. Quentin imagines that Bon only wanted his father's acknowledgment, and had he been given this, he would have walked out of the lives of the Sutpen family forever. Although the various narrators want to believe in his love for Judith, there is not a word of dialogue between these two in the novel. Nor is there any evidence of his feelings for or treatment of his son or his octoroon mistress. The only hard evidence, and all that is left of Bon after he is buried on Sutpen's property, is his final letter to Judith and the metal case he carried with the picture of the mistress and his child. The language of the letter is enigmatic. Quentin and Shreve have to answer for themselves why Bon died carrying this photograph in the case Judith had given him containing her own picture.

If you have read *The Sound and the Fury*, you know that Quentin Compson will soon commit suicide. And if you have not read that novel, you will learn from Faulkner's genealogy at the conclusion of *Absalom, Absalom!* that Quentin dies in Cambridge in 1910. This may color your view of Quentin as a narrator. He is not a disinterested observer of the

Sutpen family. In their story, he finds echoes of his own. When Quentin comes face to face with the dying Henry Sutpen, it is like a meeting between Quentin and his own ghost. Just before Quentin replies to Shreve's final question, "Why do you hate the South?" with his impassioned, "I don't hate it . . . I don't. I don't! I don't hate it! I don't hate it!" (303), Shreve tries to make an accounting of how the Sutpen family destroyed itself. He concludes that the account is still open because Jim Bond is left, and he predicts that "the Jim Bonds are going to conquer the western hemisphere" (302). Because Shreve frames his argument as being between the black and white Sutpens, he fails to account for Quentin. Jim Bond will still be there when Quentin is no more. It is possible that the last remaining Compson is Benjy, Quentin's retarded younger brother. The last Sutpen is Jim Bond, and he is the last participant in the Sutpen story.

Rosa Coldfield is a character who bears some resemblance to Emily Grierson, the protagonist of Faulkner's "A Rose for Emily." In the eyes of the people of Jefferson, both women are spinsters, gentle and harmless eccentrics. But the reader learns that this conception of them is incredibly limited. Rosa wants to tell her story to Quentin, though Quentin himself can find no reason she should choose to talk to him. She says that she imagines he might become a writer one day; but is her true motive to entrust a future writer with her story? Not only does she want him to know what happened in the past, she also wants him to confront what is happening in the Sutpen house now.

Sample Topics:

1. Thomas Sutpen: What is your view of Thomas Sutpen?

> The answer to this question, whatever it is, can serve as your thesis. Your essay will need textual evidence to support your argument. If you argue, along with Rosa, that Sutpen is a monster, there is evidence in the text to support this reading, but you would need something more than Rosa's view to build a strong argument. If you were to argue something less obvious, for instance that Sutpen's failings were of a particularly American sort, the paper would be more interesting. After all,

what did he want but to obtain a life beyond the poverty he was born into, a level of prosperity and a son to ensure the future of his plans?

2. **Charles Bon:** How can the reader know Charles Bon, when only partial accounts of him remain?

To Quentin and Rosa, Charles Bon seems the very type of a romantic hero. Do you believe in their conception of Bon? Rosa's view of him is similar to a teenager with a crush on a pop star. Quentin's view is little better. Are Bon's motives understandable? Does he engage your sympathy? Why do you think Faulkner does not allow Bon to speak for himself?

3. **Quentin Compson:** Does Quentin hate the South?

To some extent, *Absalom, Absalom!* is Quentin's story. If you enjoyed this novel and have not yet read *The Sound and the Fury*, you will want to read that novel to see how Faulkner enlarges upon that story and how these two novels are in a sense companion pieces. The question above might not be answerable in a short essay, but it could move you to begin considering Quentin's role in the novel. What sort of narrator is he? Why is he so disturbed by the story he tells? Why, when Shreve asks him to tell about the South, does Quentin tell the story of the Sutpens?

4. **Rosa Coldfield:** How would you characterize Rosa Coldfield?

Rosa gets as much time as she needs to tell her story to Quentin, but some mysteries still remain. Why does she agree, so easily and seemingly against character, to marry Thomas Sutpen? (Keep in mind that there were not the same prohibitions then about a sister marrying her deceased sister's husband as there are now.) What is her relation to her own father, who starves in the family's attic under her watch? Why does she go to the Sutpen home, find Henry obviously dying, and then return to her home to wait three more months before summoning an ambulance? Why does she choose Quentin to accompany her?

History and Context

Absalom, Absalom! is a novel about history. History is one of its thematic concerns, along with the question of how people live with its burdens, particularly in the American South. Some people, those as sensitive as Quentin Compson, might find the weight of that history to be too much. You may notice that the characters in *Absalom, Absalom!* who live through the war are less concerned with its meaning than those who come after. The novel also seems to say that history is to some extent unknowable. How is it possible to understand the motivations and feelings of people who are long dead?

In *Absalom, Absalom!* the history is specifically southern. The difficulties, the extreme problems of race and class are particular to this place and time. And yet, the story resonates with Shreve, though he is Canadian. The difference between him and Quentin is that this history is not Shreve's. He does not feel doomed to retell it or to live it over again, as Quentin does.

Thomas Sutpen returns from the war a broken man. His family is in ruins, as is his house and land. He returns to rebuilding both, but it is too late, and he does not have it in him to make things as they were before. He is unable, for instance, to sire another son. The male heir that will survive them all is Jim Bond. By the time Faulkner was born, the idea of the South as a genteel and favored land was contrary to reality.

It is also helpful to view *Absalom, Absalom!* in the context of its biblical source. The exclamation in the title is there to underscore that fact that it is a lament, the lament of a father for his lost son. The second book of Samuel has those elements that are not taught in Sunday school: betrayal, rape, incest, and murder. In that story, Absalom is the heir apparent to King David. But after killing his half brother, who has raped their sister, Tamar, Absalom plots against David. David's general kills Absalom, and the king cries out in grief for his dead son.

In the context of Faulkner's work, *Absalom, Absalom!* holds a significant place because two of the characters, Mr. Compson and Quentin Compson, appear in his earlier work *The Sound and the Fury*. Shreve is also in the earlier work. At the end of *The Sound and the Fury*, Quentin and his father are dead. *Absalom, Absalom!* takes the reader back to a time earlier than that work and provides a more complete picture of the Compson family and the troubles that will also befall them. Their story is like another version of the Sutpen story; there is no hope for the future of the Compsons.

Sample Topics:

1. **History:** What is the significance of history in this novel?

   Shreve finds it odd that Quentin is upset by the death of Rosa Coldfield, someone who is not his relative. He finds it so odd that he continually refers to her as "Aunt Rosa." After a while, Quentin no longer bothers to correct him. Why should Quentin mourn the death of this woman? Is Faulkner suggesting that there is a familial link among southerners? Consider the unusual alliances and progeny in the novel, and how difficult it is to distinguish who is related and how.

2. **The South:** Is the novel distinctively southern?

   Faulkner does seem to draw a line between Quentin and Shreve, as if Shreve, a Canadian, could not be affected or have stories like Quentin's. But there are other societies that have tolerated slavery, certainly other societies that have fought and lost devastating wars. What makes the American South different? Is that difference only a myth and perhaps a source of false pride?

3. **The Bible:** Examine the significance of the title of the novel, *Absalom, Absalom!*

   Faulkner's titles are a good entryway into his work because they are always heavy with significance. This could be a starting place for an essay on this novel. You would want to read the book of Samuel where the story of Absalom is told. How does this novel retell that story? How does *Absalom, Absalom!* differ from the biblical story? Henry is not killed in battle. Sutpen is not a king. Are they only a shadow of David's great family?

4. **Faulkner's work:** What can be said about *Absalom, Absalom!* in the context of Faulkner's work?

If you have read widely in Faulkner, you might be able to make an argument for its position in his canon. The section below on Compare and Contrast essays suggests other single works you might read for comparison to this one. You might also consider what it meant to Faulkner and his readers to resurrect major characters from an earlier novel and have them also be major characters in *Absalom, Absalom!*

Philosophy and Ideas

Sutpen's life is spent in the pursuit of his "design." As he attempts to overcome the class structure of the South that allowed him to be sent as a young man to the back entrance of the great house, he allows nothing to interfere with his goal. He sacrifices his first marriage (perhaps not a tremendous sacrifice, as it seems none of his marriages involved feelings of love) and his firstborn son. The cold calculation Sutpen brings to achieving his plan is particularly evident in the comments he makes to Rosa Coldfield and then later to Milly Jones. Both women are seen as vehicles; their only worth is that they may provide Sutpen with a son.

In the larger sense, Sutpen could be seen as representative of the southern slaveholder who fails to see the slaves who work for him as people. To Sutpen, all people are viewed in terms of how they forward his plan. This includes the slaves who built his plantation and extends to his wives and children. When he fails to recognize the humanity of those around him, his own humanity is compromised.

One idea that seems to be inherent in Sutpen's story is the corrupting influence of holding other people as property. When Sutpen is turned away from the front door of the great house as an adolescent, he becomes determined, ironically, to become the sort of person who would turn a young boy away. His condescending behavior toward Milly Jones, so ugly that it causes Wash Jones to kill him, is not unlike that of a slaveholder toward his slave.

Sutpen's house represents his dream, and it is burned down by Clytie, who is at once his daughter and his servant. After the house is no more, Sutpen's last living descendant, Jim Bond, lives wild among the plantation's ruins. He becomes a monstrous presence, known mainly by his howl. Like Benjy Compson, Quentin's brother, Jim Bond is mentally handicapped. That he is no longer seen, only heard, and then in a voice that does not speak but only howls, suggests a presence that is less human than monstrous and almost mythic.

Others might argue that Sutpen's story is one of chance and fate. Can Thomas Sutpen, after all, be blamed for a decision made in hurt and anger when he was a child? And, perhaps, Sutpen's problem is that he is the product of the American South. The model he takes for his behavior is that of the southern gentleman. His goal is to dominate in that system. The system, we now know, was corrupt and rooted in sin. But what other model was available for young Thomas Sutpen? When Mr. Compson narrates the story, he is more forgiving than the other narrators, putting down what happens to Sutpen as fate.

But Sutpen's story seems to defy such an explanation, especially as its affects those who are touched by it, even if only by hearing it. The tragedies that befall Sutpen's children bring to mind the idea of the sins of the father being passed on to the sons. Sutpen's house is built on slavery, violence, and misogyny. Even the way he acquires the land for Sutpen's Hundred represents the misappropriation of land that rightfully belonged to the Native Americans. And so the very land Sutpen possesses seems to be cursed. Sutpen's design seems to ruin the lives of all it touches: children, grandchildren, great-grandchildren, Rosa Coldfield, and, finally, Quentin Compson. Like the Ancient Mariner of Coleridge's poem, Quentin seems doomed to tell the story, though the knowledge of the story has removed him from the world of the living. Quentin believes Rosa wants him to tell the story so that people will "know at last why God let us lose the War" (6).

Sample Topics:

1. **Design:** What is Sutpen's "design"?

Describe Sutpen's "design," imagining how he himself projected it. How great is it? Why is a male child a necessary component of the design? You might go further and consider what role love plays in design. Who is responsible for the failure of what Sutpen hoped to achieve? Where and when does the design go wrong?

2. **Justice:** Is Sutpen's failure justified?

Sutpen's death at the hands of Wash Jones, a man whose presence had been tolerated on the Sutpen land, though he was obviously thought inferior to the Sutpen family, could be seen as poetic justice. Sutpen has condescended to the Jones family. They were, as Sutpen was as an adolescent, treated as one step beneath the position of the Sutpen servants. Taken further, an essay could consider the end of the Sutpen dynasty. Is Jim Bond the just end of Sutpen? Consider his racial makeup, his handicaps, and his behavior.

3. **Fate:** How can it be said that Thomas Sutpen's story is fated to turn out as it does?

You might consider to what extent fate governs the lives in *Absalom, Absalom!* In the largest sense, is Thomas Sutpen the product of an environment that robbed him of his chance to live other than he did? Or you might examine the role fate plays in the lives of one of the other characters. Was Rosa Coldfield fated to be a spinster? Why does Charles Bon seem unable to make any decision but those that will cost him his life? What about Quentin Compson? Why is he compelled to look upon Henry's face, all the while knowing that this meeting will have devastating consequences for him?

4. **Inherited sin:** Is it right that the sons in the novel pay for the sins of their fathers?

There are many ways to approach as essay on the topic of inherited sin in *Absalom, Absalom!* For instance, you could answer the question above. All of the sons in the novel die early. You might argue that this is an appropriate punishment; it does effectively stop the family by not allowing it to continue and reproduce. You might argue that Quentin is the son of the South still punished for the sins of his fathers. But you might also argue that the punishment is too great.

Form and Genre

The narrative structure of *Absalom, Absalom!* is exceedingly complex. It is incumbent on the reader to follow the story as it is told by different narrators, all of whom bring their own biases and limitations to what they tell and how they tell it. Through this complex structure, Faulkner tells more than the story of Thomas Sutpen. The novel is at once his story and the story of the narrators. So the reader is following many stories at once, fully aware that no story is being presented in its entirety. As with the character of Charles Bon, there are entire and important aspects of the story that are left in shadow. There might be a suggestion in this method that no story can be completely told or known.

Part of what the reader must untangle is the question of how much to trust the various narrators. Are they each attempting to tell the truth as they believe it to be, or is it possible that their narratives have been consciously manipulated? Perhaps each narrator, without realizing it, emphasizes the parts of the story that are of particular interest to him or her. Of course, time also plays a part. Over time, some of the story is altered or forgotten.

For the most part, the story is told by Quentin Compson, Mr. Compson (Quentin's father), and Rosa Coldfield. The story is told in pieces. It is not in chronological order, and most of it comes in flashbacks, presented as they occur to the narrator. Although a great deal of the story is told in the first chapters of the novel, it is only toward the novel's end that the reader has learned enough to understand those events. Readers who enjoy Faulkner will appreciate his ability to place one into the world of Yoknapatawpha County with very little guidance and allow the reader to discover its stories.

One label that adheres to *Absalom, Absalom!* is that it is an example of the "southern gothic." Writers such as William Faulkner and Flannery O' Connor are representative of this genre. Think of some of the aspects of this lurid tale: secrets, incest, death, sexual corruption, darkness, and the general sense of foreboding. At some points, the novel seems to be a horror story. Up in the empty and rotting house (symbolic of an empty and rotten man) there are mysterious things happening. The appearance of a ghost would not be surprising; that the ghost is alive makes it perhaps more frightening.

Absalom, Absalom! might also be called a tragedy. Mr. Compson makes this comparison himself (48–49). He notes that Sutpen named Clytie for Clytemnestra, though Mr. Compson liked to think he meant to call her Cassandra (48). The novel could be read as the tragedy of the Sutpen family, or in a larger sense as the tragedy of the South. And it could also be read as the tragedy of Thomas Sutpen, with Sutpen as its tragic hero. The hero in such a story should have a flaw, from his youth, that will project his end. The hero will rise to great heights of success, only to be brought low through his own actions. The hero will lose everything: a kingdom, those he loves, what he loves in himself. His story will act as a warning to others.

Sample Topics:

1. **Narrators:** Who do you judge to be the most reliable narrator in *Absalom, Absalom!*?

A consideration of the novel's narrators could be the starting point for any number of essays. You could answer the question above and create an argument that attests to the reliability of your chosen narrator. This would involve discussion of the other narrators in the novel. You could argue that none of the narrators are reliable. You could also argue that one of the narrators was more sympathetic or interesting to you. You could discuss the role each narrator plays: For instance, why is Shreve an important narrator? What does he bring to the novel?

2. **Complex narrative:** Do you feel that the complex narrative is an essential part of *Absalom, Absalom!*?

The essay written on this question would defend the complexity of this novel. You might think in terms of the detective story, where the pleasure is measured by how much you enjoy putting a narrative together by the clues slowly gathered. What other form could this story have taken? Would it have been as effective? How would you defend this novel to a friend who says that it is hopelessly convoluted?

3. **Southern gothic:** How is the southern gothic genre different from a horror story?

Consider how *Absalom, Absalom!* is different from a horror story. You might discuss places in the novel where you expected the novel to turn toward horror, but this did not happen. For instance, early on Rosa Coldfield is engaged to Sutpen, but no marriage ever takes place. The reader may wonder if some outrage took place, maybe a physical assault. When one learns the truth of what happened, it is more shocking than what one imagined and entirely in keeping with this story and its characters. Likewise, what Rosa and Quentin find at the house is particularly frightening, but not in the usual sense.

4. **Tragedy:** Is Thomas Sutpen a tragic hero?

An essay on this topic might want to look at the definition of tragedy and the hero. Is Sutpen the victim of his own design? Does his single-minded dedication to his goal cause him to discount the lives of those around him, or is he, at core, an objectionable human being? If he is a tragic hero brought low by a fatal flaw, it must also be true that he has some redeeming, even admirable, qualities that allow him to succeed in so much. Can you argue that this is true? Or, alternatively, is Quentin Compson the hero of this novel?

Language, Symbols, and Imagery

One fascinating thing Faulkner does, which might add to the reader's confusion, is to create characters that somehow mirror each other. These "doubles" seem to tell us more about each character involved, somehow amplifying the characteristics of each and revealing more than they would have revealed singly. In some cases, the relationship is explicit, as that between Henry and Bon. Henry consciously emulates Bon in dress and behavior before they learn they are brothers. The romantic triangle of Henry, Bon, and Judith suggests that the attraction Judith feels for Bon is the result of the attraction Henry feels for Bon. There is perhaps the suggestion of homoerotic interest on Henry's part. But Henry and Bon are not the only doubles in *Absalom, Absalom!*

Quentin sees himself in Henry, as this passage of dialogue between them makes clear:

Waking or sleeping it was the same: the bed, the yellow sheets and pillow, the wasted yellow face with closed, almost transparent eyelids on the pillow, the wasted hands crossed on the breast as if he were already a corpse; waking or sleeping it was the same and would be the same forever as long as he lived:

And you are—?
Henry Sutpen.
And you have been here—?
Four years.
And you came home—?
To die. Yes.
Yes. To die.
And you have been here—?
Four years.
And you are—?
Henry Sutpen. (298)

When Quentin and Henry meet, it is so like looking in a mirror to Henry that their dialogue is an almost perfect mirror. Perhaps less obvious is the way Quentin and Shreve resemble Henry and Bon, but they, too, are college roommates, one weaker than the other, brought together by the story of Thomas Sutpen.

A recurring motif in *Absalom, Absalom!* is family. What does it mean to be family? Why is family important? How should family members treat one another? A symbol of this relationship is the Sutpen gravesite. Quentin describes it to Shreve: Sutpen and Ellen with marble tombstones, but also Charles Bon, Charles Etienne St. Valery Bon, and Judith. The gravesite puts the family together in a way they were not in life. Charles Bon lies with Sutpen, his father. Judith is near Charles Bon, but as sister or widow? Bon's son, Charles Etienne St. Valery Bon, gains a legitimacy he did not have in life. Does he stand in for the child Judith and Bon never had? Another way family is highlighted is how Shreve continually calls Rosa Coldfield, "Aunt Rosa." Throughout the novel, Quentin corrects Shreve, telling him it is "Miss Rosa." But by the novel's end, he gives up correcting and allows Shreve to call her "Aunt Rosa." Not only does this imply a familial relationship between Quentin and Rosa, but it also implies that all southerners are related. The Sutpen family is a testament to the tangled relationships that might make up a family and to the fact that some family members are hidden or unrecognized.

Faulkner's working title for this novel was *Dark House.* The cover of the Vintage paperback shows a colonnaded mansion in shades of blue and gray that seems to represent the Sutpen house. The first step of Sutpen's design is to acquire the land and build his house. The house becomes the symbol of his design. It is built by the black men he brings with him to Jefferson. At the novel's end, it burns spectacularly.

Sample Topics:

1. **Doubling:** Choose any doubles in the novel and discuss the way they reflect and enlarge upon your understanding of each.

   An essay on this topic might focus on any of the doubles discussed above: Henry and Bon, Henry and Quentin, or Quentin and Shreve. It might also focus on less obvious pairings, such as Rosa and Ellen, Judith and Clytie, or Rosa and Quentin.

2. **Family:** What does family mean in *Absalom, Absalom!*?

   Faulkner includes a genealogy at the end of this novel to make explicit how these characters are related. He likely would not have done this if the relationships were clear. Sutpen begets at least four lines: the first with Bon's mother, the next with

Clytie's mother, then the "legitimate" family he has with Ellen Coldfield, and finally the one he begins with Milly Jones. One way to approach an essay on this topic would be to compare these families. What makes Henry and Judith his legitimate children? Why is Clytie's mother unnamed? Why is a having a son so important to Sutpen?

3. **The idiot:** Examine the character of Jim Bond. Why should he be the result of Sutpen's design?

If you have read *The Sound and the Fury*, this topic might be particularly interesting because Jim Bond is in some ways a reflection of Benjy Compson. Both prove to be the final member of their illustrious families. An essay on this topic would look particularly at the final pages of the book and Shreve's predictions about the future of mankind.

4. **The house:** What is the importance of the Sutpen house in *Absalom, Absalom!*?

One approach to this topic might be to consider that it is Jim Bond who burns the house down, although it is Clytie who instructs him to do so. But you might also consider how the house is built. There are the descriptions of the building both before and after the war. Other important moments: Charles Bon is killed at the gates of the house. Henry has ridden with Bon to this point, knowing he will not let him cross the gates. Henry himself returns to the house to die. Clytie becomes mistress of the house after Judith's death. Rosa avoids the house as if it is the embodiment of Thomas Sutpen.

Compare and Contrast Essays

Faulkner revisited many of his characters in other short stories or novels. *Absalom, Absalom!* was an important book for him, and the characters of this novel appear in numerous other places. Faulkner's short story "Wash" is narrated by Wash Jones, who at times in *Absalom, Absalom!*

is Sutpen's squatter, closest friend, and finally the great-grandfather to his last daughter when Sutpen has a child with Milly Jones, Wash's 15-year-old granddaughter. This short story reveals a very different Thomas Sutpen, thoroughly in his decline but still remembered by Wash as a great man. This story is shocking in its brutality and ends with Wash burning down the cabin he has occupied on Sutpen's Hundred for many years.

If you have read or have time to read *The Sound and the Fury*, you will have an even greater understanding of *Absalom, Absalom! The Sound and the Fury* tells the story of the Compson family. The novel witnesses the end of the Compson family. As in the Sutpen family, there is a strong daughter who is more capable than the male heirs. This daughter is the subject of her brother Quentin's incestuous interest. Benjy, the mentally feeble brother, will represent their family's end. And you learn that Quentin commits suicide not so long after he tells the Sutpen story to Shreve.

The two sets of college roommates, Henry and Bon and Quentin and Shreve, are also doubles for one another. Since the relationship between Quentin and Shreve is also important in *The Sound and the Fury*, you can learn more about them by reading that book. However, that would not be necessary for writing an essay that compared them to Henry and Bon in *Absalom, Absalom!* Quentin tells Rosa's story to Shreve, who is strangely fascinated by it. But this is not strictly a relating of the tale because the two friends supply the information that was missing from Rosa's version, and they elaborate on the thoughts and motivations of Bon, as Rosa did not.

In *Light in August*, Joe Christmas is tormented by the possibility that he has "black blood." His mother is Caucasian, but his father is a traveling performer. Possibly he is Mexican, but Doc Hines, Joe's grandfather, believes he is part Negro and kills him. Joe Christmas, like Charles Etienne St. Valery Bon, appears to be white, but the belief that he is black torments him. He does not feel he fully belongs in either community, and so he uncomfortably moves between both, suffering in both. Like Charles Bon, Christmas is murdered. Both deaths seem to be the fulfillment of self-destructive tendencies, a final act of self-hatred.

Sample Topics:

1. *Absalom, Absalom!* and **"Wash":** How does "Wash" enlarge upon the themes and the story of *Absalom, Absalom!*?

"Wash" should be considered required reading alongside *Absalom, Absalom!* The story provides a different perspective on Thomas Sutpen, and Wash Jones as narrator gives a very different understanding of his character. You might compare Sutpen's treatment of Milly Jones with his treatment of Rosa Coldfield. You might also discuss the boy Thomas Sutpen, who came from circumstances little better than Wash Jones's. Has Sutpen, the wealthy landowner, betrayed that boy by treating the Jones family no better than the livestock on his plantation? You might also compare the burning of the great Sutpen house with Wash Jones's burning of his cabin.

2. *Absalom, Absalom!* and *The Sound and the Fury:* Compare the character of Quentin Compson in these two novels.

Quentin's story is central to both these novels. One question you could attempt to answer in a paper is whether the knowledge of Quentin's imminent suicide changes your reading of *Absalom, Absalom!* Was it wrong for Rosa to tell him her story? Why does Quentin identify so strongly with Henry Sutpen? Faulkner does not tell the reader of *Absalom, Absalom!* the troubles that obsess Quentin in *The Sound and the Fury.* Why not?

3. **Henry and Bon versus Quentin and Shreve:** How does Quentin seem to embody Henry, while Shreve seems to embody Bon?

As in any good comparison, there are ways that these resemble each other and ways that they differ. That is, the relationship is not a perfect one. However, Quentin and Shreve are necessary to ensure the story of Henry and Bon is told. The final exchange between Quentin and Shreve would be a good place to begin thinking about this essay topic, as Shreve considers the future of the human race and Quentin insists that he does not hate the South.

4. *Absalom, Absalom!* **and** *Light in August:* Consider the effect of racial prejudice in these two novels.

Why do Judith and Clytie insist on raising Charles Etienne St. Valery Bon as black? Wouldn't his life have been easier in this time and place if he were raised as a white man? Why do you think he returns to Jefferson with a bride who is decidedly black, instead of, for instance, an octoroon? You might want to consider the South's definition of "one drop," wherein anyone who possessed one drop of black blood was considered black.

Bibliography and Online Resources for *Absalom, Absalom!*

Betz, B. G. Till. "*Absalom, Absalom!* and *The Sound and the Fury*: Quentin's Failure to Create a Mythic Reconstruction." *University of Mississippi Studies in English* 11–12 (1993–1995): 438–54.

Bloom, Harold, ed. *William Faulkner's Absalom, Absalom!* New York: Chelsea House, 1987.

Brooks, Cleanth. *William Faulkner: The Yoknapatawpha Country.* Baton Rouge: Louisiana State UP, 1990.

———. *William Faulkner: Toward Yoknapatawpha and Beyond.* Baton Rouge: Louisiana State UP, 1990.

Cowley, Malcolm. "*Absalom, Absalom!* as a Legend of the Deep South." *Readings on William Faulkner.* Ed. Clarice Swisher. San Diego, CA: Greenhaven, 1998. 142–48.

Cullick, Jonathan S. "'I Had a Design': Sutpen as Narrator in *Absalom, Absalom!*" *Southern Literary Journal* 28.2 (Spring 1996): 48–58.

Faulkner, William. *Absalom, Absalom!* New York: Vintage International P, 1990.

Ford, Daniel G. "Comments on William Faulkner's Temporal Vision in *Sanctuary, The Sound and the Fury, Light in August, Absalom, Absalom!*" *Southern Quarterly* 15 (1977): 283–90.

Fowler, Doreen, and Ann J. Abadie, eds. *Faulkner and Religion.* Jackson: UP of Mississippi, 1991.

Goldman, Arnold, ed. *Twentieth Century Interpretations of Absalom, Absalom!* Englewood Cliffs, NJ: Prentice-Hall, 1971.

Irwin, John T. *Doubling and Incest/Repetition and Revenge: A Speculative Reading of Faulkner.* 1975. Expanded ed. Baltimore: Johns Hopkins UP, 1996.

Justus, James H. "*Absalom, Absalom!* as an Epic Novel." *Readings on William Faulkner.* Ed. Clarice Swisher. San Diego, CA: Greenhaven, 1998. 149–58.

Kartiganer, Donald M., and Ann J. Abadie, eds. *Faulkner and Ideology.* Jackson: UP of Mississippi, 1995.

Kinney, Arthur F. *Critical Essays on William Faulkner: The Compson Family.* Boston: G. K. Hall, 1982.

———. *Critical Essays on William Faulkner: The Sutpen Family.* Boston: G. K. Hall, 1996.

Krause, David. "Opening Pandora's Box: Re-Reading Compson's Letter and Faulkner's *Absalom, Absalom!*" *Centennial Review* 30 (1986): 358–82.

———. "Reading Bon's Letter and Faulkner's *Absalom, Absalom!*" *PMLA* 99 (1984): 225–41.

———. "Reading Shreve's Letters and Faulkner's *Absalom, Absalom!*" *Studies in American Fiction* 11 (Autumn 1983): 153–69.

Muhlenfeld, Elisabeth, ed. *William Faulkner's Absalom, Absalom!: A Critical Casebook.* New York: Garland, 1984.

O'Donnell, Patrick. "Faulkner and Postmodernism." *The Cambridge Companion to William Faulkner.* Ed. Philip Weinstein. New York: Cambridge UP, 1995. 31–50.

Padgett, John B. "*Absalom, Absalom!*: Commentary." *William Faulkner on the Web.* 17 Aug. 2006. Ed. John B. Padgett. UP of Mississippi. 16 Nov. 2007. URL: http://www.mcsr.olemiss.edu/~egjbp/faulkner/n-aa.html.

Parker, Robert Dale. *Absalom, Absalom!: The Questioning of Fictions.* New York: Twayne, 1991.

Porter, Carolyn. "*Absalom, Absalom!*: (Un)Making the Father." *The Cambridge Companion to William Faulkner.* Ed. Philip Weinstein. New York: Cambridge UP, 1995. 168–96.

Ragan, David Paul. *Annotations to William Faulkner's Absalom, Absalom!* New York: Garland, 1991.

————. *William Faulkner's* Absalom, Absalom!: *A Critical Study.* Ann Arbor, MI.: UMI Research Press, 1987.

Reuben, P. "Chapter 7: William Faulkner." PAL: Perspectives in Literature—A Research and Reference Guide. Accessed March 20, 2008. URL: http://web. csustan.edu/english/reuben/pal/chap7/faulkner.html.

Schmidtberger, Loren F. *"Absalom, Absalom!*: What Clytie Knew." *Mississippi Quarterly* 35 (Summer 1982): 255–63.

————. "Names in *Absalom, Absalom!" American Literature* 55 (March 1983): 83–88.

Sundquist, Eric J. *Faulkner: The House Divided.* Baltimore: Johns Hopkins UP, 1985.

"BARN BURNING"

READING TO WRITE

"**B**ARN BURNING" was first published in *Harper's* in June 1939. Although Faulkner sometimes made dismissive remarks about his short stories, saying that he wrote them for the money they would bring, "Barn Burning" includes many of the concerns that mark his full-length fiction. The story centers on the family of Abner Snopes. It is some years after the Civil War. Abner has told his family stories of his exploits in the war, but his war wound is in fact where he was shot while stealing horses. As the story makes clear, he was not a soldier but a profiteer, stealing from both sides with impunity.

In the absence of slavery, there are families like the Snopeses who live by sharecropping the fields of large landowners. Faulkner makes it clear that their position is a hard one. They have no stable home, moving from cabin to cabin with the harvest. They are at the mercy of the men they work for, and they are doing work that once would have been done by slaves. They are just surviving. Yet, Abner Snopes's anger seems out of proportion. He does not take responsibility for the actions that might have put his family in this position, and he does not try to lift them out of it.

His youngest son, Colonel Sartoris "Sarty" Snopes possesses a clearer sense of right and wrong, even though, or perhaps because, he is a child of 10. As you read this story and consider how to write about it, try to mark the varied directions in which Sarty's loyalties are pulled as they move between such large concepts as blood and truth and justice.

The story in its outlines becomes a part of Faulkner's novel *The Hamlet*. *The Hamlet* is a part of his Snopes trilogy: *The Hamlet*, *The Town*, and *The Mansion*. Whenever you meet a Snopes in Faulkner's writing, watch for thievery, dishonesty, and sneaky behavior.

TOPICS AND STRATEGIES
Themes

"Barn Burning" could be seen as a coming-of-age story, with Sarty having to choose between family loyalty and morality. The choice he makes could determine the direction of his entire life. Abner Snopes attempts to control his family by insisting upon the ties of family. In his view, blood demands loyalty. And yet, loyalty to a father like Abner requires complicity in his criminal acts.

"Barn Burning" paints a stark picture of the gulf between the Snopes family and Major de Spain. Sarty's vision of the white house, just after locating the squatter's cabin that the Snopeses will be residing in, reveals the class differences between them. Abner Snopes is keenly aware of class. He resents the black man who opens the door at the de Spain house because this man exhibits refinement and holds a better position in the hierarchy of workers employed by Major de Spain than he will as a sharecropper.

It is difficult to think of young Sarty Snopes, just 10 years old, having to make his way in the world alone. But he has made a choice that was quite possibly fatal to his father and brother, and there is no turning back. The story suggests that Sarty resembles his mother and aunt more in character than the rest of his family. And yet, his mother and aunt, adults, do not stand up to his father. The rest of his family's complicity pushes him to act.

It might be argued that it is natural for a child to have a clear sense of justice, clearer than the adults who surround him. His loyalty to his father pulls him in another direction. Thinking of the verdicts handed down by the two courts, and the many chances that Abner Snopes is given to make his trespasses right, how can one argue against the justice of it? Abner sees injustice everywhere, but it is difficult to feel much sympathy for him.

Sample Topics:

1. **Loyalty:** How is loyalty a thematic concern in "Barn Burning"?

> Sarty displays obvious family loyalty when he engages in a fight with the boys outside the store who call his father a barn burner. There is every indication that Sarty would defend his

father endlessly were he falsely accused. Knowing that the accusations against his father are true, what concepts or person is Sarty loyal to?

2. **Class:** How do class differences influence the action in "Barn Burning"?

One possible way to approach this story is with Sarty's reaction to the white house. He believes, mistakenly, that his father has now encountered something so beyond him that it cannot be hurt. Is Abner Snopes more concerned with class than the judge or Major de Spain?

3. **Passage into adulthood:** How is this the story of a boy becoming an adult?

Sarty makes a choice that separates him from his family. Where could he have gotten his sense of right and wrong? What is his future? Is it believable that a 10-year-old boy would be able to make such a definite break from all that he has known?

4. **Justice:** Is the world depicted in "Barn Burning" a just one?

Could you argue with the sentences imposed on Abner by the courts he is brought before? Is there a surprising amount of leniency? If you were asked to point out the injustice in the world of "Barn Burning," what would you point to?

Character

In this story, you could choose to write about any single character, or you could choose to write about the characters as a whole and the traits that they share. For instance, there is a sharp sense of alienation in "Barn Burning." The character who most brings this isolation to life is probably Sarty, but it is an important aspect of the other characters as well. The source of Sarty's alienation is his family. By the end of the story, Sarty is very literally alone. Throughout the story, he and his family are alone even thought they are together. There is very little conversation or other interaction among the Snopeses. Abner believes that everyone outside the family is the enemy, and this belief has infected the others. The family's constant movement from place to place makes it impossible for them to develop any ties.

There are five women in "Barn Burning," the mother and her sister, the two daughters, and Mrs. de Spain. They are not terribly active characters. Faulkner seems to indicate that Sarty's positive traits come from his mother's side, and there is the memorable scene of the mother and aunt restraining him and then letting go. His mother and her sister seem to lack the courage to do what they know is right. They know, as Sarty does, that it might mean the dissolution of their family. Mrs. de Spain is an undeveloped character, but her appearance, as seen through Sarty's eyes, is not unremarkable. Sarty's two sisters seem to share more of their father's traits. They provide some comic relief in the story, described as they are as remarkably like two cows.

Abner's name is very close to the word *anger*, and anger is one of his chief characteristics. He is at the lowest rung of society, and much of his resentment seems to be aimed at those in a better economic situation than he is. But look just a bit closer, and it begins to be clear that his anger is not linked solely to class; he seems to be angry at everyone. There is not a moment of tenderness or kindness on his part in "Barn Burning." (Think of his treatment of the butler at the de Spain house or of his own family.)

Sarty Snopes is the story's protagonist. He is also the character whose perspective the reader shares. Where does his sense of right and wrong come from? His name sets him apart from his family. As "Colonel Sartoris" he stands for courage and good deeds, distinction and wealth; as a Snopes he has inherited other circumstances.

Sample Topics:

1. **Alienation:** Why is alienation an important aspect of the way the Snopeses live?

   Where does this alienation come from? To what extent is it wrapped up in the notion of home, a place where the family belongs? Their itinerant existence means they do not form connections to their community. Community is a powerful concept in Faulkner. It can go a long way toward forging a person's identity.

2. **Women:** How does Faulkner characterize the women of "Barn Burning"?

An essay on this topic might argue that the women are characterized as helpless. The men of the story act and speak for them. In the Snopes family they are subject to the orders of Abner. But Mrs. de Spain is similarly voiceless. Curiously, the women are closely associated with the objects they own.

3. **Abner Snopes:** Would Abner be a different character in different circumstances?

It is shocking for the reader, as it is for Sarty, to realize that Abner will not behave any differently with the de Spain family than he has with others. Can you imagine a circumstance that would change him? To what do you attribute his anger?

4. **Sarty:** Analyze the character of Sarty Snopes; do his final actions surprise you?

At the beginning of "Barn Burning," Sarty is very conflicted. It seems he would tell the truth about his father if asked, but he fights with another boy to defend his father moments later. Trace Sarty's changing views through the story, perhaps finding one scene that marks his course, such as his first view of the de Spain house.

History and Context

"Barn Burning" is set in Mississippi in the time of Reconstruction after the Civil War. Slavery has been abolished, but the South is slow to move forward. This seemed particularly apparent in areas of the economy, education, and race relations. Abner Snopes's character represents the worst of these qualities. He is shiftless and bigoted, and he considers the war to have been his finest hour.

The story provides a glimpse of an economy that you might not find altogether familiar. As a sharecropper, Abner Snopes farms a portion of the landowner's land. The landowner is allotted a portion of the crops, and the sharecropper keeps the remainder. However, while the sharecropper worked, the landowner is providing food, shelter, and other basic needs, often by way of the community store or commissary. At the season's end, there will be a settling of the books that may leave the sharecropper with virtually nothing. The sharecropper's life was one of subsistence.

With the loss of the free labor provided by slavery, those without skills and education and possibly luck stepped in to fill that void. This gave rise to a class of sharecroppers, often poor whites who now competed with blacks economically. This was a new source of racial tension, which is illustrated in Abner Snopes's encounter with the de Spain's butler. This also created a new class: the poor whites, now in a worse position, in some respects, than the slaves were before them, because no one forced their way of life upon them.

The setting of Mississippi in the 1930s shows a place still trying to maintain the economy it had before the war but without the labor force to do it. The Snopeses are a part of the class that has taken the place of the slaves. Previously, even though families like these were impoverished, they were accorded more respect by virtue of their skin color. But that is over. As itinerant sharecroppers, they are also without the support of a community. In Faulkner, the community and the idea of home are extremely important. To move as the Snopes do severs all ties to other people. The things they carry with them are all that they have to tie them to the past or to an extended family. But without the relationships these represent, the objects lose their meaning.

Sample Topics:

1. **After the war:** How has the South of "Barn Burning" changed and not changed after the Civil War?

"Barn Burning" is set after the war between the states. Looking at such imagery as the clock the Snopeses carry with them, you could argue that the problem with the Snopeses is that they are not moving ahead as time dictates. That is, they are still stuck in a time, before or during the war. They have not recognized or adapted to the changes.

2. **The economy:** Is the economy of "Barn Burning" sustainable?

Imagine the resentments that might, legitimately, grow in a laborer like Abner Snopes. Using evidence from the story, particularly the general store/courtroom scenes, discuss why this system would prove untenable.

3. **Class:** How do class distinctions fuel Abner Snopes's rage?

What does Abner have against Major de Spain? Does your understanding of the sharecropping system help to explain why Abner would want to soil the white rug? Would Abner have been better regarded during the war? Can Sarty escape his class, now that he has left his family behind?

4. **Setting:** How does the setting of "Barn Burning" contribute to the story?

One approach to a paper on this topic is to look closely at the cabin the Snopeses occupy on the de Spain property, likely only for one night. How does it compare to the de Spain house? What does it mean not to own any home? Sarty says that they have lived in 12 places he remembers in his 10 years.

Language, Symbols, and Imagery

"Barn Burning" is a relatively straightforward tale for Faulkner. It could be described as realistic; it is not heavy with symbolism. And yet, there are some powerful symbols present. One of these is blood. Abner Snopes is constantly reminding his family of the importance of blood. This is his way of forcing the family to cling to one another. It is another way of enforcing his alienation upon them. In Abner's schema, blood is all. But this is also his way of controlling his family. In Abner's world, not to be with him is to be against him. At the story's end, it seems likely that Sarty may be responsible for shedding Abner's blood (if the shots he hears have wounded or killed his father), in addition to turning away from the ties that have bound him.

Fire takes on symbolic meaning in this story as an agent of destruction. For Abner Snopes, it acts as a leveler; no one has power over him as long as he can wield it. The reader knows that even though burning a barn can threaten a farmer's existence by destroying his livelihood, it does not make Abner the equal of his victims. Instead, his acts seem cowardly. Anyone can set fire to a barn. The scene where Abner builds the campfire and Sarty reflects on the smallness of it offers some insight into Abner's relationship with fire.

Sarty Snopes is terribly impressed by the de Spain house, which to him resembles a courthouse. Abner Snopes sneers at it, so "pretty and white." He tells Sarty it was built on "sweat, nigger sweat. Maybe it ain't white enough yet to suit him. Maybe he wants to mix some white sweat with it." It is likely that the labor of slaves built the house. And yet, it does not seem likely that it is this injustice that provokes Abner's anger. After all, the previous barns he burnt were connected to small farmhouses, and they drew his anger as well. But for Sarty, the whiteness of the house is important. He hopes that it somehow puts the house and the people in it out of his father's reach.

Approaching the house, Abner purposefully steps into manure and then smears the manure into the de Spain's rug and onto their porch. Before meeting the de Spains, he attempts to muddy the whiteness of their house. The imagery of "Barn Burning" recalls the body: blood, sweat, tears, and excrement.

Sample Topics:

1. Blood: What does Abner believe about blood?

> Do you think he has any strong belief about blood, or is this just a lie he uses to control his family? Do you think Sarty holds any belief about blood?

2. Fire: What is the symbolic importance of fire?

> Consider the various descriptions of fire in "Barn Burning." How do these descriptions reflect Abner Snopes's character? Fire, when controlled, is a positive and necessary element. Is

there anything redeeming to be found in Abner? An essay on this topic would pay particular attention to Sarty's reflections on the campfire Abner builds.

3. **Whiteness:** What does "whiteness" represent in "Barn Burning"?

Race is a central concern in Faulkner's work. Although it may not be a central concern in this story, the idea of whiteness is powerful one in "Barn Burning." To Abner Snopes the whiteness of the de Spain house means "nigger sweat." What does whiteness mean to Sarty?

4. **Dirt:** What does dirt represent in "Barn Burning"?

The converse of the whiteness above, dirt has a meaning larger than itself in this story. The cabins the Snopes family live in cannot be kept clean. Dirt is the medium they work as farmhands. And for Abner, dirt is the way he shows the de Spains that he will not be owned. It is a symbol of his defiance. But it takes on different meaning to Sarty when he sees it smeared across the whiteness of the rug, and a paper on this topic would discuss all possible meanings.

Bibliography and Online Resources for "Barn Burning"

Billinglea, Oliver. "Fathers and Sons: The Spiritual Quest in Faulkner's 'Barn Burning.'" *Mississippi Quarterly: The Journal of Southern Culture* 44.3 (Summer 1991): 287–308.

Bradford, M. E. "Family and Community in Faulkner's 'Barn Burning.'" *The Southern Review* 17.2 (April 1981): 332–39.

Cackett, Kathy. "'Barn Burning': Debating the American Adam." *Notes on Mississippi Writers* 21.1 (1989): 1–17.

Carruthers, James B. *William Faulkner's Short Stories.* Ann Arbor, MI: UMI Research Press, 1985. 61–67.

Faulkner, William. *Collected Stories of William Faulkner.* New York: Vintage International P, 1995.

Fowler, Virginia C. "Faulkner's 'Barn Burning': Sarty's Conflict Reconsidered." *College Language Association Journal* 24.4 (June 1981): 513–22.

Franklin, Phyllis. "Sarty Snopes and 'Barn Burning'." *Mississippi Quarterly: The Journal of Southern Culture* 21 (1968): 189–93.

Hiles, Jane. "Kinship and Heredity in Faulkner's 'Barn Burning.'" *Mississippi Quarterly: The Journal of Southern Culture* 38.3 (Summer 1985): 329–37.

Loges, Max L. "Faulkner's 'Barn Burning.'" *Explicator* 57.1 (Fall 1998): 43–45.

Moreland, Richard C. "Compulsive and Revisionary Repetition: Faulkner's 'Barn Burning' and the Craft of Writing Difference." *Faulkner and the Craft of Fiction.* Faulkner and Yoknapatawpha Conference, 1987. Eds. Doreen Fowler and Ann J. Abadie. Jackson: UP of Mississippi, 1989. 48–70.

Nicolet, William P. "Faulkner's 'Barn Burning.'" *Explicator* 34 (1975): Item 25.

Padgett, John B. "'Barn Burning': Commentary & Resources." *William Faulkner on the Web.* 17 August 2006. 19 December 2007. URL: http://www.mcsr.olemiss.edu/~egjbp/faulkner/r_ss_barnburning.html.

Volpe, Edmond L. "'Barn Burning': A Definition of Evil." *Faulkner: The Unappeased Imagination: A Collection of Critical Essays.* Ed. Glenn O. Carey. Troy, NY: Whitston, 1980. 75–82.

Yunis, Susan S. "The Narrator of Faulkner's 'Barn Burning.'" *Faulkner Journal* 6.2 (Spring 1991): 23–31.

Zender, Karl F. "Character and Symbol in 'Barn Burning.'" *College Literature* 16.1 (Winter 1989): 48–59.

"THE BEAR"

READING TO WRITE

"THE BEAR" is considered a masterpiece of short fiction. It is the heart of Faulkner's novel *Go Down, Moses* but is often taught alone, and it stands alone without difficulty. It is fine to consider it first as a hunting story, though there is a lot more going on in it. *Go Down, Moses* tells the story of the family engendered by Lucius Quintus Carothers McCaslin, called Carothers McCaslin. The McCaslin plantation is of such importance to the story that it might be called another character. This interest in land is also present in "The Bear." Carothers McCaslin is not a character in "The Bear"; he is long dead. The central character is his grandson, Isaac McCaslin. But his grandson is very much affected by his grandfather's life and such questions as how his grandfather obtained their land, his participation in slavery, and the acts of miscegenation that created another branch of the McCaslin family that is mixed race and does not enjoy the rights or status of the white line.

The relationship of man and nature might be said to be the central concern of "The Bear." Old Ben is the bear of the title. Over the years that he is hunted, the bear becomes a creature of mythical proportions in the minds of the hunters. He seems invulnerable. To some extent, even while hunting him, there is the sense that they do not want to kill him and that they are aware that his passing will mark the passing of something greater than themselves or the bear. Still, they come yearly to hunt, and Old Ben is the prize that they find just out of their reach. When he passes, along with Lion and Sam Fathers, it seems to mark the end of the natural world as they have known it.

TOPICS AND STRATEGIES
Themes

"The Bear" explores a number of themes that are important to Faulkner. One concern that moves beyond the themes of ownership and slavery and miscegenation is the theme of accounting. When Isaac reads the family ledgers, he finds an account in the truest sense of what his family has wrought. He believes, moreover, that it is his duty to make it right. He believes that what he finds there is the story of how his grandfather impregnated one of his slaves and then, in turn, impregnated the daughter he and that slave produced together. Isaac believes this sin to be the fruit of slavery and the institution that would allow one man to own another. Because the plantation was built upon that slavery, he rejects his inheritance.

Isaac's reading of the ledgers marks one rite of passage he goes through as he moves from being a boy to being a man. The hunts mark another. He first goes to the woods with the men when he is 10 years old. At 12 he kills his first deer. Sam Fathers seems to impart to him a mystical sense of the woods and a regard for it that is as reverential as a religion.

The continuing effects of slavery are an important theme of "The Bear." Isaac McCaslin feels responsible for the wrongs done by his family. Isaac's renunciation of his inheritance does not wipe the slate clean, however. Readers learn that the family is still shaped by the actions of Carothers McCaslin. Isaac's understanding of those wrongs does not move him to embrace his mixed-race family members. The problems of race in this story are not limited to those between the white and black races but include the Native Americans as well. Sam Fathers illustrates some of the difficulties that have befallen the Indians. In Isaac's mind, and perhaps Faulkner's as well, the land is by birthright Sam Fathers's.

Sample Topics:

1. **Accounting:** Is there any way to balance the accounts in the McCaslin ledgers?

   When Isaac reads the plantation ledgers, he learns a great deal about the history of his family. He attempts to right it, first by making sure that the inheritance that belongs to the Beauchamp children reaches them, and then by refusing his inheritance. But is that enough to wipe the slate clean?

2. **Initiation:** Is there any singular event that marks Isaac McCaslin's passage into adulthood?

An essay on this topic could argue that any number of events stands as an initiation for Isaac McCaslin. Some possibilities are the killing of his first deer, seeing Old Ben for the first time, reading the ledgers, or the deaths of Old Ben, Sam Fathers, and Lion.

3. **Man and nature:** How does the theme of man in nature or man versus nature work in "The Bear"?

What is the role man should assume in the natural world? Is he an adversary, attempting to capture, kill, and tame? Or is nature the realm he should feel most comfortable in? Can the two be reconciled? What does Isaac McCaslin feel is his proper place in the order of the woods? Would the other hunters agree with him? What about Sam Fathers?

4. **Race:** What does "The Bear" suggest about the differences between the races?

One thing "The Bear" does is to show how arbitrary the categories of race were in Mississippi at the time. Is Sam Fathers, for instance, a king or a slave? Why are the descendants of Carothers McCaslin who live in the slave cabins given fewer rights than those who live in the main house?

Character

Isaac McCaslin is the central character of "The Bear" and the novel *Go Down, Moses,* of which "The Bear" is a part. Isaac, sometimes called Ike or Uncle Ike, is the heir to the McCaslin plantation. Isaac was born to older parents and orphaned early. He is raised by a number of father figures, primarily his cousin McCaslin Edmonds and Sam Fathers. Sam

Fathers is the son of an Indian chief and an African-American slave girl. He was sold by his father into slavery with his mother, but he retains a Native American wisdom. He imparts to Isaac a mystical relation to the woods and the creatures who dwell there.

Isaac refuses his inheritance and makes his meager living as a carpenter in town. He believes he lives in emulation of Jesus. But Isaac does nothing to change the history of his family or to speak out about the crimes of the South. His protest is a completely individual one, and the reader might see it as ineffective. His attempts to give Tomey's grandchildren their inheritance are not entirely successful. He marries a woman who resents his decision not to take his rightful place on the McCaslin plantation, and in her anger she refuses to give him a child.

"The Bear" could be considered the story of the death of Sam Fathers. It is hard to talk about Sam Fathers without talking about all he represents. He is a symbolically loaded character. His passing is linked to the passing of the wilderness they hunt. And his death is also at one with the deaths of Lion and Old Ben. Sam's lineage makes him a curious product of the American South. He is the son of the Chickasaw chief Ikkemotubbe and an African-American slave girl. His father sells him, with his mother, into slavery. He grows up on the McCaslin plantation but has a dignity that marks him as different from their other slaves. To Isaac McCaslin, he is a father figure. Also, like Isaac, he has no children.

Boon Hogganbeck stands somewhat in contrast to Sam. He is also of mixed race, but his family tree is not as illustrious. He is an alcoholic and no hunter. His position in the camp is somewhere between servant and difficult family member. His relationship with Lion seems to be the strongest relationship he has. But he also has an unusual bond with Sam Fathers. It is the image of Boon and the tree of squirrels that closes the story.

Throughout the years they hunt Old Ben, they say that they must wait for the right dog. Lion is the dog who will finally allow them to kill Old Ben. Like Old Ben, he is described in terms that are almost mythical. He seems less a dog than some sort of mongrel creature out of mythology. Boon has a strange relationship to the dog, feeding him and sleeping with him almost in the way of a servant. When Lion encounters the Bear, it ends the idyll in the woods, along with his own life, Old Ben's, and Sam Fathers's.

Sample Topics:

1. **Isaac McCaslin:** Is Isaac an admirable character? Why or why not?

An essay on this topic might choose to differentiate between the younger and the older Isaac. The question of whether or not the reader admires him can be answered in any way, as long as the appropriate supporting evidence is given. Isaac wants to lead an exemplary life; there is some question about whether he succeeds.

2. **Sam Fathers:** Is Sam Fathers's role in the story realistic or symbolic?

The reader learns little about Sam Fathers himself. Is his character more important for what he does in the story or for his effect on the others? A writer might start with his name. "Sam" is a simple name, with connotations perhaps of "Uncle Sam." "Fathers" tell the reader most of what we learn about his life, that he is the son of two fathers and, in a sense, no father. Why does he want an Indian burial?

3. **Boon Hogganbeck:** Why would Boon kill Sam Fathers?

It seems odd that Boon is likely the instrument of the death of Old Ben and Sam Fathers. What does Boon see in Lion that makes him so entranced with him? What is the significance of Boon being such a poor hunter?

4. **Lion:** The title of the story when it first appeared in *Harper's* in December 1935 was "Lion." Why would Faulkner consider this a good title? Why would he change it instead to "The Bear"?

An essay on this topic might argue for Lion's place as a central character in "The Bear." The men have waited a long time for the dog they could match to Old Ben. By the time Lion is found, he has already achieved a mythic stature as the dog they have waited for.

History and Context

When Isaac reads the ledgers, he learns that many of his family's slaves, when freed, chose to remain with them. This may seem strange at first glance. But for many slaves, the family who owned them was all they knew. And even after the Emancipation Proclamation of 1862, opportunities for freed slaves were meager. The people raised in slavery had not had access to the education or training that would have allowed them to move on from the labors they were accustomed to. What is evident in Isaac's family and the South of "The Bear" is a culture that has done away with slavery but has retained culturally the artifacts and customs of slavery. The African-American or mixed-race characters are still treated as second-class citizens.

The industrialization of the North eventually lured former slaves and their children away from the South and the agrarian economy it was based on. "The Bear" illustrates the beginning of this trend. The effects of industrialization are also seen in the diminishing of the de Spain woods. Faulkner wrote "The Bear" during the depression, a time when the country's economy mirrored that of the South after the war. The hunters are southern aristocrats. Their hunt is more for sport than for need. But Isaac lets the reader know that the men who join in the hunt for Old Ben (those who come to see it, really) are of a different class.

Isaac tries to live like those men after he has rejected his inheritance. Though he chooses to live simply, he is never so far removed from his birthright as to be impoverished. The section of "The Bear" that recounts Isaac's argument with Cass Edmonds is rich with references to other texts and to history. It is interesting to see how both men are well versed in the Bible and the history of the South, reaching back to the time before European colonization. Isaac's rejection is in part a rejection of the history of mankind as he embraces biblical teaching.

Isaac's argument also includes his distinct views about the future of the black, white, and Native American races in America. He makes it clear that he views slavery as a grave sin that gave way to even greater sins against African Americans. It is unclear whether these sins can ever be expiated. Isaac's steps toward righting the wrongs of his family include his rejection of his inheritance and his attempts to deliver to his black family members their inheritance. And, perhaps, interpreting the ledgers and opening up a discussion of what they hold.

Sample Topics:

1. **Emancipation:** How did emancipation affect the slaves on the McCaslin plantation?

Fonsiba's story is representative of the kind of life that might await a child born to former slaves who struck out to live a life independent of the plantation. Even though Fonsiba is born after emancipation, her learned husband feels he must present himself to Cass Edmonds (the plantation owner at the time) before taking her away. When Isaac delivers her share of the inheritance, he sees that her life is a harder one than she would have had on the plantation.

2. **Economic depression:** What does "The Bear" have to say about the economic troubles the characters face?

The hunting party is a mix of the affluent (white) hunters and the poor (mixed-race) men who are dependent upon them. The selling of the woods gives some indication of how the aristocratic southerner was less economically sound as the years went on. Isaac renounces his inheritance and lives in a way that resembles Sam Fathers, though his position is perhaps more a choice. An essay on this topic might argue that it shows a South less bound by class divisions as it moves into the 20th century.

3. **The history and context of Isaac's decision:** How does Isaac defend his rejection of his inheritance?

One possible thesis for this topic would be that Isaac uses the Bible to justify the refusal of his inheritance. An essay on this topic might focus on the dialogue between Isaac and Cass and attempt to identify the references made. The writer might want to read the biblical passages Isaac uses. An essay could also be written that looked at other references, such as the story of John Brown.

4. The future: What does the story predict is the future of the races?

In some ways, Isaac seems very progressive in his thinking about race. He forecasts a future when race will be less of an issue. And yet, at other times he is seems to subscribe to the same prejudices held by his contemporaries. In light of his own attitudes, what faith can be put in his predictions for a future that will be color blind?

Form and Genre

It is important to note the point of view of the story. "The Bear" is told from Isaac's perspective, and often in Isaac's voice. You might consider whether or not the story would be changed if told from another point of view. For instance, what is learned from the ledgers is interpreted by Isaac. Is there any possibility that Isaac is wrong in his interpretation? The reader needs to be able to trust Ike as narrator but also to question him and hold him accountable. The reader may also recognize that Isaac at times withholds information.

"The Bear" is set upon a small section of land over a very long period of time, basically the whole of the 19th century. The story it tells begins in 1772 with the birth of Lucius Quintus Carothers McCaslin and ends with Isaac's last visit to the hunting camp in 1882. Isaac, with the help of the ledgers, is able to see a great deal of the history of his family. "The Bear" could be seen as a story about the end of things: the end of a family, the end of slavery, the end of the wilderness, and still other endings, not the least of which are the ends of the lives of Lion, Old Ben, and Sam Fathers.

These endings are strongly foreshadowed throughout "The Bear." From Isaac's earliest hunts the men talk of the dog that will eventually allow them to kill Old Ben. They repeatedly say that this dog will come in time. And there is always a sense of melancholy attached to the idea of the passing of the bear.

"The Bear" is a good example of modernist techniques. Until section four of the story, the events have been related in a straightforward and realistic manner. But in section four this changes. The time is uncertain. Events referred to range from the distant past to the future. Speakers are unidentified at times. And the ledgers are introduced as they appear to Isaac, with only the explanations Isaac arrives at. This requires a lot of thought by the reader but also allows a greater intimacy with the thoughts and speech of the characters. This is the type of writing that earned Faulkner a reputation as a difficult writer.

Sample Topics:

1. **Point of view:** How would "The Bear" be a different story if told from a different perspective?

   This is always a useful exercise in thinking about a work of literature. Another way of looking at it is to consider how Isaac, with his own views and limitations, shapes the story.

2. **Setting:** What is important about the setting of "The Bear"?

   To some extent, the setting is the story in this case. Without the wilderness or the McCaslin plantation, the center of "The Bear" is gone. That is one argument that could be made in an essay. You might alternatively discuss setting in other ways. One possibility would be to focus on Isaac learning to find his way in the woods. Isaac comes to know the woods better than other men while he is still a boy. Is there some equation made between knowing the land and knowing one's self?

3. **Foreshadowing:** Why does Isaac say he "should have hated and feared Lion?" (218).

   Where are the surprises in "The Bear"? Is there ever any doubt that they will eventually trap Old Ben? Why not? What does Lion also foreshadow in Isaac's mind?

4. **Modernism:** How does section four of "The Bear" compare to the story's other sections?

   Section four is an example of modernist technique. To answer the question above you might consider what section four adds to the story, not simply the new information that is presented but how it is presented. How does it change what you know of Isaac so far? How does it change your perception of the hunting party, particularly Sam Fathers and Tennie's Jim's place in it?

Bibliography and Online Resources for "The Bear"

Ackerman, R. D. "The Immolation of Isaac McCaslin." *Texas Studies in Literature and Language* XVI.3 (Fall 1974): 557–65.

Adams, Richard P. "Focus on William Faulkner's 'The Bear': Moses and the Wilderness." *American Dreams, American Nightmares.* Ed. David Madden. Southern Illinois UP, 1970. 129–35.

Aiken, Charles S. "A Geographical Approach to William Faulkner's 'The Bear'." *Geographical Review* 71.4 (October 1981): 446–59.

Backman, Melvin. "Wilderness and the Negro in Faulkner's 'The Bear'." *PMLA* 76 (December 1961): 595–600.

Baumgarten, Murray. "The Language of Faulkner's 'The Bear'." *Western Humanities Review* XV.2 (Spring 1961): 180–82.

Beauchamp, Gorman. "The Rite of Initiation in Faulkner's 'The Bear'." *Arizona Quarterly* 28 (Winter 1972): 319–25.

Bradford, Melvin E. "Brotherhood in 'The Bear': An Exemplum for Critics." *Modern Age* 10 (Fall 1966): 278–81.

———. "The Gum Tree Scene: Observations on the Structure of 'The Bear'." *Southern Humanities Review* 1 (Summer 1967): 141–50.

Brooks, Cleanth. *William Faulkner: The Yoknapatawpha Country.* Baton Rouge: Louisiana State UP, 1963.

Claridge, Laura P. "Isaac McCaslin's Failed Bid for Adulthood." *American Literature* 55 (May 1983): 241–51.

Faulkner, William. *Three Famous Short Novels.* New York: Vintage International P, 1961.

Gelfant, Blanche H. "Faulkner and Keats: The Ideality of Art in 'The Bear'." *Southern Literary Journal* 2 (Fall 1969): 43–65.

Gilley, Leonard. "The Wilderness Theme in Faulkner's 'The Bear'." *Midwest Quarterly* 6 (July 1965): 379–85.

Gold, Joseph. "'The Bear' as Allegory and Essay." *Readings on William Faulkner.* Ed. Clarice Swisher. San Diego, CA: Greenhaven, 1998. 78–83.

Grimwood, Michael. "Faulkner and the Vocational Liabilities of Black Characterization." *Faulkner and Race.* Eds. Doreen Fowler and Ann J. Abadie. Oxford: UP of Mississippi. 1987, 255–71.

Kern, Alexander C. "Myth and Symbol in Criticism of Faulkner's 'The Bear'." *Myth and Symbol.* Ed. Bernice Slote. Lincoln: U of Nebraska P, 1963. 252–62.

Lewis, R. W. B. "The Hero in the New World: William Faulkner's 'The Bear'." *Kenyon Review* 13 (Autumn 1951): 641–60.

Lydenberg, John. "Nature Myth in Faulkner's 'The Bear'." *American Literature* 24 (March 1952): 62–72.

McGee, Patrick. "Gender and Generation in Faulkner's 'The Bear'." *Faulkner Journal* 1 (Fall 1985): 46–54.

Merton, Thomas. "'Baptism in the Forest': Wisdom and Initiation in William Faulkner." *Mansions of the Spirit: Essays in Religion and Literature.* Ed. George A. Panichas. New York: Hawthorn Books, 1957. 19–44.

Rudich, Norman. "Faulkner and the Sin of Private Property." *Minnesota Review* 17 (Fall 1981): 55–57.

Simpson, Lewis. *Nine Essays on Modern Literature.* Ed. Donald E. Stanford. Baton Rouge: Louisiana UP, 1965.

Sundquist, Eric J. "The True Inheritance of Ike McCaslin." *Critical Essays on William Faulkner: The McCaslin Family.* Ed. Arthur F. Kinney. London: G. K. Hall, 1990.

Utley, Francis Lee, Lynn Z. Bloom, and Arthur F. Kinney, eds. *Bear, Man, and God: Seven Approaches to William Faulkner's "The Bear."* New York: Random House, 1964.

Welty, Eudora. "Faulkner's 'The Bear'." *On Short Stories.* New York: Harcourt, Brace, 1949. 39–47.

Willis, Susan. "Aesthetics of the Rural Slum: Contradiction and Dependency in 'The Bear'." *Faulkner: New Perspectives.* Ed. Richard H. Broadhead. New York: Prentice-Hall, 1983.

GO DOWN, MOSES

READING TO WRITE

Go Down, Moses is a novel that spans a great deal of time and includes many characters. It may seem at first more like a collection of seven short stories than a novel. The unifying factors are the presence of one character, Isaac McCaslin, and the book's thematic concerns.

Go Down, Moses tells the story of the McCaslin family over the course of nearly a century. In the larger sense, what happens in the McCaslin family could be viewed as also happening to the South as a whole. The book's title refers to the spiritual "Go Down, Moses," with its chorus:

> Go down, Moses,
> 'Way down in Egypt's land.
> Tell ole Pharaoh,
> Let my people go.

As in the spiritual, the book's central theme is slavery and its affect on people, both white and black, and even upon the land itself.

One of the more vexing problems when reading *Go Down, Moses* will be to keep the large cast of characters clear in your mind (Padgett provides a helpful genealogy at his Web site). In many cases, names are similar enough to cause confusion. The family tree that begins with Lucius Quintus Carothers McCaslin, called Old Carothers, is split into two segments: his white family, his legitimate heirs in the eyes of the law, and his black or mixed-race family, fathered upon his slaves. Isaac McCaslin, his white grandson, repudiates his inheritance. After he comes to know the family history from reviewing the ledgers of his family's plantation, he believes his inheritance to be corrupted by the sin of slavery. He also thinks that just as no man can own another, no man can really profess to own the land.

The first story in the novel is called "Was," and it takes place before the birth of Isaac McCaslin. McCaslin Edmonds is the boy of the story. He lives with Uncle Buck and Uncle Buddy. On its face, the story is comical. The boy and his uncles go to track the slave Tomey's Turl, who has run away to the Beauchamp plantation to see Tennie. The difficulties between the Beauchamp and McCaslin plantations will be decided in a poker game. This story introduces some of the major themes of *Go Down, Moses*, the theme of the hunt, and of ownership, kinship, and slavery. The story is less comical when one considers the humanity of the people being bartered (although this effect is somewhat mitigated by the fact that Uncle Buck's bachelor status is also at stake in the game) and even more so when the reader later discovers that Tomey's Turl was actually the half brother of Uncle Buck and Uncle Buddy. As you read each of these stories in preparation for writing about this novel, try to keep in mind that every action will have consequences beyond its initial mention.

"The Fire and the Hearth" tells the story of Lucas Beauchamp's attempts to conceal the still he is operating on the McCaslin plantation. This story illustrates the disparity between the black and white descendants of Carothers McCaslin. The story is filled with comical turns. George Wilkins and Lucas's daughter, Nat, attempt to outsmart Lucas. Lucas attempts to have George Wilkins incarcerated for making whiskey illegally. While burying his own still, Lucas finds some gold and becomes obsessed with finding the treasure that is rumored to be buried on the plantation. His obsession nearly costs him his marriage, but the importance of his family is made clear by the story's end.

"Pantaloon in Black" is the story of Rider, who lives on the McCaslin plantation but is not directly related to the family. Rider's grief at the death of his wife is uncontrollable. In a rage, he kills a white man, and Rider is found hanged two days later. This story highlights the distance between the races. Rider's grief is seen as unnatural, animalistic. Faulkner closes the story by having a white sheriff tell the story to his wife. The lack of compassion or understanding is profound.

"The Old People" highlights the relationship of Sam Fathers and Isaac McCaslin, a relationship that is central to the story "The Bear." Sam is named as he is because he is said to have had "two fathers." Isaac, by the novel's end is said to be "father to none." Sam is a bridge between two worlds: He is the son of an Indian chief and a Negro slave girl. The chief, his father, sold him and his mother into slavery. Ikkemotubbe, the Indian chief, once ruled over the land that they hunt, but he sold the land to the white people. What Isaac learns from Sam will form the basis of his belief system. The story touches on the themes of the importance of family and the land. Isaac learns how to hunt and also when not to shoot. Sam teaches Isaac to respect the land and all who inhabit it. When Sam addresses the buck as "grandfather," he opens up to Isaac the idea of a patrimony between the boy and the land.

This story continues in "The Bear" as these same characters attempt to hunt Old Ben, a bear whose size, strength, and ability to elude hunters have given him a mythical status. They do eventually succeed in killing Old Ben, but Lion, the hunting dog that has been raised for the purpose of this hunt, and Sam Fathers are also killed. They are buried in the same clearing where Ben fell. This story contains the entries in the plantation's ledgers that are read by Isaac. Using the ledger entries, he pieces together the history of the plantation that is his patrimony. What he reads there confirms the white and black branches of the McCaslin family, and seems to reveal to Isaac not just the miscegenation that was a by-product of the evil of slavery but also incest between Carothers McCaslin and his daughter and slave Tomey, the child of Carothers and his slave Eunice. Isaac rejects his inheritance.

"Delta Autumn" continues the story begun in "The Bear." Isaac McCaslin is now an old man. The land that he used to hunt has diminished as developers have purchased and built upon it. Roth Edmonds, now the last in the family of white McCaslins, asks Isaac to deliver a mysterious message. He gives him an envelope filled with money. When the woman comes with her child, Isaac learns that the black and white McCaslins have met and procreated again, as she is a descendant of the black McCaslins. The woman's infant child is the future of the McCaslin family, though he will not bear his father's name. The future of the family is much like its past: There is miscegenation, incest, secrets, and an uncertain patrimony.

The novel's final story is also called "Go Down, Moses." It takes place during the census of 1940. The story centers on Molly Beauchamp and Gavin Stevens, as Gavin Stevens attempts to bring her grandson's body back after he is executed in Illinois. The novel was published on May 11, 1942, so *Go Down, Moses* the novel spans nearly a century and ends by depicting current times.

As you begin to read *Go Down, Moses*, do not overlook Faulkner's dedication. It reads: "To Mammy Caroline Barr, Mississippi [1840–1940]: Who was born in slavery and who gave to my family fidelity without stint or calculation of recompense and to my childhood an immeasurable devotion and love."

TOPICS AND STRATEGIES
Themes

The stories of *Go Down, Moses* are held together, in part, by their themes, and there are a number of themes addressed in this novel. "Pantaloon in Black" is a good story to look at to identify some of the themes, as it is the story least connected to the McCaslin family. Why does it belong in the novel? It explores the gulf between the black and white races. The deputy illustrates how little understanding and empathy there is between the two. This story also explores the meaning of family and the devastation of grief. As the deputy tells the story of Rider to his wife, it becomes clear that to this white man Rider's actions are proof of a lack of humanity in the black man.

The hunt is another theme of *Go Down, Moses*. Rider is hunted and lynched for killing a white man. Throughout the novel various hunting expeditions take place. In the first story, Tomey's Turl is tracked like an animal. There is little understanding of why Turl runs to Tennie, of the possibility of love existing between these characters. To be fair, Sophonsiba's attempts to trap Uncle Buck are similar. The hunting party is an essential part of the novel. As Isaac learns to hunt, he learns others lessons about how to be a man. The hunt for Big Ben marks a transition for all the people involved.

"The Bear" is important enough as a story or novella to stand alone, and so it is discussed in this book in its own chapter. But of the stories in *Go Down, Moses*, "The Bear" illustrates best the theme of man and nature. The novel is populated by characters that are at home in the natural world. Those who are not, like Samuel Beauchamp, come to grief. Faulkner seems to suggest that as the century of the novel goes by and the characters became more alienated from the land, they also lost sight of other important aspects of their selves.

The character of Isaac illustrates another theme of this novel: questions of patrimony. What is passed down from father to son? Isaac rejects his inheritance, but in doing so he is also rejecting his patrimony in a larger sense. He attempts to reject what Carothers McCaslin represents to him. And there are other major themes explored in the novel, such as death, initiation, family, and grief.

Sample Topics:

1. **Race:** Does the novel suggest that one day, in the future, race relations will change?

   There are many ways to think about race in *Go Down, Moses.* The question above only points to one, and the question could be answered in the affirmative or in the negative, depending upon your view and the evidence you choose to support your position. The novel spans approximately a century in time, but it may seem that little has changed from the view of the deputy in "Pantaloon in Black" to Gavin Stevens in "Go Down, Moses." On the other hand, Isaac expresses the belief in "Delta Autumn" that the world will be ready for interracial love someday, though it is not at present.

2. **The hunt:** What meaning does the hunt take on in *Go Down, Moses*?

   If you were to write about the hunt as a theme of *Go Down, Moses,* you might focus on Isaac and Sam Fathers and the idea of the hunt as an initiation or passage into adulthood. You might write a very different paper on the hunting of people throughout the novel, such as the hunts for Tomey's Turl or Rider.

3. **Man and nature:** What is the relationship between man and nature depicted in *Go Down, Moses*?

   As the novel progresses in time, nature becomes a less important feature in the stories. A writer on this topic might talk about the consequences such an estrangement brings. The McCaslin plantation no longer holds the family together. Even Isaac rejects that land and lives in the town. Samuel Beauchamp rejects rural Mississippi altogether and goes to Chicago. What changes seem to be forecast for the future where land is not a common denominator? A paper could also be written defining what nature means to someone like Sam Fathers.

4. Legacy: What is passed down in *Go Down, Moses*?

The novel has a great deal to say about inheritance, whether it be the McCaslin plantation or the McCaslin blood or some other element. Isaac attempts to reject his inheritance. Lucas Beauchamp clings to his. Sam Fathers presents Isaac with another possible inheritance. Consider some of those things that are passed down: land, gold, a name, characteristics, blood, a horn, a curse, a history, or an experience.

History and Context

"Delta Autumn" begins with Isaac McCaslin arguing with Carothers Edmonds about America's involvement in World War II. This war, like the one before it, does not feature Mississippi as a prominent player, as the Civil War did. Life has become much less local and more global. And the wilderness they are driving to has become a destination instead of a place they live with and near daily. It has diminished over the course of the novel. The prediction seems to be that it will soon disappear.

One argument Faulkner seems to make is that slavery will forever mark the South. As he writes on page 280 of the novel, the history of slavery is "that record which two hundred years had not been enough to complete and another hundred would not be enough to discharge; that chronicle which was a whole land in miniature, which multiplied and compounded was the entire South." The effects of slavery are everywhere in the novel, marking the black and the white characters.

Miscegenation is part of the evil of slavery. Near the novel's end, the black and white branches of the McCaslin family tree have reunited in the child of Carothers Edmonds and the granddaughter of Tennie's Jim. It is hard to imagine that good will come from a situation where the child's father pays the mother to disappear, considering the importance the novel places on patrimony. And although the child will carry the McCaslin blood into the future, he will not carry on the McCaslin name.

In a sense, one theme of the novel is that he who does not remember the past is doomed to repeat it. Remember, the novel begins with a chapter called "Was." Think of all that title implies.

Sample Topics:

1. **Slavery:** Actual slavery is only present at the beginning of the novel; how does slavery remain a concern throughout the book?

   Uncle Buck and Uncle Buddy play poker for the possession of Tennie at a time when she and her lover are still property to be wagered over. How are characters like Rider or Samuel Beauchamp any freer? The same question could be asked of Isaac McCaslin, who spends his life in reaction to the sin of slavery. Why does Mollie Beauchamp spend all of her life on the McCaslin plantation?

2. **The South:** How would you define the "South" in reference the *Go Down, Moses*?

   If you were to explain the American South given only this novel, how would you characterize this place? This topic is very broad. It could encompass a discussion of slavery, or industrialization, or the Civil War, just to name a few possibilities. Faulkner shows so much of the South that is damning, yet he still manages to convey love for it. What is redeeming about the South of *Go Down, Moses*?

3. **Miscegenation:** How does miscegenation affect the lives of the characters in *Go Down, Moses*?

   The mixing of races affects not only the characters who are both black and white but also characters such as Sam Fathers. He is the son of an Indian chief, yet he is sold with his African-American mother into slavery. He exists between worlds. Lucas Beauchamp is the grandson of the master of a large plantation, but his status is very different.

4. **The importance of the past:** How does the past affect the lives of the characters in *Go Down, Moses*?

This question could be addressed in a number of ways. For instance, you might write about how history seems to repeat itself in the novel. Characters (sometimes with very similar names) pursue similar paths and can sometimes cause confusion in the reader. Carothers McCaslin fathers a shadow family; Carothers Edmonds does the same. Isaac McCaslin chooses a life similar to Jesus Christ and Sam Fathers, but he seems to fall short of both. The ledgers are an important document that influences all of Isaac's life. Why does he choose to let the actions of a grandfather he never knew dictate his life?

Philosophy and Ideas

The ties of family are emphasized in *Go Down, Moses,* and also how those ties are expressed when the common familial relationships break down. One of the greatest difficulties of Faulkner's fiction is understanding the genealogy of his characters. Here McCaslin Edmonds is raised by Uncle Buck and Uncle Buddy. Isaac is raised by McCaslin and eventually becomes known as Uncle Ike. Carothers Edmonds is nursed by Molly alongside her own child.

Particularly in "The Old People," the relationship between mankind and the land is explored. Sam Fathers attempts to teach Isaac a different way of being in the woods and relating to the animals they are tracking. His lessons shape all of Isaac's life. Isaac comes to believe that the land cannot be owned. Some of his experiences are mystical, such as his close meetings with the deer, the snake, and Old Ben.

The novel looks closely at a number of marriages, such as Rider's with his wife or Lucas's to Molly Beauchamp. Others are only glimpsed, but that glimpse tells the reader a lot. Think about Isaac McCaslin's marriage or Sophonsiba Beauchamp's and the devastating portraits of each drawn in one quick scene. There is also the story of how Isaac comes to be born, with his mother seeking to entrap his father into a marriage and finally succeeding. The majority of the men in the novel seem to choose to be alone. All the children we see brought up are boys.

Sample Topics:

1. **Family:** Is family fluid in *Go Down, Moses*, or is it completely binding?

   This novel has a great deal to say on the subject of family. It may at times seem that everyone in the novel is related to everyone else. Does the novel finally make a statement about family? For instance, is there a definition? Is family real or a construct? Is it genetics or acknowledgment? What does it finally mean?

2. **Relationship to the land:** What is man's proper relationship to the land, according to *Go Down, Moses*?

   A paper on this topic might discuss respect or the proper role of the hunter. Sam Fathers leaves Isaac with a reverence of the natural world. Is this a distinctly Native American way of looking at the earth?

3. **Marriage:** Does marriage mean something different to the white and black families in *Go Down, Moses*?

   An essay on this topic could look at all the marriages in the novel or choose one to focus on. Is Faulkner making a statement about marriage? Is marriage taken more seriously by the black families and, if so, is this another consequence of slavery?

4. **Patrimony:** What is passed from father to son?

   Isaac wants a son but does not have one. Carothers Edmonds has a son he renounces. Looking at the various sons and fathers in the novel, what is the importance of patrimony? Isaac gives the horn to the mother of Roth's child. This is his patrimony. Isaac has attempted to renounce his. Lucas feels he is a stronger individual because he is from the male branch of the family tree, even though his patrimony is unacknowledged.

Form and Genre

Foremost among questions of form and genre for this novel is the question of whether it is a novel or a book of short stories. An argument could be made that Isaac is the figure that ties the stories together. Another argument could be that it is the land that ties the stories together. The McCaslin plantation, even before it was the McCaslin plantation and belonged to the Indians who lived there, unifies all the stories. Various themes also unite the whole. Still, there is the possibility that some belong only tenuously, such as "Pantaloon in Black."

The novel's title is shared with the final story in the volume. This makes the reader anticipate that this final story will have a special relevance to what has gone before. Also, readers should know that the title is taken from the spiritual song of the same name. These are the lyrics to "Go Down, Moses":

>When Israel was in Egypt's land,
>   Let my people go.
>Oppressed so hard they could not stand,
>   Let my people go.
>
>Chorus
>   Go down, Moses,
>   'Way down in Egypt's land.
>   Tell ole Pharaoh,
>   Let my people go.
>
>We need not always weep and mourn,
>   Let my people go.
>And wear these slav'ry chains forlorn
>   Let my people go.
>
>The devil thought he had us fast
>   Let my people go.
>But we thought we'd break his chains at last,
>   Let my people go.

Thus saith the Lord, bold Moses said,
    Let my people go.
If not I'll smite your first born—dead,
    Let my people go.

No more shall they in bondage toil,
    Let my people go.
Let them come out with Egypt's spoil,
    Let my people go.

When Israel out of Egypt came,
    Let my people go.
And left the proud oppressive land,
    Let my people go.

O 'twas a dark and dismal night,
    Let my people go.
When Moses led the Israelites,
    Let my people go.

The Lord told Moses what to do,
    Let my people go.
To lead the children of Israel thro',
    Let my people go.

As Israel stood by the water side,
    Let my people go.
By God's command it did divide,
    Let my people go.

When they reached the other shore,
    Let my people go.
They sang a song of triumph o'er,
    Let my people go.

Molly's complaints that Roth Edwards has sold her child echo these lyrics. Many other events in the novel echo them as well. For instance, when you hear the line "If not I'll smite your first born—dead," you might be reminded that Roth's firstborn son will not be raised by him and will not bear his name. The McCaslin family freed their slaves, but the family still labors under the curse of having first owned them.

Names are important in *Go Down, Moses*. It is confusing that so many characters are given the same or remarkably similar names. If you take the time to untangle the genealogy and reflect upon why they are named as they are, it may be less confusing and you may find that the name reveals something about the character. In the ledgers of "The Bear," there is some discussion of the names of the black branch of the McCaslin family. Many of those children are given the same names as the white family members. But these are often truncated or slightly changed, so that "Lucius" becomes "Lucas." Sam Fathers's name announces the history of who Sam Fathers is and reveals a great deal about the life he has lived as a result.

Sample Topics:

1. **The novel:** What makes this book a novel instead of a collection of short stories?

   One could make this argument by focusing broadly on the stories and what links them. One could argue that various elements repeat throughout the book. It might also be useful to look at the publication history of the stories, when and how they were published alone.

2. **The title:** Why did Faulkner title the book as he did?

   An essay on this topic might look at the spiritual by the same name or at the final story of the volume. Who is the Moses of the title? Do you find him anywhere in the book? Where is it he must go "down" to?

3. **The spiritual:** How is the spiritual related to the novel?

   If you choose to write on this topic, you would carefully analyze the lyrics to the spiritual for the echoes found in the novel. You might want to listen to a recording of the spiritual or research the role this type of song had for communicating among slaves.

4. Names: What is the importance of names in *Go Down, Moses*?

The novel closes at the 1940 census, an attempt to count the people but also to record their names, ages, race, and occupations. This takes on extra meaning in families as convoluted genealogically as the McCaslin family. When the census taker comes to Samuel Beauchamp, he gives a name different from the one he is held under. His grandmother calls him by another name; the people of Jefferson by still another. In a world where the name is important, not having a name is especially important.

Bibliography and Online Resources for *Go Down, Moses*

Bluestein, Gene. "Faulkner and Miscegenation." *Arizona Quarterly* 45.2 (Summer 1987): 151–64.

Brooks, Cleanth. "The Story of the McCaslins (Go Down, Moses)." *William Faulkner: The Yoknapatawpha Country* (1963): 244–78.

Buell, Lawrence. "Faulkner and the Claims of the Natural World." *Faulkner and the Natural World.* Faulkner and Yoknapatawpha Conference, 1996. Eds. Donald Kartiganer and Ann J. Abadie. Jackson: UP of Mississippi, 1999. 1–18.

Canfield, J. Douglas. "Faulkner's Grecian Urn and Ike McCaslin's Empty Legacies." *Arizona Quarterly* 36.4 (Winter 1980): 359–84.

Duvall, John N. "Doe Hunting and Masculinity: Song of Solomon and Go Down, Moses." *Arizona Quarterly* 47.1 (Spring 1991): 95–115.

Early, James. *The Making of Go Down, Moses.* Dallas: Southern Methodist UP, 1972.

Faulkner, William. *Go Down, Moses.* New York: Vintage International P, 1990.

Hoffman, Daniel. *Faulkner's Country Matters: Folklore and Fable in Yoknapatawpha.* Baton Rouge: Louisiana State UP, 1989.

Kinney, Arthur F. *Critical Essays on William Faulkner: The McCaslin Family.* Boston: G. K. Hall, 1990.

————. *Go Down Moses: The Miscegenation of Time.* New York: Twayne, 1996.

O'Donnell, Patrick. "Faulkner and Postmodernism." *The Cambridge Companion to William Faulkner.* Ed. Philip Weinstein. New York: Cambridge UP, 1995. 31–50.

Padgett, John B. *"Go Down, Moses:* Commentary." *William Faulkner on the Web.* 17 Aug. 2006. Ed. John B. Padgett. U of Mississippi. 19 Dec. 2007. URL: http://www.mcsr.olemiss.edu/~egjbp/faulkner/n-gdm.html.

Polk, Noel. "Noel Polk's Study Guide for *Go, Down Moses.*" Accessed July 17, 2008. URL: http://www.mississippireads.org/Articles/Mississippi_Reads_Web_Site___GDM_Study_Guide ___Polk.doc

Powers, Lyall H. "The Structure of Go Down, Moses." *Readings on William Faulkner.* Ed. Clarice Swisher. San Diego, CA: Greenhaven, 1998. 159–67.

Prewitt, Wiley C., Jr. "Return of the Big Woods: Hunting and Habitat in Yoknapatawpha." *Faulkner and the Natural World.* Faulkner and Yoknapatawpha Conference, 1996. Eds. Donald Kartiganer and Ann J. Abadie. Jackson: UP of Mississippi, 1999. 198–221.

Rowe, John Carlos. "The African-American Voice in Faulkner's Go Down, Moses." *Modern American Short Story Sequences: Composite Fictions and Fictive Communities.* Ed. J. Gerald Kennedy. Cambridge: Cambridge UP, 1995. 76–97.

Schreiber, Evelyn Jaffe. "'Old Carothers' Doomed and Fatal Blood': The Layers of the Ledgers in Go Down, Moses." *Faulkner Journal* 12.2 (Spring 1997): 87–88.

Taylor, Nancy Drew. *Annotations to William Faulkner's Go Down, Moses.* New York: Garland, 1994.

Trilling, Lionel. "Race as a Theme in Go Down, Moses." *Readings on William Faulkner.* Ed. Clarice Swisher. San Diego, CA: Greenhaven, 1998. 168–71.

Wagner-Martin, Linda, ed. *New Essays on Go Down, Moses.* New York: Cambridge UP, 1996.

Zender, Karl F. "Faulkner and the Politics of Incest." *American Literature* 70.4 (December 1998): 739–65.

INDEX